Buy to Let
Property
Hotspots

Other related titles published by How To Books

Buy to Let Handbook
*How to invest for profit in residential property
and manage the letting yourself*

How to Make Money from Property
The expert guide to property investment

Property Hotspots in London
Where in our capital city to buy and let property for profit

Buy to Let in France
How to invest in French property for pleasure and profit

howtobooks

Please send for a free copy of the latest catalogue:

How To Books
3 Newtec Place, Magdalen Road,
Oxford OX4 1RE, United Kingdom
email: info@howtobooks.co.uk
http://www.howtobooks.co.uk

Buy to Let
Property
Hotspots

Where to buy property
and how to let it for profit

Ajay Ahuja

Nick Rampley-Sturgeon

howtobooks

Published by How To Books Ltd,
3 Newtec Place, Magdalen Road,
Oxford OX4 1RE, United Kingdom.
Tel: (01865) 793806. Fax: (01865) 248780.
email: info@howtobooks.co.uk
http://www.howtobooks.co.uk

First published 2003
Reprinted 2003

British Library Cataloguing in Publication Data
A catalogue record for this book is available from the British Library

Cover design by Baseline Arts Ltd, Oxford
Produced for How To Books by Deer Park Productions
Typeset by Pantek Arts, Maidstone, Kent
Printed and bound in Great Britain by Cromwell Press, Trowbridge, Wiltshire

NOTE: The material contained in this book is set out in good faith for general
guidance and no liability can be accepted for loss or expense incurred as a result of
relying in particular circumstances on statements made in the book. The laws and
regulations are complex and liable to change, and readers should check the current
position with the relevant authorities before making personal arrangements.

I dedicate this book to my mother.
Thanks to Giles and Nikki for their belief.
Thanks to Nick for his foresight and Ellie for her inspiration.
Special thanks to Nicola for her research.

Ajay Ahuja

I am very grateful to have received the help and support of our editor Nikki
Read at How To Books, and for the wisdom of my Literary Agent Frances
Kelly. Beyond these two people there are many landlords, agents and
investors who have shared their thoughts, ideas and time with me around the
country. Very grateful thanks also go out to Nicola Hayne and to Steve
Hasler for their 'behind the scenes' research work.

Closer to home I would like to say a big thank you to Joanna and our two
boys Henry and Johnny for keeping themselves busy so that I could find the
time to finish the book.

Nick Rampley-Sturgeon

Contents

A Note from the Authors ix

How the Book Works xiii

Property Viewing Record xxiii

How to Use the Property Hotspot Profiles xxvii

A–Z of property Hotspots 1

Index of Property Hotspots 223

A Note from the Authors

Ajay Ahuja

I started with nothing. I bought my first property when I was 24 with £500 and now I am 30 and I own 60 properties and earn an income in excess of £250,000p.a. It's not difficult but requires DEDICATION, PERSISTENCE and DISCIPLINE. If you lack any of the above then forget it. However, if you have all of the above then welcome. I bought my first property in 1996 for myself to live in. I couldn't get used to it, so I let it out. I soon realised that the tenant was paying my mortgage as well as my beer money (about £120 per month), and required minimal effort from myself. I thought, 'this is easy!', so I bought another one and did the same. 58 properties later ... you get the idea.

The dedication, persistence and discipline I had to becoming rich was not driven by money, but by freedom – the freedom to do what I like, when I like, without restriction from my boss or my wallet. Freedom does not have to be your driving factor, it could be a brand new Ferrari, private schooling for your children or simply financial security. Whatever it is, it's this that will keep you going. With the right properties, financial products and tenants, there is no doubt you will succeed. Property has made more millionaires than any other type of business or investment over the last 100 years. This is fact. When you understand property properly it will be obvious that this type of investment is a sure way to long term wealth.

So why choose property? Why not invest in stocks and shares? I'll tell you why. The first reason is that property carries an inherent low risk factor. Houses will not go out of fashion or become obsolete like services or products. They are an essential for us all. That's why house prices have consistently doubled every 10–15 years in the last century. Coupled with the fact that monthly rental values rise with wages (which is a function of inflation) and that the mortgage payment is relatively fixed (only altering with interest rate fluctuations) the profit element always rises. In addition, after the mortgage has been paid, the rent is all profit. That's why many people see investing in property as their pension fund.

The second reason is basic economics. With an expanding population, fragmenting families, an ever moving workforce, fewer properties for sale and fewer council owned properties, THE DEMAND FOR RENTAL PROPERTIES EXCEEDS SUPPLY.

The third reason is an inherent attribute in all of us – we are lazy! To play the stock market properly requires lengthy research, ongoing monitoring and nerves of steel for the duration of the investment. That's why 3 out of 4 private investors lose money. When a property is set up properly, you just sit back and watch the money roll in.

I am a chartered accountant (I left employment when I was 27 to concentrate on the property business) and I must admit, the training I received in accountancy and more importantly, in business, has helped me in my success. Through my experience I am able to isolate the key variables in investing in property and present them in this book. No list is ever complete, but these key variables will help you determine which area or areas are right for you. I hope you find this book useful whatever your goals are – this may be to buy a second home to earn a little additional income, or to build a multi-million pound empire.

For further information with help in building your portfolio you can contact me on: Telephone: 0800 652 3979; Fax: 01277 362563 or visit my website: www.accdirect.co.uk.

Nick Rampley-Sturgeon

I became a Landlord almost by accident in 1989 when my experience of negative equity encouraged me to take a lodger and then to let out the whole house. Since then I have built a strong property portfolio, and gained a wealth of knowledge as both a landlord and investor during the process. Through my work with individual entrepreneurs and family business owners I have become convinced of the value and importance to my clients of developing personal financial strategies for investing in residential property.

Through my Buying to Rent business I run a range of events designed to help new and existing landlords to grow and develop their portfolios. These include an individual coaching service; weekend 'property bootcamp' seminars; and an active property buying syndicate.

The basis of my work is that by creating and working with an individual strategy the landlord and investor can create opportunity regardless of the direction of the market.

In Spring 2003 the property buying syndicate invested successfully in more than £16 million of new builds, both houses and apartments around the country. This process continues and is backed by good research and time spent on analysis of opportunities. The acquisitions and style of the syndicate have featured very positively in the national press.

As a member of the Professional Speakers Association, I work with Event Organisers in the property and finance industries, bringing extra insight to investors and finance teams alike through my keynote talks and presentations.

For further information with help in building your portfolio you can contact me on: Telephone: 01327-706622; Fax: 01327-706623 or visit my website: www.buyingtorent.com.

How the Book Works

What is a Hotspot?

A hotspot is an area where there are properties available for sale that fall into one of these categories:

Category	Description
A	Property prices are predicted to rise at a greater rate than the national average AND the rental yield is greater than the national average.
B	The rental yield is greater than the national average.
C	Property prices are predicted to rise at a greater rate than the national average.

We have ranked the categories, with category A being the most desirable as it enjoys the best of both worlds – capital growth and yield, thus spreading the return and overall risk. Category B is ranked second as the yield is a definite outcome, whereas capital growth is categorised as C because it is a less certain outcome.

We've found in our experience that investors choose category A, B or C on personal circumstances but more so on gut reaction. Our advice is to choose all of them! There is no need to place all your eggs in one basket. Property is a relatively safe investment but there is a degree of uncertainty, so if possible, by investing in all the categories above, you eliminate some of the business risk.

Identification of a Hotspot

So how did we identify the hotspots listed? Well the categories are based on two factors:

1. Actual rental yields
2. Predicted property prices.

1. Actual Rental Yields

The first factor, actual rental yields, was easy to do. Actual rental yield is:

$$\frac{\text{ACTUAL YEARLY RENT}}{\text{ACTUAL PROPERTY PRICE}}$$

Since these figures are actuals, we collated all the rental figures from local letting agents in the UK and all the local property prices in the UK from the Land Registry and calculated all the yields being offered from all UK locations. We then eliminated all the poor yielding locations and where we thought tenant demand was low (even if they were high yielding).

2. Predicted Property Prices

Here we did not predict property prices as this is impossible to do. If we could do this we would not be writing this book, but buying everything we could in a hotspot area! All we did was to look at what would make an area's property price rise above the national average. We came up with the following:

- Proposed transportation link improvements, such as: improved road and rail links, expansion of local airports and improved public transport.
- Proposed inward investment from private companies, government and trusts.
- Proposed improvements to leisure facilities, such as: sport centres, parks and shopping centres.
- The likelihood of holiday seasons being lengthened for holiday areas.
- Our own experience gathered from being in this industry and from comments from letting and estate agents.

What Type of Investor Are You?

So you know you want to invest in property. However, why and how are you going to invest in property? Well there are many ways to invest in property, but we have narrowed these ways down to seven types. Investors can be broadly categorised into the following and it is up to you to decide which category or categories you fit into:

Type	Objective	Description
Cash&Equity Investor	To maximise rental income and capital growth combined. Will also sell home when this further achieves this objective.	This approach is a semi-business approach. The investor has no love for the property but is only interested in the overall money the property is going to make. He will sell if the market is high or hold if the rental income is good. His intentions are to re-invest any monies gained back into another property or properties. This type of investor will have a greater degree of interest in property than other investors as he will stay abreast of the market.
Pension Investor	To cover all costs involved with the house by the rental income and have the house paid off by retirement age. The rental income (or return on sale) thus providing an income thereon.	This investor will be at least 15 years off retirement age. He will look for a property that will always have good rental demand as he intends to live off this rental income when he retires. He may also consider selling the property and using the monies raised to purchase an annuity. If so, he will also look for a high capital growth area. As good practice this type of investor should always evaluate whether their equity in the property can purchase an income greater than the rental income being generated currently.
Holiday Investor	To cover some of the costs of owning the house by letting it out but ultimately to get a holiday home that can be enjoyed by family and friends.	Typically an investor with a family who wishes to save on holiday costs and to eventually pass down the property to his children, or release the value of his nest egg. Saving money rather than making money is the motivation for this investor. He will seek non-conventional investment properties such as cottages, properties far from the city centre and stations and restricted occupancy homes.
Retirement Investor	To cover all costs involved with the house by the rental income and have the house paid off by retirement age. Then sell own home to move into the investment home.	Again non-typical investment properties will be sought and he will probably seek properties in a surrounding village of a main town or city. A key concern for this investor is tenant demand so he may well be steered towards villages surrounding main towns and cities. The investor will use the proceeds from the sale of his original home to clear outstanding mortgages and purchase an annuity.

▶

Type	Objective	Description
University Investor	To provide a home for son/daughter while at university for 3 years. Sell/hold after 3 years.	The aim of this investor is to purchase a 4+ bedroomed home near the university and get the son or daughter to live in one room and rent the other rooms to his or her friends. The rental income will cover all costs involved with the house and then the house can be sold on for profit or held and rented out again through the university. The overall profit on the investment is the boarding fees saved in the 3 years and the gain on the sale of the property.
Downshifter Investor	To sell existing home and buy a lifestyle property (i.e. B&B) with no outstanding mortgage.	This investor will realise the gain in their home free from tax and purchase a property which will change both their location and their job. Typical properties are B&Bs and shops with living accommodation above.
Business Investor	To maximise rental income to replace salary from full-time employment.	The investor will look for high yielding properties so as to replace the lost income from leaving their job. He will invest in only high tenant demand areas as he relies on this income to pay his day-to-day bills. He will be interested in the property market hence he will be abreast of the latest prices, mortgage rates and rental figures. This way he can ensure that his net income is maximised.

From reading this list you will be able to decide what type of investor you are and more importantly what you want to get from your investment. Once you are clear what you want, then the whole process becomes easier as you know exactly what you are looking for.

So Which Hotspot Should You Choose?

It is not for us to tell you where to specifically invest. We have short-listed areas where to invest, but the rest is up to you. We think you should consider some or all of the following, depending on what type of investor you are:

1. In or out of your home town?
2. Proximity to a university
3. Proximity to a motorway junction
4. Fashionable addresses

5. Public transport links
6. Ex-council properties
7. School and catchment areas
8. Shopping facilities and local leisure facilities
9. Parking
10. Hospitals
11. Flooding

In Your Home Town

The advantages of buying property locally are many. You know the area well and may be able to hear of property coming up for sale before it goes to the estate agents. Because of local knowledge you have a 'gut feel' or sixth sense about whether a house in such and such an area will attract which sort of tenants.

Perhaps you can tell which side of the estate or which side of the road is easiest for getting into work or shopping areas using public transport. You don't have to take the word of the estate agent on everything and I think this gives you more strength sometimes in making your offering to buy. The chances are strong that you can put together a small team of builders, decorators and repairers to look after the property or portfolio of properties you end up buying.

The final benefit of having property close to you is that you can be on hand quicker and for many landlords this is particularly important. If you are collecting money yourself there are clear benefits. If you are using the services of a letting agent then the location does not matter and you can choose more broadly.

Away From Your Home Town

If you have a house in an area which commands good rent and live yourself in an area where either mortgages or rent are low by comparison, then it is possible for you to benefit strongly by receiving a rental income – even on just one property – that is greater than your own accommodation cost.

One small property in a fashionable part of London grosses more rent than a country farmhouse in rural Nottinghamshire. Might this be something for you to explore? Could your lifestyle benefit from a rental income which covered your own biggest bill each month? With the use of telephones and e-mail, particularly if you are self-employed, work in creative or people focussed businesses, there is far more opportunity than ever before for you to work from home say three days a week and go to see work colleagues and clients on the other two.

Look at this location topic from a different angle. As a rule of thumb, the further away you are from London the lower the price of most properties. The further you are from an area of a town which is fashionable or desirable, the less you are likely to pay for a property. However, the closer you are to good train networks between cities, or to decent bus and train networks in and around cities, the more attractive your property becomes, no matter how unfashionable the area.

The real value to you in understanding this process is that you can use your money to buy property in towns where property could cost around half of what it might cost to buy in your own area.

Proximity to a University

If the campus is within a mile or two from your flat then you will probably score well here. There will be a strong demand for property that is well maintained, clean, dry and has a good landlord – you! Keep in with the student accommodation office and you could have a steady stream of revenue.

On the other hand, what happens during the ten weeks of summer holiday? Do you spend two weeks decorating it every summer and eight weeks wishing you had full-time tenants, or do you offer the students a slight reduction in rental over the summer period so as to ensure your house is always occupied by someone? Think it through, but the location overall could mean you are onto a winner.

Proximity to a Motorway Junction

Provided it is within ten or fifteen minutes' drive this can have a great beneficial impact on your house or flat. Many busy, working people want to be able to get on the road quickly each day for their jobs and this accessibility means you can be assured of a quick turnaround time between tenancies. Generally a plus point and a good move.

Two minutes' drive from the same junction and you should be worrying. If a tenant is renting in a place where they feel the local environment is either too noisy, too smelly or too dangerous they will not stay in your property for long. By inspecting a property at different times of the day you can become aware of the impact of the rush hour on local traffic conditions, whether people are using the street as a 'rat run'. But if your tenant market is busy, professional people then buy property where they can have quick access to the road networks without living on top of them!

Fashionable Address

Watch out for this one. The more you have to pay for a property the more nervous you get watching the gap between tenancies and the smaller the return on your investment generally. You can get tenants to fill these properties but they have to find the money and corporate lets are only feasible in certain postcode areas. For the majority of the country this is not relevant.

If you want to experience the benefit of capital appreciation, but are a little short of the readies to begin with, buy in an adjacent area where the tenants are still close to these fashionable and trendy postcodes, but without you having to pay stupid prices for your bricks and mortar. If you can get a rent of £1,000 on an ex-council flat close to a city centre and still retain a healthy profit, why would you want to pay through the nose for only a marginally better rent and use up much of your own investment funds on a heavy deposit? Remember your strategy and stick to it!

Public Transport Links

This is a big one! If your tenants can be on a bus or a train within ten minutes' walk of the property they will be keen to take the property on. Five minutes is of course even better. In the London market anything within five to ten minutes' walk from a tube station will command a better premium for the advantage of that proximity. The same is true of any of the bigger cities with their tram link services across the central routes.

If there are few transport links then ask yourself seriously who you are trying to attract as a tenant. If they do not use transport will they have their own car? Are they working and able to commute to earn their money in order to pay your rent. Will they be so far removed in your property from friends and workmates that after three months they become lonely and move out? Be careful on this one.

Ex-council Properties

Where, for many private buyers, this does not appeal as a place to make their homes, these are often a landlord's dream. Normally built to a good standard you can buy a lot of bedroom for your pound! Semi-detached and terraced properties are plentiful and rent well to people who want to live and work in an area where they perhaps grew up, or where they can stay close to friends and family. In urban areas, ex-council high rise blocks provide the best views around. Your working tenants will get as much space on the city skyline as in many expensive warehouse and industrial building conversions that have cost three or four times as much. Unemployed tenants on the same estate may provide you with an income that – although slow to get started with the Benefit Office – can be as reliable or more reliable than the income from a working tenant.

On the downside you may have one of just a few privately purchased properties within a very large and run down estate. Avoid these. Instead look to buy flats or maisonettes on the outer edges of such big estates, close to public transport, schools and shopping facilities.

School and Catchment Areas

Where a school has been judged to be of a high standard, parents will move as close as possible to be able to get their child into the school without having to pay for private education. This demand can be very strong and push house prices up significantly close to the school. This means that if you can rent out a property close to such a school you can expect demand to be high from professional people, perhaps on a corporate let. The implication is that you can stand to receive good capital appreciation on your original investment, while the tenants cover the mortgage until you want to sell.

Pricing around good schools can be prohibitive to the flow of investing landlords, given they know what margins they want and can see what the rental sector will stand.

Shopping Facilities and Local Leisure Facilities

Big brand fast food restaurants, out of town shopping centres and good designer pubs within a few miles of your property will again make the rental easier. Where the amenities are of good quality there will be good demand from tenants who want to be able to shop, dine and socialise within a short distance of their new home in your flat or house.

Where there is a lack of such facilities, or where shopping is unsafe and streets are awkward after dusk, you will find the rentals equally unattractive. Take care to think why a property is so cheap in the agent's window? Why is it such an apparent bargain at auction?

Parking

With cars so cheap and finance so easy to come by, most of your tenants will be drivers with at least one car. If you are letting to a couple or to a group of friends who share the tenancy, there may be two or three cars that need to park nearby. This is fine if you have a large driveway to the property, or if there is plenty of land around the house. But being realistic this may not be the case. Get properties where parking outside is straightforward – either on a driveway or at the roadside.

Where parking is difficult, where roads are narrow and driving is cramped, things can work against the rental of the property. People are territorial animals and like to park their cars within a hundred yards of their house, if not right outside. Narrow streets and few parking bays simply cause more aggravation. No one wants to go to their car in the morning and find a wing mirror smashed, or a body panel scratched.

Hospitals

Just like having a university near to your investment, a hospital on your doorstep can be a great source of tenants and the effective route to some consistent rental cash flow. Hospitals have their own accommodation teams to help staff find a place to sleep, so make friends with such people and keep your properties in good condition.

The fastest way to be thrown off the list of a hospital accommodation office is to misrepresent your property, or to not maintain it once you have hospital staff renting from you. No-one likes a bad landlord and the message spreads fast.

Flooding

The memory of recent downpours and the sight of Britain underwater has forced the introduction of flood risk insurance premiums. In such areas you will not get insurance for properties and in certain postcodes you are even less likely to get a mortgage at the terms you want one. Check that your intended property is not in a flood zone and if in doubt err on the side of caution and avoid the purchase altogether.

Property Viewing Record

We have created a Property Viewing Record that can be a useful aide-memoire to have with you when going to look at potential investments:

Property Viewing Record
Estate Agent/Auctioneer
Address of the property
Type of Property
Asking Price
Date of first viewing
Date of second visit
Comments about the Surrounding Area
Schools   Traffic Noise   Shops   Public Transport   Business Units
Outside
Garden and Driveway
Garage
Window Frames/Glass
Walls
Drains/Guttering
Roof
Neighbouring Properties

Inside
Hallway
Lounge
Dining Room
Kitchen
Utility Room
Bedroom 1 (Sizes)
Bedroom 2
Bedroom 3
Bedroom 4
Bathroom
Loft
Potential Work Required
Heating and Plumbing
Electrical Repair
Decoration
Damp Patches
External Lighting
General Observations/Things to Remember

And Finally...

These are a few little pointers that we have learned that should help you along the way:

- Avoid the common mistake of purchasing a property because you like the look of it, or think it is cute! Instead, put your money into one which will appeal strongly to tenants.

- Buy the local newspapers and gazettes on the day they advertise local property. If you don't live in the area ask them to send you this on a weekly basis.

- Telephone all the agents and ask them to recommend the areas which rent the best and the most consistently.

- Get on the agent's mailing list as a potential investor and ask for their landlords pack. This will include details of property they have for rent and property suitable for a rental investment. This way you can do your homework from one mailing.

- Tell the agent you work to strict pricing/bedroom criteria and hold your ground. Most agents will always send you the properties at the top end of your budget because they make more commission this way. Find an agent you can trust to bring you good deals. Watch out for them trying to promote all the one bed studio flats and maisonettes they can find. This is fine if you are looking at a city with a very fluid population and you are buying in the central district because you want to rent to urban dwelling city workers seeking tiny *pied-à-terre* properties. Elsewhere however think carefully about this type of unit and the difficulties that come with it.

- At the other end of the scale don't be tempted into buying one enormous house or a flat with four bedrooms because in most circumstances they will be slow to let and even slower to relet. Instead consider investing in three two bed flats or two bed terraced properties.

- Using your criteria for return on investment select a half dozen properties and tour round them with your agent. Don't be afraid to take photographs or video, or to use a small dictating machine to record your impressions of each property.

- Make notes about the street it is in as well as about neighbouring properties.

- Never visit any property outside of full daylight. This is safer for you but it also means you see things as they are. You have every right to take a friend or adviser with you on these property tours. They will see things you never notice. This could save you a lot of time and money wasted. Always have either a camera or a video camera with you when you go to see properties. By the time you are ten minutes away from the house you have just seen, you will have forgotten the features, or be unable to recall the colour of the woodwork.

Good Luck!

Nicholas Rampley-Sturgeon and Ajay Ahuja

How to Use the Property Hotspot Profiles

Before you explore all the property hotspot profiles we've prepared for you, here is an explanation of what headings we used for each hotspot, what they mean and why we've included them.

Heading	Description	Why included
Area:	The area in the UK where the hotspot is.	You need to know where the hotspot is!
Category:	The quality of the hotspot – see above under heading 'What is a Hotspot' for definitions.	Some hotspots are better than others. We have graded them to help you fit them in with your own personal goals.
Investor profile:	The investor profiles which the area is suited to. The seven types of investor are above – see 'The Seven Types of Investor' for definitions.	There's no point looking at a hotspot if it doesn't fit the type of investor you are. Ensure that the hotspot is relevant to you.
Population aged 15+:	The population aged over 15 in the hotspot.	Gives you an idea of the size of the area based on population of people.
Percentage class ABC1:	The percentage of the population aged over 15 within the social group ABC1.	Gives you an idea of how affluent the area is based on the type of people in the area.
Crime:	*Violence* – Acts of violence against a person *Sexual* – Sexual assaults on a person *Burglary* – Burglaries from dwellings *Motor* – Theft of motor vehicles	Gives you an idea of the scale of crime in the area across the key types of crime that can affect property prices.
Per 1000 population:	The number of reported crimes defined above per thousand population.	

▶

Heading	Description	Why included
Yield range:	The range of yields that can be expected from this area. Yield being: (Annual Rental Income) divided by (Purchase Price of Property) x 100.	At a glance to see if the area can offer you the yields you require based on your investment plan.
Price ranges – *Low*	The lowest purchase price expected for the type of property in question.	A guide price for the cheapest property available in the area.
Price ranges – *Hi*	The highest purchase price expected for the type of property in question.	A guide price for the most expensive property available in the area.
Price ranges – *Low £pw*	The lowest rental figure per week expected for the type of property in question.	A guide price for the cheapest rental figure available in the area.
Price ranges – *Hi £pw*	The highest rental figure per week expected for the type of property in question.	A guide price for the most expensive rental figure available in the area.
Price ranges – *Low*	The lowest yield expected for the type of property in question.	What you can expect in the worst case scenario.
Price ranges – *Hi*	The highest yield expected for the type of property in question.	What you can expect in the best case scenario.
Flats & maisonettes	Studio and 1+ bed flats. These are typically leasehold properties without gardens.	We have segregated the types of property for you to closer identify and analyse the property prices. Some yields are better for the different types of properties. This can then direct you to these type of properties thus maximising your possible yield.
Terraced	1+ bed properties that are homes in a row greater than 2 homes.	
Semi-detached	A row of 2 homes only and being either the left or the right home.	
Detached	A home that is not attached to any other home.	
Percenage above the national average:	The valuation of the homes in the area relative to the rest of the UK. The calculation being: (Average Price of Property in Area – Average Price of Property in UK) divided by (Average Price of Property in UK) x 100	It's a good benchmark to see how good the area is. If the valuation is above the national average then the area will tend to be a better area.
Capital growth last 12 months:	(Average Price for Quarter 4 2002 – Average Property Price for Quarter 4 2002) divided by (Average Property Price for Quarter 4 2001) x 100	Its good to see the growth that has occurred in the last 12 months – has it seen a boom? Has it not grown and is ready to boom? Is it on the way down? But remember that past performance is no indication of future performance.

▶

Heading	Description	Why included
Capital growth last 4 years: Note: when data permits the 5 year growth is stated	(Average Price for Quarter 4 2002 − Average Property Price for Quarter 4 1998) divided by (Average Property Price for Quarter 4 1998) x 100	It's good to see the growth that has occurred in the last 4 years property is a long term investment. However you can still ask − has it seen a boom? Has it not grown and is ready to boom? Is it on the way down? But remember that past performance is no indication of future performance.
Large employers in the area:	Significant employers that employ people in that area.	It's good to know that there are medium to large sized companies in the area to provide jobs and hence strong tenant demand.
Demand For letting:	In our own professional opinion what we think the likely demand is for rental properties.	If you want a non-quantative opinion then here it is!
Average void period:	In our own professional opinion what we think the likely time the property will be un-let between tenancies.	If you want a quantative opinion then here it is!
Capital Growth (out of 5)	Our own total score out of five for the area based on predicted capital growth.	It's why we invest − we want our money to grow. A simple score out of 5 should help you.
Yield (out of 5)	Our own total score out of five for the area based on actual yield.	Another reason why we invest − we want money now! A simple score out of 5 should help you.
Out of 10	Our own total score out of ten for the area based on capital growth and yield. See below.	Everyone loves a score out of 10. It gives you an idea of the quality of the hotspot in numerical format.
Summary:	A brief summary of the area without needing to read the whole description below.	For the lazy. The area summed up in a nut shell.
Description:	A full description of the area and why it is a hotspot.	For the serious. The detail for the area to help you make a more informed choice.
Mainline railway station:	The mainline railway station that serves the area and travelling times to major destinations.	You need to know how well it's connected.
Road access:	The main road routes in to the area.	You need to know how well it's connected.
Local newspaper:	The local newspaper that serves the area.	Once you've found the place you need to know where to advertise.

Heading	Description	Why included
Estate agents:	The estate agents that serve the area.	So you like the area – this is where you find the properties!
Letting agents:	The letting agents that serve the area.	So you've got the property – you need to let it! These organisations will help you.

A–Z of Property Hotspots

Area:	**Alnwick, Northumberland**			
Category:	C			
Investor profile:	Retirement, Cashflow Investment, Capital Appreciation Investment and Holiday Lettings			
Population aged 15+:	24,303			
	Actual		**National Average**	
Percentage Class ABC1:	45%		44%	
Crime:	Violence	Sexual	Burglary	Motor
Per 1000 population:	5	1	2	1
Yield range:	3.5% – 10.0%			

Price ranges:	Low £	Hi £	Low £pw	Hi £pw	Low	Hi
Flats & maisonettes	34,400	51,600	66	89	9.0%	10.0%
Terraced	57,600	86,400	76	103	6.2%	6.9%
Semi-detached	77,600	116,400	84	113	5.0%	5.6%
Detached	122,400	183,600	92	125	3.5%	3.9%

Percentage above the national average:	0%	
	Actual	**National Average**
Capital growth last 12 months:	19%	18%
Capital growth last 4 years:	47%	74%
Large employers in the area:	Mainly tourist related small businesses and local government, i.e. schools, hospitals and councils. Few large employers locally.	
Demand for letting:	Good	
Average void period:	4 weeks	

	Capital Growth (out of 5)	Yield (out of 5)	Total (out of 10)
Our rating:	3	3	6

Summary:	Where your long term strategy involves downshifting to a good small town, then this will bring you rewards way beyond the rent roll, yet funded by your passive income.
Description:	If a quiet life is what you want then this may be the ideal location. Recently voted the most desirable place in Britain in terms of 'quality of life', Alnwick tops the charts for peace and tranquillity, access to the countryside, proximity to the sea, small market town identity, etc.
	The town has a strong sense of identity and people choose to live here to be part of a community. Rising above the town is the castle home of the Duke of Northumberland. Ancient buildings are no restriction to

▶

modern technology and the local business community is flourishing. For a small business owner seeking an active community this town of 8,000 people offers great promise

As a retirement location it offers great opportunities for leisure activities in and around the town. Local produce is easily bought here as well as at Morpeth, Wooler, Berwick and Coldstream with Farmers' Markets adding value to your table. The sea is as close as 3 miles with the historic attraction and beauty of Holy Island just 20 miles up the coast. The town is just on the edge of the Cheviot Hills with Northumberland National Park being on your doorstep.

If securing a property for a retirement which involves hill walking and country pursuits then look to the communities inland and just to the North of the town. Good value holiday property is abundant in the area, whether this is inland cottages or properties close to the coast. Each of these can attract good rentals for the spring and summer months as well as many shorter weekend breaks for walkers and fishermen (both salmon and trout in good supply) across the year.

For many, Alnwick is an ideal commuter base being just 35 miles from Newcastle upon Tyne, or an hour and a half from Edinburgh for the big shops and the cultural activity. Large properties are at a premium as are those with a combination of village location or country views. Prices here are much lower than you will expect and you receive a lot of space for your money. A key reason for this is that Northumberland has the lowest predicted inflow of population for any English county over the next twenty years.

Look also to the properties just south of Alnwick in communities such as Acklington, Felton, Widdrington, and Longhurst. Other communities around Ashington are popular for the north side commute into Newcastle.

Well served North–South by the A1, the route across the Pennines to the West is far more difficult and you will need to use the slower A69 across to Carlisle. The local train station is just three miles away. Local and international flights can be accessed from Newcastle airport, conveniently situated on the North side of the city.

Mainline railway station:	35 minutes to Newcastle			
Road access:	Main access A1 35 miles north of Newcastle-upon-Tyne 1 mile from A1			
Local newspaper:	Newcastle Journal 0191 232 7500			
Estate agents:	Name	Address	Tel	Web
	Parker Stag State Agents	41 Bondgate Within Alnwick Northumberland NE66 1SX	01665 603202	www.parkerstag. co.uk/

Estate agents:	Name	Address	Tel	Web
	Rook Matthews Sayer	5 Market Street Alnwick Northumberland NE66 1SS	01665 510044	www.rook matthews sayer.co.uk
	Clark Scott-Harden	36 Narrowgate Alnwick Northumberland NE66 1JQ	01665 606777	Website currently under development

Letting agents:	Name	Address	Tel	Web
	Proper Let	99 Station Road Ashington Northumberland NE63 8RS	01670 854000	www.properlet. co.uk
	Northern Coalfields Property	37 Pont Street Ashington Northumberland NE63 0PZ	01670 811092	Website currently under development
	Phoenix Properties	71 Station Road Ashington Northumberland NE63 8RS	01670 522822	Website currently under development

Area:	**Anglesey**					
Category:	A					
Investor profile:	Student Rentals, Holiday Lets and Retirement					
Population aged 15+:	52,983					
	Actual			National Average		
Percentage Class ABC1:	48%			44%		
Crime:	Violence		Sexual	Burglary		Motor
Per 1000 population:	10		1	2		2
Yield range:	5.2% – 13.2%					
Yield range:	Low £	Hi £	Low £pw	Hi £pw	Low	Hi
Flats & maisonettes	24,800	37,200	63	86	12.0%	13.2%
Terraced	40,800	61,200	66	89	7.6%	8.4%
Semi-detached	52,000	78,000	85	115	7.7%	8.5%
Detached	88,000	132,000	97	132	5.2%	5.7%
Percentage above the national average:	0%					
	Actual			National Average		
Capital growth last 12 months:	15%			18%		
Capital growth last 4 years:	17%			74%		
Large employers in the area:	Mainly tourist related small businesses and local government, i.e. schools, hospitals and councils. Few large employers locally.					
Demand for letting:	Excellent					
Average void period:	3 weeks					
	Capital Growth (out of 5)		Yield (out of 5)		Total (out of 10)	
Our rating:	2		5		7	
Summary:	Strong university exerts an influence over the whole community and absorbs most of the available housing. Breathtaking location with the mountains and the sea all around. Highest yield comes from older stock which may require further investment in maintenance.					
Description:	Anglesey fully justifies its Welsh designation as one of the five Areas of Outstanding Natural Beauty. As a working community with the thriving modern industry of Bangor just across the Menai Strait, or as a location for retirement and holiday lettings, Anglesey has a lot to attract the investor who will live with their investment.					
	The economy of Anglesey has been aided by a number of projects intended to bolster or enhance the challenges that have faced the					

	island which features the heavy traffic of Holyhead at its Western edge. The projects have included the industrial parks at Mona and also at Bryn Cefni; the Coleg Menai Centre for Food Technology and Food Industrial Park; Eastman Technology Centre; and the enhanced rail facilities at Holyhead.
	Financial initiatives from government and county bodies have helped to give new momentum to businesses in the area and more companies in recent years have been drawn to Bangor and Caernarfon for the quality of life afforded them by the location. These businesses have workforces who need rented accommodation. On the island at Beaumaris and Rhosneigr there is a demand for quality property for sailors and regular holiday makers.
	The University of North Wales at Bangor enjoys an outstanding location with coastal and mountain views, making it a popular choice for undergraduates with a love of the countryside. The university works extremely hard to provide enough first year accommodation for its annual September intake, and has more than 2,500 places in halls of residence. Demand for good standard accommodation among students is high from their second year on.
	Within twenty miles of the Menai Strait tourism creates a strong demand for rented and mostly seasonal accommodation. Look to the Cambrian Mountains and Snowdon for a year round source of climbers, walkers and cavers always looking for cottages, barns and traditional housing for rental. Beddgelert, Capel Curig and Betws-y-Coed and neighbouring communities enjoy strong rental demand from leisure visitors.
	Also look to the Lleyn Peninsular for holiday lettings in Pwllheli, Abersoch and Porthmadog, and also the village of Barmouth. These and many other coastal sites enjoy strong loyalty from holiday makers. As with any new and particularly rural location you are well advised to holiday in an area several times before making the move to retirement. What you see on a sunny day is no representation of any area in the deep of winter.
	Easily reached by the A55 Expressway running in from the Wirral and Cheshire, approaching Anglesey or any part of Snowdonia from the South or South East of Wales is slow. Even the enhancements to the A5 have not taken away the frustration of following the heavy lorry traffic as its makes it way to Holyhead and then on to Dún Laoghaire by ferry.
Mainline railway station:	2 hour 40 minutes to Liverpool Central
Road access:	Main access A55, then A5 96 miles west of Liverpool 81 miles from M56
Local newspaper:	Holyhead Mail 01492 584321

Estate agents:	Name	Address	Tel	Web
	Mon Properties	The Property Centre 2–4 Market Street Holyhead Isle of Anglesey LL65 1UL	01407 763377	www.property-wales.co.uk/ monproperties
	Burnells	9 Stanley Street Holyhead Isle of Anglesey LL65 1HG	01407 762165	www.northwales-property.co.uk
	Dafydd Hardy	12 Church Street Llangefni Isle of Anglesey LL77 7DU	01248 723322	www.dafydd hardy.co.uk
	Morgan Evans & Co	28–30 Church Street Llangefni Isle of Anglesey LL77 7DU	01248 723303	www.morgan evans.co.uk
Letting agents:	**Name**	**Address**	**Tel**	**Web**
	Williams & Goodwin The Property People	23 Church Street Llangefni Isle of Anglesey LL77 7DU	01248 751000	www.tppuk.com
	Rowan Residential Letting & Property Management	21 William Street Holyhead Isle of Anglesey LL65 1RN	01407 761900	Website currently under development

Area:	**Ashford, Kent**					
Category:	A					
Investor profile:	Pension, Retirement, Downshifter, Business and Cash&Equity					
Population aged 15+:	47,154					

	Actual			National Average		
Percentage Class ABC1:	49%			44%		

Crime:	Violence		Sexual	Burglary		Motor
Per 1000 population:	9		1	5		3

Yield range:	6.2% – 8.5%					

Price ranges:	Low £	Hi £	Low £pw	Hi £pw	Low	Hi
Flats & maisonettes	49,600	74,400	81	110	7.7%	8.5%
Terraced	84,800	127,200	112	151	6.2%	6.9%
Semi-detached	89,600	134,400	120	163	6.3%	7.0%
Detached	144,000	216,000	195	264	6.4%	7.0%

Percentage above the national average:	11%					

	Actual			National Average		
Capital growth last 12 months:	17%			18%		
Capital growth last 4 years:	78%			74%		

Large employers in the area:	Van den Bergh Foods, Letraset, Quest International, Techpro, Coty Manufacturing UK, Stena Line, Computer Crafts and Alliance & Leicester Girobank
Demand for letting:	Good
Average void period:	2 weeks

	Capital Growth (out of 5)	Yield (out of 5)	Total (out of 10)
Our rating:	5	4	9

Summary:	This will be an international address in 10 years' time. The Channel Tunnel Rail Link will really put this place on the map and being only 36 mins to London and 90 mins to Europe – it will be the capital of Kent.
Description:	This town has really seen a dramatic change in the last 100 years. It has grown from a small railway town to now a gateway to the whole of Europe for the south east of England.
	What I expect to see is the location of many medium to large sized European export businesses locating to this area due to the opening of the Channel Tunnel Rail Link which will only increase the population

and hence demand for rental properties. There is a fully functional International Passenger Station at Ashford which can only mean that governmental investment in to the town will be consistent for the next 10 years at least.

The high speed railway link to London will now make Ashford (59 miles from London) a commuter town, being only 36 mins to the city of London. I do not know of any other town being nearly 60 miles away, yet a travelling time of just over half an hour to the city! Residents here will get the best of all worlds – close to the countryside, close to Europe and close to London.

The proximity to Europe would make Ashford an ideal retirement home for those who wish to travel. Knowing that you can be in virtually any part of Europe within the day you travel will make this town a jumping ground for those who are regular travellers but still love being UK residents.

The influx of tourists will also make the demand for hotel accommodation rise. I suspect that quaint, very English B&Bs will be sought from the tourists as Ashford will become the alternative place to visit from our capital city, London.

Due to the Channel Link the roads have seen major improvements. The M20 is completed (and to be honest is very under-used) and the M2 is undergoing a road widening programme. Road travelling times are going to be heavily reduced which will open up the whole of Kent, but especially Ashford.

Mainline railway station:	35 minutes to London Charing Cross 45 minutes to Cannon Street, London
Road access:	Main access M20 54 miles south east of London 2 miles from M20
Local newspaper:	Kentish Express Series 01233 623232

Estate agents:	Name	Address	Tel	Web
	Gould & Harrison	1 Middle Row High Street Ashford Kent TN24 8SQ	01233 646411	www.gould harrison.co.uk
	Hunters Estate Agents	73a High Street Ashford Kent TN24 8SF	01233 643535	www.hunters estates.co.uk
	Connells Estate Agents	77 High Street Ashford Kent TN24 8SF	01233 622206	www.connells. co.uk

Estate agents:	Name	Address	Tel	Web
	Milton Ashbury Ltd	102 Manorfield Ashford Kent TN23 5YP	0800 970 7349	Website currently under development
Letting agents:	**Name**	**Address**	**Tel**	**Web**
	Connells	77 High Street Ashford Kent TN24 8SF	01233 634156	www.connells. co.uk
	Countrywide Residential Lettings	Mann Countrywide 45–47 High St Ashford Kent TN24 8TF	01233 639934	www.mann countrywide. co.uk
	Bradford & Bingley Geering & Colyer	Bank St Ashford Kent TN23 1BP	01233 640200	www.bbg.co.uk
	Calcutt Maclean Standen Lettings	The Granary Bridge St Wye Ashford Kent TN25 5ED	01233 812606	www.calcutt maclean standen.co.uk
	Your Move	55 High St Ashford Kent TN24 8SG	01233 645588	www.your-move.co.uk

Area:	**Bath, Somerset**					
Category:	C					
Investor profile:	Pension, Retirement, Holiday, University, Downshifter and Cash&Equity					
Population aged 15+:	83,782					

	Actual			National Average		
Percentage Class ABC1:	58%			44%		

Crime:	Violence		Sexual	Burglary		Motor
Per 1000 population:	10		1	9		8

Yield range:	2.2% – 4.6%					

Price ranges:	Low £	Hi £	Low £pw	Hi £pw	Low	Hi
Flats & maisonettes	104,800	157,200	91	124	4.1%	4.5%
Terraced	132,000	198,000	117	158	4.1%	4.6%
Semi-detached	153,600	230,400	127	172	3.9%	4.3%
Detached	257,600	386,400	119	161	2.2%	2.4%

Percentage above the national average:	42%					

	Actual			National Average		
Capital growth last 12 months:	18%			18%		
Capital growth last 5 years:	113%			80%		

Large employers in the area:	Mainly tourist related small businesses and local government, i.e. schools, hospitals and councils. few large employers locally.
Demand for letting:	Good
Average void period:	2 weeks

	Capital Growth (out of 5)	Yield (out of 5)	Total (out of 10)
Our rating:	4	2	6

Summary:	One of those pretty cities, that although the property prices are not cheap, represent a safe place to put your money.
Description:	The golden city of Bath has been welcoming visitors for over 2,000 years. Designated by UNESCO as a World Heritage Site, Bath presents some of the finest architectural sights in Europe, such as the Roman Baths & Pump Room, the Royal Crescent, Pulteney Bridge and the Circus. In between 2 Areas of Outstanding Beauty, the Cotswolds and the Mendips, Bath has been the obvious choice for people wishing to take a mini break in the west part of the UK.

	B&B demand is high due to the number of visitors at the weekend as well as during the week from the corporate sector. The University also places a demand on the rental market with the university offering a free service to landlords that match students to properties. Room rates are around £60 per room, so if you can get your hands on a 4+ bedroomed house with 2/3 reception rooms then the returns make sense.
Mainline railway station:	15 minutes to Bristol Temple Meads
Road access:	Main access A4, A46 & M4 13 miles east of Bristol 10 miles from M4
Local newspaper:	Bath Chronicle 01225 322322

Estate agents:	**Name**	**Address**	**Tel**	**Web**
	Andrews Estate Agents	8 Wellsway Bath Avon BA2 4QL	01225 310570	www.andrews online.co.uk
	Smith-Woolley	24 Barton Street Bath Avon BA1 1HL	01225 427000	www.smith-woolley.co.uk
	Pritchard & Partners	11 Quiet Street Bath Avon BA1 2LB	01225 466225	www.pritchard-partners.co.uk
	Allen & Harris	1 Balustrade Bath Avon BA1 6QA	01225 482244	www.sequence home.co.uk
	David Earle-Brown	7 Chapel Road Queen Square Bath Avon BA1 1HN	01225 484484	www.davidearle-brown.co.uk
	Connell Estate Agents	1 Wood Street Queen Square Bath Avon BA1 2JQ	01225 336522	www.connells.co.uk

Letting agents:	**Name**	**Address**	**Tel**	**Web**
	Castle Estates	31 Monmouth St Bath Avon BA1 2AN	01225 337673	www.castle-estates.co.uk

Letting agents:	Name	Address	Tel	Web
	Cluttons	9 Edgar Buildings Bath Avon BA1 2EE	01225 469511	www.cluttons. co.uk
	Andrews Letting & Management	1 Princes Buildings George St Bath Avon BA1 2EY	01225 329909	www.andrews online.co.uk
	Executive Property Services	2 Brock St Bath Avon BA1 2LN	01225 464224	www.epservices. co.uk
	Bath Property Services	17 Charles St Bath Avon BA1 1HX	01225 314055	www.bibs.co.uk
	Bradford & Bingley Alder King	4 Princess Buildings George St Bath Avon BA1 2ED	01225 469882	www.bbg.co.uk

Area:	**Beckenham, Kent**						
Category:	C						
Investor profile:	Pension, Business and Cash&Equity						
Population aged 15+:	38,316						
	Actual			**National Average**			
Percentage Class ABC1:	71%			44%			
Crime:	Violence		Sexual	Burglary		Motor	
Per 1000 population:	13		1	6		7	
Yield range:	2.4% – 5.4%						
Price ranges:	Low £	Hi £	Low £pw	Hi £pw	Low		Hi
Flats & maisonettes	116,800	175,200	120	163	4.8%		5.3%
Terraced	160,800	241,200	166	225	4.6%		5.4%
Semi-detached	206,400	309,600	170	230	3.9%		4.3%
Detached	338,400	507,600	175	238	2.4%		2.7%
Percentage above the national average:	60%						
	Actual			**National Average**			
Capital growth last 12 months:	19%			18%			
Capital growth last 5 years:	105%			80%			
Large employers in the area:	Many tourist related small businesses and local government, i.e. schools, hospitals and councils. Few large employers locally.						
Demand for letting:	**Excellent**						
Average void period:	1 week						
Our rating:	**Capital Growth** (out of 5) 4			**Yield** (out of 5) 2		**Total** (out of 10) **6**	
Summary:	Great value and great location – what more do you want?						
Description:	This is only one of two areas I have chosen within the M25 and I've chosen this area because its one of the few areas that represents good value. You can see from the guide prices above that you can purchase a home fit for a family at a reasonable price and still be only 10 miles away from London Bridge.						
	The flats also represent good value to would-be young professional sharers who work in the city looking to rent hence the rapid building and renovating of 2-bed apartments at the top end of the market.						
	As a place to live it has what you would expect of suburban living – a well stocked shopping centre, sports clubs, parks, restaurants etc. and is						

	also only a short distance away from Bluewater, the massive retail park just outside the M25.			
Mainline railway station:	25 minutes to Cannon Street, London			
Road access:	Main access A205 8 miles south east of Central London 11 miles from M25			
Local newspaper:	Bromley Express 020 8269 7000			
Estate agents:	**Name**	**Address**	**Tel**	**Web**
	George Proctor & Partners	90 Elmers End Road Beckenham Kent BR3 4TA	020 8676 0093	www.george-proctor.co.uk
	Charles Eden	1 Kelsey Park Road Beckenham Kent BR3 6LH	020 8663 1964	www.charles eden.co.uk
	Curtis Haines	257 Croydon Road Beckenham Kent BR3 3PS	020 8650 1000	www.curtis haines.co.uk
	Hicklin & Hicklin	233 High Street Beckenham Kent BR3 1BN	020 8650 0011	Website currently under development
	Andrew Kingsley	62 Bromley Road Beckenham Kent BR3 5NP	020 8650 1886	Website currently under development
	Acorn Estate Agents	428 Croydon Beckenham Road Kent BR3 4EP	020 8650 0060	www.acorn.ltd.uk
Letting agents:	**Name**	**Address**	**Tel**	**Web**
	Kinleigh Folkard & Hayward	50 High St Beckenham Kent BR3 1AY	020 8658 8443	www.kfh.co.uk
	Andrews Reeves	114 High St Beckenham Kent BR3 1EB	020 8658 8566	www.andrews reeves.co.uk

Area:	**Bedford, Bedfordshire**					
Category:	B					
Investor profile:	Pension, Retirement, University, Business and Cash&Equity					
Population aged 15+:	85,195					

	Actual			National Average		
Percentage Class ABC1:	55%			44%		

Crime:	Violence		Sexual		Burglary	Motor
Per 1000 population:	11		1		6	6

Yield range:	5.3% – 8.8%					

Price ranges:	Low £	Hi £	Low £pw	Hi £pw	Low	Hi
Flats & maisonettes	48,000	72,000	81	110	7.9%	8.8%
Terraced	77,600	116,400	97	132	5.9%	6.5%
Semi-detached	95,200	142,800	107	146	5.3%	5.8%
Detached	137,600	206,400	191	258	6.5%	7.2%

Percentage above the national average:	0.5%		

	Actual	National Average
Capital growth last 12 months:	17%	18%
Capital growth last 5 years:	91%	80%

Large employers in the area:	Autoglass, Charles Wells, Box-Clever and Unipath
Demand for letting:	Good
Average void period:	2 weeks

	Capital Growth (out of 5)	Yield (out of 5)	Total (out of 10)
Our rating:	3	4	7

Summary:	A good centrally located town with excellent links with the rest of the UK.
Description:	Bedford is a beautiful, buoyant market town and regional centre for shopping, leisure and tourism with a buzzing business community. It is caked with history, being one of the oldest boroughs in England. The main attraction is the attractive River Great Ouse which flows through the heart of the town and is famous for being one of the UK's best river views.
	Bedford is a very popular location for people to come and settle as the quality of life is very high. The town is well planned – with most homes within half a mile from a town park, superb schools with good academic

▶

	results (pupils 10% above national average for 5 GCSE grades A–C) and plenty of activities provided by the council and private companies. If you are looking for a long term investment, which I personally consider property to be, then Bedford is your place as people rarely tend to leave out of choice.
	Bedford is home to a lot of successful national and international players. The reason Bedford is popular with these types of businesses is its mid-England position and great road links connecting them with the national and international markets. Bedford is very close to both the M1 and A1 and 5 international airports – what more do you need? Bedford has a workforce of over 75,500 and this is to rise by 8% by 2011. there have been 5,000 houses recently constructed to cater for this.
	The pedestrianised town centre has all the usual high street shops as well as an open-air market held twice a week in the town centre. There are plenty of small shops and arcades mixed with a large, modern, indoor shopping centre – The Harpur Centre – which attracts over 6 million shoppers a year.
Mainline railway station:	45 minutes to Kings Cross Thameslink
Road access:	Main access A428, A6 & M1 60 miles north of Central London 11 miles from M1
Local newspaper:	Northants Evening Telegraph 01536 506100

Estate agents:	Name	Address	Tel	Web
	Walton Property	103 High Street Bedford Bedfordshire MK40 1NE	01234 272662	www.walton property.net
	Country Properties	1 Church Street Ampthill Bedford Bedfordshire MK45 2PJ	01525 403033	www.homeson view.co.uk
	Martin & Co	60 Bromham Road Bedford Bedfordshire MK40 2QG	01234 300445	www.martinco. com/bedford
	Compass Estate Agents	Compass House 8–16 Bramham Road Bedford Bedforshire MK40 2QA	01234 214234	www.compass propertygroup. co.uk

▶

Estate agents:	Name	Address	Tel	Web
	Porters Estate Agents	78 Bromham Road Bedford Bedfordshire MK40 2QH	01234 270055	www.porters estateagents. co.uk
	Taylor Brightwell	40 Allhallows Bedford Bedfordshire MK40 1LN	01234 326444	www.taylor brightwell. co.uk
Letting agents:	Name	Address	Tel	Web
	Bradford & Bingley Letting Agents Wilson Peacock	29 Market Square Biggleswade Bedfordshire SG18 8AQ	01234 213646	www.bbg.co.uk

Area:	**Billericay, Essex**					
Category:	A					
Investor profile:	Pension, Retirement and Cash&Equity					
Population aged 15+:	31,401					
	Actual			National Average		
Percentage Class ABC1:	69%			44%		
Crime:	Violence		Sexual	Burglary		Motor
Per 1000 population:	8		1	5		9
Yield range:	5.9% – 8.5%					
Price ranges:	Low £	Hi £	Low £pw	Hi £pw	Low	Hi
Flats & maisonettes	96,800	145,200	158	215	7.7%	8.5%
Terraced	120,000	180,000	187	253	7.3%	8.1%
Semi-detached	142,400	213,600	189	256	6.2%	6.9%
Detached	237,600	356,400	297	402	5.9%	6.5%
Percentage above the national average:	57%					
	Actual			National Average		
Capital growth last 12 months:	22%			18%		
Capital growth last 4 years:	73%			74%		
Large employers in the area:	Mainly tourist related small businesses and local government, i.e. schools, hospitals and councils. Few large employers locally.					
Demand for letting:	Good					
Average void period:	2 weeks					
	Capital Growth (out of 5)		Yield (out of 5)		Total (out of 10)	
Our rating:	4		2		6	
Summary:	The next Chigwell!					
Description:	Billericay is a mid Essex town that is booming. It is an affluent area and has continued to grow and develop, with new housing and commercial properties being built. The train station is a direct link to Liverpool St. which makes Billericay a prime commuter town.					
	As you drive through the town there is a multitude of large detached houses all individually designed. There are a number of apartment complexes dotted around this essentially small town all mainly near the station. Billericay was known to have at least two prosperous periods within its colourful history: Tudor and Georgian. These styles are still visible today with historically rich buildings in and around the High Street.					

	There have been more leisure sector businesses locating to the area such as bars, restaurants and gyms rather than commercial industries, because it's really a place to live rather than a place to live and work.
	It's the choice of the middle class family! All the right shops are here and there is also the picturesque Lakemeadows Park which is a large park area for families wishing to spend a day out in greener surroundings. This is my wildcard entry for this book as the prices are not cheap as you can see from above, but if there is any town in Essex that can rival Chigwell for celebrity status then this is the one.

Mainline railway station:	30 minutes to Liverpool Street, London

Road access:	Main access A12 & A127 36 miles north east of Central London 8 miles from M25

Local newspaper:	Brentwood Gazette Mid Essex Recorder 01277 219222

Estate agents:	Name	Address	Tel	Web
	Beresfords	129 High Street Billericay Essex CM12 9AH	01277 632948	www.beresfords group.co.uk
	Quirks Estate Agents	108a High Street Billericay Essex CM12 9BY	01277 626541	www.quirksand partners.co.uk
	Holmes Pearman Estate Agents	148 High Street Billericay Essex CM12 9DF	01277 622466	www.holmes pearman.co.uk

Letting agents:	Name	Address	Tel	Web
	Beresfords Lettings Division	129 High Street Billericay Essex, CM12 9AH	01277 658666	www.beresfords group.co.uk
	Countrywide Residential Lettings	Estate House 108 High St Billericay Essex CM12 9BY	01277 633044	www.right move.co.uk

Area:	**Birmingham City Centre, West Midlands**					
Category:	A					
Investor profile:	Pension, University, Downshifter, Business and Cash&Equity					
Population aged 15+:	738,643					
	Actual			**National Average**		
Percentage Class ABC1:	39%			44%		
Crime:	**Violence**		**Sexual**	**Burglary**		**Motor**
Per 1000 population:	23		1	14		11
Yield range:	6.3% – 12.7%					
Price ranges:	**Low £**	**Hi £**	**Low £pw**	**Hi £pw**	**Low**	**Hi**
Flats & maisonettes	52,000	78,000	75	167	7.5%	11.1%
Terraced	61,000	85,000	110	207	9.3%	12.7%
Semi-detached	69,600	104,400	150	250	11.2%	12.4%
Detached	153,600	230,400	209	282	6.3%	7.0%
Percentage above the national average:	0%					
	Actual			**National Average**		
Capital growth last 12 months:	22%			18%		
Capital growth last 4 years:	71%			74%		
Large employers in the area:	Jaguar, MG Rover, Cadbury Trebor Bassett, Vodafone, Cap Gemini, BPS Teleperformance and Specialist Computer Holdings					
Demand for letting:	**Excellent**					
Average void period:	1 week					
Our rating:	**Capital Growth** (out of 5) 5		**Yield** (out of 5) 4		**Total** (out of 10) 9	
Summary:	The 2nd capital city of England having seen major investment in the past 5 years – it has to be a good choice.					
Description:	Birmingham is a progressive and cosmopolitan city. With its roots in the industrial revolution, it is still the powerhouse of the United Kingdom's manufacturing sector and home to internationally-known companies such as Jaguar, MG Rover and Cadbury Trebor Bassett.					
	Traditional industries remain important to the region's success, but now, through highly effective diversification, the New Birmingham is a major centre for telecommunications, information technology and the development of knowledge-based industries, with companies such as Vodafone, Cap Gemini, BPS Teleperformance and Specialist Computer Holdings.					

▶

Companies from across the globe are recognising the advantages of a base at the heart of the UK. Investment by overseas-owned companies in the city is strong, with over 300 companies choosing Birmingham as their preferred location.

Birmingham is also Britain's number one exhibition, conference and event city – having hosted the G8 Conference of world leaders and the Lions International Convention – and, served by Birmingham International Airport, is increasingly a mecca for business and leisure tourism. Twenty-two million business and leisure tourists visit Birmingham each year.

New Birmingham, home to the biggest financial and professional services community in the United Kingdom outside London, employing over 60,000 people, is, however, more than just a thriving business city. It is a vibrant, multi-cultural society, currently regenerating itself with spectacular redevelopments in Greater Birmingham worth over £11 billion. It is a city where people like to live, work and enthusiastically play. Birmingham is a city with an emphasis on youth – over a third of its population being aged 24 and under. It has a catchment area of over 500,000 people within a 25 minutes drive to the city.

Economic forecasts predict that between 2001 and 2010, economic growth in Birmingham will accelerate to 2.5% per annum. 74% of the City's employment is now in sectors where job numbers are forecast to increase over the next ten years.

The City's three universities – the University of Birmingham, Aston University and The University of Central England – have a total student population of over 56,000, and a graduate population of over 17,000 an increase of 8.7% and 16.9% respectively over the previous year.

Birmingham International Airport is one of the UK's fastest growing airports, handling 7.8 million passengers in 2001, an increase of nearly 3% over the previous year. This is despite the impact on air travel following recent terrorist attacks. The airport is the 2nd largest UK airport outside London, the 3rd largest for charter traffic and the UK's 5th largest overall. The airport's £260 million expansion programme is underway, with the second phase already complete. Facilities will handle a projected 10 million passengers by 2005. Birmingham International Airport has been voted best UK Business Airport 4 times in the past 6 years.

Mainline railway station:	1 hour 45 minutes to London Euston
Road access:	Main access M5, M6 & M40 51 miles south west of Nottingham 5 miles from M6
Local newspaper:	Birmingham Evening Mail 0121 236 3366

Estate agents:	Name	Address	Tel	Web
	Chamberlains Estate Agents	343 High Street Birmingham B17 9QL	0121 427 7442	www.chamberlains.uk.com
	Judith Hitching	57 Hewell Road Birmingham B45 8NL	0121 447 8300	www.judithhitching.co.uk
	Burchell Edwards	148 Church Road Birmingham B25 8UT	0121 783 4494	www.burchelledwards.com
	Englands Estate Agents	146 High Street Birmingham B17 9NP	0121 427 1974	www.englands.uk.com
	Cooke Rudling & Co	Queensway House 57 Livery Street Birmingham B3 1HA	0121 212 1701	www.cookerudling.co.uk
	Andrew Grant Estate Agents	98 Colmore Row Birmingham B3 2AA	0121 230 1000	www.andrew-grant.co.uk
Letting agents:	**Name**	**Address**	**Tel**	**Web**
	Pennycuick Collins	9 The Square 111, Broad St Birmingham West Midlands B15 1AS	0121 665 4150	www.pennycuick.co.uk
	Robert Powell & Co Residential Lettings	40, George Rd Edgbaston Birmingham West Midlands B15 1PL	0121 454 3322	www.robertpowell.co.uk
	Hollier Browne	1880, Pershore Rd Kings Norton Birmingham West Midlands B30 3AS	0121 458 7421	www.hollier-browne.co.uk
	Fishers	20–24, High St Harborne Birmingham West Midlands B17 9NF	0121 428 1000	www.fishers-rental.co.uk

▶

Letting agents:	Name	Address	Tel	Web
	Scriven & Co	821/829 High Street Hagley Road West Quinton Birmingham B32 1AD	0121 422 9920	www.teamprop. co.uk
	Searchers Letting Agency	1043 Stratford Rd Birmingham West Midlands B28 8AS	0121 702 2222	www.searchers homes.co.uk
	Wolfs	Weekin Works 112–116 Park Hill Rd Harborne Birmingham West Midlands B17 9HD	0121 428 3232	www.wolfs.co.uk
	Cottons	361 Hagley Rd Birmingham West Midlands B17 8DL	0121 247 2233	www.cottons. co.uk
	Curry & Partners	14, Beeches Walk Sutton Coldfield West Midlands B73 6HN	0121 354 2079	www.curry and partners.com
	Bright Willis	1323, Stratford Rd Birmingham West Midlands B28 9HH	0121 693 6000	www.brightwillis. com

Area:	**Bournemouth, Doreset**					
Category:	C					
Investor profile:	Pension, Retirement, Downshifter, Holiday, University and Cash&Equity					
Population aged 15+:	151,581					
	Actual			National Average		
Percentage Class ABC1:	57%			44%		
Crime:	Violence		Sexual	Burglary		Motor
Per 1000 population:	11		1	8		6
Yield range:	3.4% – 5.6%					
Price ranges:	Low £	Hi £	Low £pw	Hi £pw	Low	Hi
Flats & maisonettes	124,800	187,200	91	124	3.4%	3.8%
Terraced	118,400	177,600	127	172	5.0%	5.6%
Semi-detached	143,200	214,800	142	193	4.7%	5.2%
Detached	235,200	352,800	219	296	4.4%	4.8%
Percentage above the national average:	7%					
	Actual			National Average		
Capital growth last 12 months:	28%			18%		
Capital growth last 5 years:	112%			80%		
Large employers in the area:	Siemens, Unisys, The Royal Bournemouth & Christchurch Hospitals NHS Trust, American Express					
Demand for letting:	Excellent					
Average void period:	1 week					
	Capital Growth (out of 5)		Yield (out of 5)		Total (out of 10)	
Our rating:	3		3		6	
Summary:	An all-year-round resort that has everything.					
Description:	Bournemouth is a beautiful place. It is a hit with the 18–35 trendy surf dudes as well as families. I rank this alongside Brighton for credibility. Due to its strength of image it has attracted enormous investment from smaller businesses such as clubs, bars and restaurants.					
	Large firms have been relocating to Bournemouth and are attracted to the city due to its high proportion of skilled workers (mainly due to the graduates from Bournemouth University staying on) and the quality of life the city provides. I imagine that once tenants are found they will probably stay in the property for a longer period of time than normal assuming the property is maintained to a good standard.					

	Its all year round season appeals a lot to me. The city does not look like one of those ghost cities like Clacton or Margate in the Winter. People are still visiting because of the strong infrastructure of bars, clubs and restaurants and decent water sport facilities. There is the Boscombe Spa Village being created which will focus further on all year round water sports activities and the pier is being offered by the council to private investors to be taken over and redeveloped. The aim is to make the pier an all year round attraction. There is a £55 million redevelopment of the Hampshire Centre which will be a 36 acre retail park, health & fitness centre, food hall and parking centre providing a further 1,500 jobs. Marks & Spencer, Asda, Sainsburys and B&Q being the four corners of the centre. This will only increase demand for good rental properties. Completion date is Autumn 2003. Bournemouth's economy has seen rapid development over the past twenty years. World-class firms have seen the advantages in recent years of relocating to an area which combines a large pool of skilled workers with a high quality of life for their employees. The region's prosperity means that potential demand for properties is high due to businesses in the town having access to a catchment market of around 435,000 people.
Mainline railway station:	1 hour 45 minutes – 2 hours to London Waterloo
Road access:	Main access A338 or A31 (mainly dual carriageway) 33 miles west of Southampton 22 miles from M27
Local newspaper:	Bournemouth Daily Echo 01202 554601

Estate agents:	Name	Address	Tel	Web
	Mossgreen Ltd	11 Westcliff House 45 Westcliff Road Bournemouth Dorset BH4 8AZ	01202 569013	Website currently under development
	Darrell Howlett	10 Trewitham Close Bournemouth Dorset BH7 7JA	01202 480838	Website currently under development
	House & Son	11–14 Lansdowne House Christchurch Road Bournemouth Dorset BH1 3JW	01202 298044	website currently under development

▶

Estate agents:	Name	Address	Tel	Web
	Blake & Blake	707 Wimbourne Road Moordown Bournemouth Dorset BH9 2AU	01202 512621	www.teamprop.co.uk
	Bradley & Vranch	297 Charminster Road Bournemouth Dorset BH8 9QP	01202 548548	www.fish4 homes.co.uk
	Solent Estates	174 Tuckton Road Southbourne Bournemouth Dorset BH6 3JX	01202 418294	www.solent estates.co.uk
	Andrew Snape & Co	3–5 Firvale Road Bournemouth Dorset BH1 2JA	01202 296441	www.andrew-shape.co.uk
	Clatworthy & Bailey	11 Dean Park Road Bournemouth Dorset BH1 1HU	01202 316116	Website currently under development
	Nigel LeGrand	723 Christchurch Road Bournemouth Dorset BH7 6AQ	01202 300200	www.teamprop.co.uk
	Whitehouse Estate Agents	47 Poole Road Westbourne Bournemouth Dorset BH4 9BA	01202 751333	www.white house-estates.co.uk
	Churchfield Estate Agents	122 Charminster Road Bournemouth Dorset BH8 8UT	01202 779911	www.church field-uk.com
	Fox & Sons	119–121 Old Christchurch Road Bournemouth Dorset BH1 1LU	01202 554242	www.sequence home.co.uk
	Simpsons Estate Agents	85 Castle Lane West Bournemouth Dorset BH9 3LH	01202 532556	Website currently under development
	Martin & Co	182 Hinton Road Bournemouth Dorset BH1 1HU	01202 559966	www.martinco.com

Estate agents:	Name	Address	Tel	Web
	Atkins Estate Agents	272 Wallisdown Road Bournemouth Dorset BH10 4HZ	01202 548844	www.atkins estate agents.co.uk
	Athertons (Bournemouth) Ltd	508 Wimbourne Road Bournemouth Dorset BH9 2EX	01202 512348	No website
	Paul Watts Estate Agents	377–381 Charminster Road Charminster Bournemouth Dorset BH8 9QT	01202 524252	www.paul watts.co.uk
	Blackstone Estate Agents	1004b Wimborne Road Kinson Bournemouth Dorset BH10 7AS	01202 582222	www.blackston-estate-agents.co.uk
	Owens & Porter	328a Wimborne Road Winton Bournemouth Dorset BH9 2HH	01202 522012	Website currently under development
	Gaston Taylor	167 Tuckton Road Bournemouth Dorset BH6 3LA	01202 417741	www.gaston taylorstate agents.co.uk
	Tudor Estate Agents	364 Holdenhurst Road Bournemouth Dorset BH8 8BH	01202 300120	www.tudor-estates.co.uk
	Ellis & Partners	Old Library House 4 Dean Park Crescent Bournemouth Dorset BH1 1LY	01202 551821	Website currently under development
	The Bungalow Centre	163 Tuckton Road Bournemouth Dorset BH6 3LA	01202 432244	www.bungalow centre.co.uk
	Frost & Co	20 Poole Hill Bournemouth Dorset BH2 5PS	01202 31188	Website currently under development

Estate agents:	Name	Address	Tel	Web
	Headstart	672 Wimborne Road Winton Bournemouth Dorset BH9 2EG	01202 241561	www.headstart estateagents. co.uk
	Fahren Estate Agents	170 Old Christchuch Road Bournemouth Dorset BH1 1NU	01202 551022	www.fahren. co.uk

Letting agents:	Name	Address	Tel	Web
	Palmer Snell	21 Castle Lane West Bournemouth Dorest BH9 3LH	01202 424404	www.palmers nell.co.uk
	Fahren Estate Agents	170 Old Christchuch Road Bournemouth Dorest BH1 1NU	01202 551022	www.fahren. co.uk
	Countrywide Property Management	Dickens House 15 West Borough Wimbourne Dorest BH21 1LT	01202 840777	www.right move.co.uk
	Burns Property Management	Hawthorne House 1 Lowther Gardens Bournemouth Dorest BH8 8NF	01202 553335	website currently under development
	Rumsey & Rumsey	116 Poole Rd Westbourne Bournemouth Dorest BH4 9EF	01202 496206	www.bbg.co.uk
	Harker & Bullman	2 Park Lane Wimbourne Dorest BH21 1LD	01202 889088	www.homes 2let.net
	Goadsby & Harding	31 Southbourne Grove Bournemouth Dorest BH6 3QT	01202 544644	www.goadsby. co.uk

Area:	**Brentwood, Essex**					
Category:	A					
Investor profile:	Pension, Retirement and Cash&Equity					
Population aged 15+:	54,448					
	Actual			National Average		
Percentage Class ABC1:	65%			44%		
Crime:	Violence		Sexual	Burglary		Motor
Per 1000 population:	5		1	3		4
Yield range:	4.5% – 8.1%					
Price ranges:	Low £	Hi £	Low £pw	Hi £pw	Low	Hi
Flats & maisonettes	100,000	150,000	155	210	7.3%	8.1%
Terraced	124,800	187,200	166	225	6.3%	7.0%
Semi-detached	189,600	284,400	195	264	4.8%	5.3%
Detached	307,200	460,800	293	396	4.5%	5.0%
Percentage above the national average:	55%					
	Actual			National Average		
Capital growth last 12 months:	19%			18%		
Capital growth last 4 years:	75%			74%		
Large employers in the area:	Ford, BT, Amstrad					
Demand for letting:	Excellent					
Average void period:	1 week					
	Capital Growth (out of 5)		Yield (out of 5)		Total (out of 10)	
Our rating:	5		3		**8**	
Summary:	Superb commuter town with great schools, low unemployment, low crime rates and strong community.					
Description:	I want to live in this town! When I find the right property I will move to this town. It's a place where if you move to it you won't leave. I assume this will be the same for tenants as well as property owners.					
	Well let me tell you why I love this place. It has over 300 shops, boutiques and nice public houses, some of the best academic results in the country, a direct rail link to Liverpool Street station, very low crime rates and the most stunning properties in Brentwood and surrounding villages such as Shenfield and Hutton Mount – all this but only 20 miles down the A12 from London!					

	If you are like me who likes being part of an aspirational community but doesn't like being right in the centre of the hustle and bustle of a major city (like London) then Brentwood or the surrounding villages are perfect. Migration from this town is low – once you move there it's rare if you leave.
	Let me tell you a few facts about Brentwood:
	■ It has a high level of both in and out – commuting, with a net deficit of 8,000 jobs. The total net out-flow is 55% of Brentwood's workers. They commute to London, Basildon & Chelmsford which all have thriving local economies. The net deficit is completely healthy as all Essex towns experience this. However people still commute to Brentwood from areas such as Romford, Ongar & Billericay.
	■ Extremely low levels of unemployment. Brentwood's unemployment is the lowest in Essex bar one. Unemployment figures have dropped year on year to under 2% which equals only about 500 people.
	■ 80% of local jobs are service sector jobs and less than 10% of jobs are manufacturing thus overall pay is high in this area.
	Due to Brentwood's location i.e. being commutable to London and surrounded by greenbelt land I only see Brentwood growing outwards thus boosting the local economy and property prices. I think the quality of tenant will be at the top end due to Brentwood's workforce being white collar workers for the local economy or for London, Basildon or Chelmsford.
	Other areas to look at around Brentwood are:
	Warley Hill This is the area around Brentwood station which contains a large number of offices and has one of the town's largest neighbourhood shopping centres. This is near Clements Park housing estate which has just recently been built. The properties sold in record time when they were built. When properties from Clements Park do come on the market they are usually snapped up.
	Shenfield A very affluent area which also has a mainline station into Liverpool St. It has a small but very up-market shopping centre with a few offices in and around the village.
	Ingatestone Ingatestone is the largest commercial centre outside Brentwood, focused on the High Street with its blend of shops, offices, pubs and restaurants.
	Warley Home to Warley Business Park, the state of the art office development, where most of the large employers are located. Down the road is Ford's Head Office.
Mainline railway station:	35 minutes to Liverpool Street Station, London

Road access:	Main access route A12 30 miles north east of Central London 2 miles from M25			
Local newspaper:	Brentwood Gazette Mid Essex Recorder 01277 219222			
Estate agents:	**Name**	**Address**	**Tel**	**Web**
	Keith Ashton	38 Blackmore Road Kelvedon Hatch Brentwood Essex CM15 0AT	01277 375757	www.keith ashtons.co.uk
	Meacock & Jones	106 Hutton Road Shenfield Brentwood Essex CM15 8NQ	01277 218485	Website currently under development
	Hilbery Chaplin	184 Hutton Road Shenfield Brentwood Essex CM15 8NR	01277 218387	www.hilbery chaplin.co.uk
	Walkers Estate Agents	26 St Thomas Brentwood Essex CM14 4DB	01277 223388	walkersbrent wood@aol.com
Letting agents:	**Name**	**Address**	**Tel**	**Web**
	Ingleton Wood	230 Hutton Rd Shenfield Brentwood Essex CM15 8PA	01277 219775	www.ingleton-wood.co.uk
	Walkers Estate Agents	26 St. Thomas Rd Brentwood Essex CM14 4DB	01277 223388	www.itlhome search.com
	Keith Ashton Estates	24 St. Thomas Rd Brentwood Essex CM14 4DB	01277 202200	www.keith ashton.co.uk
	Hilbery Chaplin Residential	94a High St Ingatestone Essex CM4 0BA	01277 263444	www.hilbery chaplin.co.uk
	Beresfords Lettings	Hayward Chambers 22 St. Thomas Rd Brentwood Essex CM14 4DB	01277 218151	www.beresfords group.co.uk

Area:	**Brighton, Sussex**					
Category:	C					
Investor profile:	Pension, Retirement, Downshifter, Holiday, University and Cash&Equity					
Population aged 15+:	82,486					
	Actual			National Average		
Percentage Class ABC1:	59%			44%		
Crime:	Violence		Sexual	Burglary		Motor
Per 1000 population:	17		1	7		6
Yield range:	5.0% – 10.0%					
Price ranges:	Low £	Hi £	Low £pw	Hi £pw	Low	Hi
Flats & maisonettes	106,400	159,600	204	276	9.0%	10.0%
Terraced	161,600	242,400	174	235	5.0%	5.6%
Semi-detached	176,000	264,000	191	258	5.1%	5.6%
Detached	262,400	393,600	340	460	6.1%	6.7%
Percentage above the national average:	19%					
	Actual			National Average		
Capital growth last 12 months:	19%			18%		
Capital growth last 5 years:	152%			80%		
Large employers in the area:	University of East Sussex					
Demand for letting:	Good					
Average void period:	2 weeks					
	Capital Growth (out of 5)		Yield (out of 5)		Total (out of 10)	
Our rating:	4		3		7	
Summary:	The all-year-round resort that has seen a lot of people and businesses locating to this part of the UK due to the lifestyle that it can offer.					
Description:	The original trendy UK seaside resort. This place has seen itself grow from a typical English seaside town to a home to the movers and shakers of our country. Anyone that is anyone has a flat in Brighton. Prices have soared in the last five years and I suspect that this trend will continue.					
	Brighton has grown to be a major centre for financial services, new media and business. It came first in the Key British Enterprises Survey of top places to do business and it is named the most profitable place to do business in – 85% of the top businesses were in profit in 2002.					

▶

	There are 30,000 students at the local university and they add to the city's youthful appeal. Graduates tend to stay on in Brighton because the lifestyle provided by the city is so magnetic – retention of residents is not a problem in this city! Due to this, Brighton has a highly skilled, well-educated workforce with 18% of the local workforce educated to degree standard or above. Coupling this with the city having lower than average earning compared to the south east has led to large employers locating to Brighton thus keeping the local economy healthy.
	Its road link, A23 off the M25 makes it a convenient day trip for anyone within the M25 being only an hour away from the M25. Brighton has an all-year-round trade and has every shop and market known to mankind. Brighton holds the record for having the most nightclubs and bars in one city – beating even London!
	As a hotspot it is unique as it meets every type of investor. Based on this fact alone makes the city's property prices sustainable as the city appeals to a wide investor audience.

Mainline railway station:	55 minutes to London Bridge Station, London
Road access:	Main access A27 then A23 52 miles south of London 38 miles from M25
Local newspaper:	Brighton Argus 01273 544544

Estate agents:	**Name**	**Address**	**Tel**	**Web**
	Halifax Estate Agents	99 Preston Drove Brighton East Sussex BN1 6LD	01273 558661	www.right move.co.uk
	Eric Marchant	138 Old London Road Brighton East Sussex BN1 8YA	01273 508955	www.marchants-estateagents.co.uk
	Wilkinsons	24 Elm Grove Brighton East Sussex BN2 3DD	01273 626624	www.asserta home.com
	Parsons Son & Basley	32 Queens Road Brighton East Sussex BN1 3YE	01273 26171	Website currently under development
	Carr & Priddle	34 Ship Street Brighton East Sussex BN1 1AD	01273 208010	www.carr priddle.co.uk

Estate agents:	Name	Address	Tel	Web
	Tanat-Jones & Co	49 Norfolk Square Western Road Brighton East Sussex BN1 2PA	01273 207075	www.tanat-jones.com
	Bradford & Bingley Geering & Colyer	20 Gloucester Place Brighton East Sussex BN1 4AA	01273 608746	www.bbg.co.uk
	Uden Estate Agents	88 Dyke Road Seven Dials Brighton East Sussex BN1 3JD	01273 721721	www.uden estateagents. com
	Barrie Alderton	73 Southover Street Brighton East Sussex BN2 2UF	01273 570242	www.barrie alderton.co.uk
	Fox & Sons	117–118 Western Road Brighton East Sussex BN1 2AE	01273 414049	Website currently under development
	Sinclairs Estate Agents	62–64 Warren Road Woodingdean Brighton East Sussex BN2 6BA	01273 278866	Website currently under development
	Michael Joseph Estates	115 Western Road Brighton East Sussex BN1 2AB	01273 748828	Website currently under development
	Raymond Beaumont	9 Kings Parade Ditchling Road Brighton East Sussex BN1 6JT	01273 550881	www.raymond beaumont.co.uk
	Halls Estate Agents	27 New Road Brighton East Sussex BN1 1UG	01273 571955	Website currently under development

Estate agents:	Name	Address	Tel	Web
	Bonetts Estate Agents	89 St Georges Road Brighton East Sussex BN2 1EE	01273 677365	Website currently under development
	Jonathan Rolls	244 Eastern Road Kemp Town Brighton East Sussex BN2 5TA	01273 684997	www.johnathan rolls.com
	Marina Properties Village Square	Brighton Marina Brighton East Sussex BN2 5WA	01273 818 819	www.marina properties brighton.co.uk
	Bidwells	27 Ladies Mile Road Patcham Brighton East Sussex BN1 8QE	01273 553753	Website currently under development
	4 Sale Estate Agents	48 George Street Brighton East Sussex BN2 1RJ	01273 692424	www.4sale home.co.uk
	Graves Son & Pilcher	51 Old Steyne Brighton East Sussex BN1 1HU	01273 321123	www.gsp.uk.com
Letting agents:	**Name**	**Address**	**Tel**	**Web**
	Lampons Lettings	4 St George's Rd Kemp Town Brighton East Sussex BN2 1EB	01273 679679	www.lampons. com
	Leaders Limited	119–120 Western Road Brighton East Sussex BN1 2AD	01273 321721	www.leaders. co.uk
	Your Move	14–15 Queens Rd Brighton East Sussex BN1 3WA	01273 778588	www.your-move.co.uk/ lettings

▶

Letting agents:	Name	Address	Tel	Web
	Parsons Son & Basley	32 Queens Rd Brighton East Sussex BN1 3YE	01273 274000	Website currently under development
	Home Leasing	51 Queens Rd Brighton East Sussex BN1 3XB	01273 323344	www.finda property.com
	Tanat-Jones & Company	49 Norfolk Square Western Road Brighton Wast Sussex BN1 2PA	01273 207207	www.tanat-jones.com
	Spark & Sons	45 Western Rd Hove East Sussex BN3 1JD	01273 220077	www.spark andsons.com

Area:	**Bristol, Somerset**					
Category:	C					
Investor profile:	Cash & Equity investor, University investor, Business investor					
Population aged 15+:	358,348					

	Actual			National Average		
Percentage Class ABC1:	50%			44%		

Crime:	Violence		Sexual	Burglary		Motor
Per 1000 population:	18		1	21		17

Yield range:	7.0% – 12.2%						

Price ranges:	Low £	Hi £	Low £pw	Hi £pw	Low	Hi
Flats & maisonettes	69,600	104,400	163	220	11.0%	12.2%
Terraced	92,000	138,000	170	231	8.7%	9.6%
Semi-detached	100,800	151,200	188	255	8.8%	9.7%
Detached	108,000	162,000	161	218	7.0%	7.8%

Percentage above the national average:	2%		

	Actual	National Average
Capital growth last 12 months:	28%	18%
Capital growth last 5 years:	118%	80%

Large employers in the area:	Bristol City Council, North Bristol NHS Trust, Trust United Bristol Healthcare, Trust University of Bristol, British Telecom, Lloyds TSB, Nat West/Royal Bank of Scotland, Bristol & West Building Society, Somerfield Stores, Royal & Sun Alliance Insurance.
Demand for letting:	Excellent
Average void period:	2 weeks

	Capital Growth (out of 5)	Yield (out of 5)	Total (out of 10)
Our rating:	4	4	8

Summary:	We both love this town and continue to look at both newbuilds and traditional redbrick stock. Busy with professionals on reasonable to high salaries, yet with a strong student community, there is much to tempt the landlord. The area around the harbour has been well done and city centre living is supported by some fabulous shopping, dining, and entertainment facilities. A big pull for companies and professional lets given the facilities of the town without London overheads for premises.
Description:	Tremendously busy city working hard to regenerate the more difficult housing areas while running full ahead to attract upmarket corporate investment to the waterfront areas and the dockside.

▶

	With a working population where more than half consider themselves to be managerial, professional or technical, there are some good salaries in the town and the pull has been towards higher quality housing and a lot of pressure placed on the 'nice' areas of the surrounding spread of housing. In the centre there is a big demand for quality apartments, and good money can be had from the long completion of city living units here.
	Don't be put off by the crime figures here across the various wards, as there will sadly almost always be a higher concentration in certain areas.
	The same is true of the higher yields on housing stock. In terms of the programme for regeneration and redevelopment, the city council has highlighted some ten districts as meriting special attention. The priority neighbourhoods have been identified as Ashley (incorporating St Paul's, St Agnes, and St Werburghs), Barton Hill, Easton, Hartcliffe & Withywood, Hillfields, Knowle West, Lawrence Hill, Lawrence Weston, Lockleaze and Southmead. The work here includes security and safety programmes, housing refurbishment agendas and wellbeing enhancement schemes for residents. While these are ongoing it means that some landlords will be slow into these areas and miss out on currently high yields while the housing stock is underpriced for its future postion.
	The university also has a strong influence on housing sectors here with the student niche being well served but always requiring good rooms or complete houses.
Mainline railway station:	$1\frac{1}{2}$ hours to London Paddington
Road access:	Main access M4, M5 and M32. 120 miles west of Central London. 10 miles from M4, 6 miles from M5
Local newspaper:	Bristol Evening Post 0117 9343000

Estate agents:	Name	Address	Tel	Web
	Andrews Estate Agents	84 Station Road Bristol BS37 4PH	01454 322255	www.andrews online.co.uk
	Harvey James	44 High Street Thornbury Bristol BS35 2AN	01454 411505	www.harvey james.co.uk
	Draton Services	29 Bloomfield Road Bristol BS4 3QA	0845 8500123	Website currently under development
	Sue Brown Estate Agents	28 Station Road Yate Bristol BS37 4PW	01454 858858	www.team prop.co.uk

▶

Estate agents:	Name	Address	Tel	Web
	James B King	2 South Parade Chew Magna Bristol BS40 8SH	01275 333400	www.james bking.co.uk
	Anne James Estate Agents	89a Bath Road Longwell Green Bristol BS30 9DF	0117 932 8611	www.annejames. co.uk
	Oceans Estate Agents	2 Baileys Court Webbs Wood Road Bradley Stoke Bristol BS32 8EJ	0117 931 1133	www.oceans-estates.co.uk
	Kingsley Thomas	3 Whiteladies Gate Clifton Bristol BS8 2PH	0117 946 6767	ww.kingsley thomas.co.uk

Letting agents:	Name	Address	Tel	Web
	Woods Letting & Management	10a Ratcliffe Drive Stoke Gifford Bristol Avon BS34 8UE	01454 614848	www.woods estateagents. co.uk
	Executive Property Services	28 The Mall Bristol Avon BS8 4DS	0117 906 4700	www.ep services.co.uk
	Andrews Letting & Management	80–82 Gloucester Rd Bristol Avon BS40 8SN	0117 946 6566	www.andrews online.co.uk
	Chappell & Matthews	5 South Parade Chew Magna Bristol Avon BS40 8Sh	0117 946 6236	www.chand matt.co.uk
	Hooton & Partners	199a Whiteladies Rd Bristol Avon BS8 2SB	0117 973 3344	www.hootons. co.uk

Area:	**Cambridge, Cambridgeshire**						
Category:	C						
Investor profile::	Pension, Retirement, University, Downshifter and Cash&Equity.						
Population aged 15+:	113,000						
	Actual				National Average		
Percentage Class ABC1:	55%				44%		
Crime:	Violence		Sexual		Burglary		Motor
Per 1000 population:	12		1		11		4
Yield range:	4.6%–6.9%						
Price ranges:	Low £	Hi £	Low £pw	Hi £pw	Low		Hi
Flats & maisonettes	89,600	134,400	119	161	6.2%		6.9%
Terraced	129,600	194,400	145	196	5.2%		5.8%
Semi-detached	137,600	206,400	162	219	5.5%		6.1%
Detached	209,600	314,400	204	276	4.6%		5.1%
Percentage above the national average:	15%						
	Actual				National Average		
Capital growth last 12 months:	6%				18%		
Capital growth last 5 years:	164%				80%		
Large employers in the area:	Microsoft, Domino Printing Sciences, Sindalls, The Universities, Big 4 Accountancy Firms & Cambridge Science Park.						
Demand for letting:	Excellent						
Average void period:	1 week						
	Capital Growth (out of 5)		Yield (out of 5)		Total (out of 10)		
Our rating:	4		2		6		
Summary:	Pretty city with strong tenant demand and good likelihood for capital growth.						
Description:	Cambridge is really like those post cards. Plenty of old historic buildings, tree lined avenues and large Victorian semis & terraces. The city centre has had an influx of all the right shops – Pizza Express, Starbucks, Pret-á-manger – not a charity shop in sight. The student community is quite large, totalling around 20,000 (18%) of the total population and they all seem to travel by bike! As an investment you can always rely on the student market. Cambridge is one of the oldest universities of Great Britain so the inflow of students is consistent. Many private schools have been set up for foreign students wishing to learn English because these schools cash in on the 'Cambridge'						

▶

name. We also shouldn't forget the University of East Anglia, who have limited student accommodation thus further propping up demand from the student sector. Mill Road and all the roads off this street are a favourite with the students. Mill Road is a long road that leads to the city centre via Parkers Piece (cricket pitch sized green where students like to hang out) and is really the only other high street that exists other than Regents Street located in the city centre.

There are plenty of up and coming surrounding villages (4 miles max from city centre) – the ones to look for are Cherry Hinton, Sawston & Trumpington which are all idyllic villages and have strong demand from the young professional sector. One to avoid is Arbury as it is predominantly council housing and will only attract DSS claimant tenants or low paid workers.

The Cambridge Science Park (which has seen a £50m investment by Microsoft alone) is located north of Cambridge's city centre close to the notorious A14. The congestion on the A14 at rush hour to get to the park and city is reflected in both property and rental values due to the single carriageway entrance to Cambridge. Properties north of this park may be difficult to let such as Bar Hill & Swavessey.

Mainline railway station:	50 mins to Liverpool St, London (Fast Train)
Road access:	Access by M11 (majority triple carriage way) 46 miles from outer London, A14 (majority dual carriage way) 80 miles from Birmingham.
Local newspaper:	Cambridge Evening News 01223 434000

Estate agents:	Name	Address	Tel	Web
	Redmayne Arnold & Harris	2 Dukes Court Newmarket Road Cambridge CB5 8DZ	01223 323130	www.rah.co.uk
	The Rooke Wood & Miller Partnership	110 Regent Street Cambridge CB2 1DP	01223 301616	www.rwandm.co.uk
	Cheffins	49–53 Regent Street Cambridge CB2 1AF	01223 358721	www.cheffins.co.uk
	Hockeys	81 Regent Street Cambridge CB2 1AW	01223 356054	www.hockeys.co.uk
	Bidwells	Stonecross Trumpington High Street Cambridge CB2 2SU	01223 841842	www.bidwells.co.uk
	Russell Residential	100–102 Regent Street Cambridge CB2 1DP	01223 358302	www.russellres.co.uk

▶

Estate agents:	Name	Address	Tel	Web
	The Tucker Partnership	48–50 Woolards Lane Great Shelford Cambridge CB2 5LZ	01223 845240	www.tg residential.com
	Pocock & Shaw	170 Mill Road Cambridge CB1 3LP	01223 516171	Website currently under development
	Keystone Associates	Fairmead Annex Moules Lane Hadstock Cambridge CB1 6PD	01223 890049	Website currently under development
	Tylers	94 Regent Street Cambridge CB2 1DP	01223 302600	www.tylers.net
	Bush & Company	169 Mill Road Cambridge CB1 3AN	01223 246262	www.bushandco. co.uk
	Spires International	185 East Road Cambridge CB1 1BG	01223 300903	www.spires.co.uk
	F P D Savills	24 Hills Road Cambridge CB2 1JW	01223 347000	Website currently under development
	Anglia Residential Ltd	Anglia House 102 Cherry Hinton Road Cambridge CB1 7AJ	01223 412000	Website currently under development
Letting agents:	**Name**	**Address**	**Tel**	**Web**
	First Site Property Services Ltd	17 Norfolk St Cambridge CB1 2LD	01223 508020	www.firstsite. co.uk
	Covehome Ltd	Orchard House Tebbutts Rd St Neots Cambridgeshire PE19 1AW	01480 218081	www.cove home.co.uk
	FPD Savills plc	8–10 Upper Kings St Norwich Norfolk NR3 1HB	01223 347 236	www.fpdsavills. co.uk
	Ambassador Property Management	54 Cherry Hinton Road Cambridge CB1 7AA	01223 727277	www. ambassador- properties.co.uk

▶

Letting agents:	Name	Address	Tel	Web
	Spires International	The Tram Shed 185 East Road Cambridge CB1 1BG	01223 300903	www.spires.co.uk
	Vernon Property Management	7 Rookery Place Fenstanton Huntingdon Cambridgeshire PE28 9GB	01480 300992	www.vernon property.co.uk
	Carter Jonas	6–8 Hills Rd Cambridge CB2 1NH	01223 368771	www.carter jonas.co.uk
	Camflats Property Management	Elmhurst 22a Brooklands Avenue Cambridge CB2 2DQ	01223 350800	www.camflats. co.uk
	Pennington Properties	Stukeley House Stukeley Rd Huntington Cambridgeshire PE29 6HQ	01480 459999	www.penprops. co.uk
	Russell Residential	100–102 Regent St Cambridge CB2 1DP	01223 521152	www.russellres. co.uk
	Bidwells	Sheraton House Castle Park Cambridge CB3 0AX	01223 841842	www.bidwells. co.uk
	Redmayne Arnold & Harris	Dukes Court 54–64 Newmarket Rd Cambridge CB5 8DZ	01223 819300	www.rah.co.uk
	Front Door Property Management	Rowe House 4 Emson Close Saffron Walden Essex Cb10 1HL	01799 525136	www.fdpm.co.uk
	Keeley Associates	48a St Marys St Ely Cambridgeshire CB7 4EY	01353 663036	www.keeley associates.co.uk
	Saint Andrews Bureau Limited	20 St Andrew's Street Cambridge CB2 3AX	01223 352170	www.sab.co.uk

Area:	**Canterbury, Kent**					
Category:	C					
Investor profile:	Pension, Retirement, University, Downshifter and Cash&Equity					
Population aged 15+:	37,264					
	Actual			**National Average**		
Percentage Class ABC1:	57%			44%		
Crime:	Violence		Sexual	Burglary		Motor
Per 1000 population:	7		1	4		4
Yield range:	4.6% – 7.4%					
Price ranges:	Low £	Hi £	Low £pw	Hi £pw	Low	Hi
Flats & maisonettes	72,000	108,000	102	138	6.6%	7.4%
Terraced	94,400	141,600	131	178	6.5%	7.2%
Semi-detached	111,200	166,800	146	197	6.1%	6.8%
Detached	178,400	267,600	175	236	4.6%	5.1%
Percentage above the national average:	16%					
	Actual			**National Average**		
Capital growth last 12 months:	19%			18%		
Capital growth last 4 years:	77%			74%		
Large employers in the area:	Mainly tourist related small businesses and local government, i.e. schools, hospitals and councils. Few large employers locally.					
Demand for letting:	Good					
Average void period:	2 weeks					
	Capital Growth (out of 5)		**Yield** (out of 5)		**Total** (out of 10)	
Our rating:	4		3		7	
Summary:	The capital of Kent with a thriving economy and great links to London and the rest of Europe.					
Description:	This area is one of the largest economies in Kent being around 51,000 employees and over 4,800 companies in 2002, which are worth around £1.4billion. It ranks within the most economically competitive of all the local authority districts in the UK. It has a large proportion of its employees in the business services sector such as financial and legal services, which employ around 8,500 people and generate significant wealth in the local economy. Canterbury has a good manufacturing base within all the district's key business parks in Herne Bay and Whitstable, which have surprisingly					

	developed well in the last decade considering the manufacturing recession we are currently facing.		
	The University of Kent is a mile away from the city centre so the students, all 12,000 of them, give the historic city a youthful feel. Its proximity to Dover (Canterbury being the closest city to Dover) makes the city appealing being that Dover is the gateway to the rest of Europe. The M2 which takes you into London is undergoing a major improvement scheme. The M2 is easily accessible from the A2 in Canterbury.		
Mainline railway station:	2 hours to London Victoria		
Road access:	Main access A2 & A28 60 miles east of Central London 8 miles from M2		
Local newspaper:	Kentish Gazette 01227 768181		
Estate agents:	**Name** **Address**	**Tel**	**Web**
	Pearson Gore	75 St Dunstans Street Canterbury Kent CT2 8UB	01227 463709	www.pearson gore.co.uk
	John Bishop & Associates	5 Dover Street Canterbury Kent CT1 3HD	01227 764884	www.john bishop.co.uk
	Priors Estate Agents	92 High Street Bridge Canterbury Kent CT4 5LB	01227 831999	www.colebrooks turrock.co.uk
	Spicer McColl	17a Burgate Canterbury Kent CF1 2HG	01227 454577	Website currently under developmenmt
	Caxtons	1a Castle Street Canterbury Kent CT1 2QF	01227 785288	www.caxtons. com
	G W Finn & Sons	Brooklands Fordwich Canterbury Kent CT2 0BS	01227 710200	www.gwfinn. co.uk
Letting agents:	**Name** **Address**	**Tel**	**Web**
	Caxtons	4 St Margarets St Canterbury Kent CT1 2TP	01227 785288	www.caxtons. com
	Berrys Canterbury	70 Castle St Canterbury Kent CT1 2QD	01227 765268	Website currently under development

▶

Letting agents:	Name	Address	Tel	Web
	Connells	77 Castle St Canterbury Kent CT1 2QD	01227 764720	www.connells. co.uk
	Let Solutions	75 Stour St Canterbury Kent CT1 2NR	01227 456466	www.let solutions.co.uk
	Strutt & Parker	2 St Margarets St Canterbury Kent CT1 2SL	01227 451123	www.strutt andparker.com
	Your Move	3 St Margarets St Canterbury Kent CT1 2AX	01227 453662	www.your- move.co.uk/ lettings
	Countrywide Residential Lettings	St James House 79 Castle St Canterbury Kent CT1 2QD	01227 763393	www.right move.co.uk

Area:	**Cardiff, South Glamorgan**					
Category:	A					
Investor profile:	Pension, Retirement, University, Downshifter and Cash&Equity					
Population aged 15+:	276,801					
	Actual			National Average		
Percentage Class ABC1:	51%			44%		
Crime:	Violence		Sexual	Burglary		Motor
Per 1000 population:	13		1	7		10
Yield range:	4.0% – 8.8%					

Price ranges:	Low £	Hi £	Low £pw	Hi £pw	Low	Hi
Flats & maisonettes	48,000	72,000	81	110	7.9%	8.8%
Terraced	89,600	134,400	99	134	5.2%	5.7%
Semi-detached	111,200	166,800	123	166	5.2%	5.8%
Detached	149,600	224,400	127	172	4.0%	4.4%

Percentage above the national average:	0%	
	Actual	National Average
Capital growth last 12 months:	23%	18%
Capital growth last 5 years:	80%	80%
Large employers in the area:	Mainly tourist related small businesses and local government, i.e. schools, hospitals and councils. Few large employers locally.	
Demand for letting:	Good	
Average void period:	2 weeks	

	Capital Growth (out of 5)	Yield (out of 5)	Total (out of 10)
Our rating:	3	4	7

Summary:	The safest place in Wales to put your money.
Description:	Cardiff is home to the largest university in Wales and came 7th out 106 universities for research. The university is considered as a major engine for economic development for Wales. The Cardiff University Innovation Network has helped at least 250 companies to the skills and resources the university offers. The University's transfer activities, from the success of start-up companies and the licensing of new products, have contributed over £20 million to the economy yearly. Cardiff University is a major player and has close links with business. I predict that property prices will play catch up with the South East of England as Cardiff is making itself into one of the key cities for research and business.

	There are also two key developments occurring in Cardiff at the moment: **St Davids Centre Phase II** – This project will be a key opportunity to improve the environment of the Cardiff City Shopping Centre and the quality of the overall city centre generally. It will also heighten Cardiff's image and place it in the retail shopping league of shopping centres. St Davids Centre Phase 2 is a regeneration plan approved by the council for Cardiff's City Centre in 2005. Phase 2 will increase the retail space by 750,000sq ft and add to the original St Davids Centre. It will be crammed with stores, leisure centres, restaurants and bars. The centre will also include public open spaces and squares and a public covered mall. **Callaghan Square** – An office development grouped around a beautiful landscaped square next to the city centre. It offers high spec offices and unrivalled services. It totals 52,500 sq m (565,110 sq ft) in floor space area and could end up poaching many businesses from surrounding areas. Both these developments will certainly attract people towards the city and hence increase demand for good rental properties.
Mainline railway station:	40 minutes to Bristol Parkway 2 hours to London Paddington
Road access:	Main access M4, A470 & A48(M) 45 miles west of Bristol 6 miles from M4
Local newspaper:	South Wales Echo 02902022 3333

Estate agents:	Name	Address	Tel	Web
	Mansells Estate Agents	3 Heol y Deri Rhiwbina Village Cardiff CF14 6HA	029 2052 1600	www.mansells.net
	Peter Mulcahy	64 Albany Road Cardiff CF2 3RR	029 2049 6452	No website
	Peter Alan	86 Albany Road Cardiff CF24 3RF	029 2046 2246	www.peteralan.co.uk
	Chris John & Partners	95 Pontcanna Street Cardiff CF1 9HS	029 2039 7152	www.chrisjohn.co.uk
	John Williams	18c High Street Llandaff Cardiff CF5 2DZ	029 2055 2666	www.teamprop.co.uk

▶

Estate agents:	Name	Address	Tel	Web
	Michael Jones & Co	70 Whitchurch Road Cardiff CF14 3LX	029 2034 2331	www.michael jonesandco.com

Letting agents:	Name	Address	Tel	Web
	Thomas George	32Churchill Way Cardiff South Glamorgan CF10 2DZ	029 2039 5563	www.thomas george.net
	Chris John & Partners	95 Pontcanna St Cardiff South Glamorgan CF11 9HS	029 2039 7152	www.chrisjohn. co.uk
	Allen & Harris	46 Merthyr Rd Whitchurch Cardiff South Glamorgan CF14 1DJ	029 2022 5660	www.sequence home.co.uk
	R H Seel & Co	The Crown House Wyndham Crescent Canton Cardiff South Glamorgan CF11 9UH	029 2037 0100	www.rhseel.co.uk

Area:	**Cardigan, Dyfed**					
Category:	C					
Investor profile:	Holiday investor, Downshifter investor, Business investor					
Population aged 15+:	18,000					
	Actual			**National Average**		
Percentage Class ABC1:	51%			44%		
Crime:	**Violence**	**Sexual**		**Burglary**	**Motor**	
Per 1000 population:	10	1		1	1	
Yield range:	4.7% – 8.5%					
Price ranges:	**Low £**	**Hi £**	**Low £pw**	**Hi £pw**	**Low**	**Hi**
Flats & maisonettes	42,400	63,600	61	82	6.7%	7.5%
Terraced	49,600	74,400	66	89	7.6%	8.4%
Semi-detached	61,600	92,400	85	115	7.7%	8.5%
Detached	99,200	148,800	99	134	4.7%	5.2%
Percentage above the national average:	0%					
	Actual			**National Average**		
Capital growth last 12 months:	6%			18%		
Capital growth last 4 years:	87%			74%		
Large employers in the area:	Mainly tourist related small businesses and local governent, i.e. schools, hospitals and councils. Few large employers locally.					
Demand for letting:	Good					
Average void period:	6 weeks					
Our rating:	**Capital Growth** (out of 5) 3		**Yield** (out of 5) 3		**Total** (out of 10) 6	
Summary:	Pure lifestyle and downshifting Cardigan offers a good lifestyle as the fortunate ones on a rent roll. Rents are reasonable and the demand for housing strong. Buy prudently and it won't take long to build a good portfolio here or further down the coast in Fishguard.					
Description:	Just over a mile from the sea Cardigan is a lifestyle investment as most landlords who go there for the first time learn to their cost. Some will stay on holiday and fall in love with the place, while others stay because they have fallen in love.					
	A tourist centre and a place of pilgrimage, for hundreds of years it has been the home of kings as evidenced by the many castle sites close by. Globally it is famous for the National Eisteddfod festival that takes					

▶

place each year to grateful audiences and participants. The broad Cardigan Bay contains a large seal population and also plays host to dolphins, attracting yet more seasonal visitors.

With a population of barely 5,000 that swells during the spring and summer seasons Cardigan offers several niche opportunities to landlords as well as investors. The first is the provision of housing to the permanent community with steady rents and equal capital growth. There is a surrounding community of perhaps 30,000 – 40,000 who look to Cardigan for shopping, leisure facilities, market day, etc.

The second is the opportunity to focus on seasonal lets of holiday property that command premium rental incomes. For the best returns on these self-management is the strongest option and hence it is possible to live locally and manage a portfolio of perhaps a dozen or so houses yourself. On the other hand you may prefer to keep your distance in which case there are many good specialist holiday accommodation agencies who can manage the places for you, allowing you to receive the rent rolls while focussing on other interest or activities. The third is to go the Bed & Breakfast route where you make a choice to move here and 'work over the shop' effectively as you do everything yourself, and experience several months at a time of endless guests and work, and then follow this with months of quiet inactivity.

The same distinct routes are available to you in Fishguard some 20 miles to the SouthWest on the far side of the beautiful Pembrokeshire Coast National Park and again in Aberystwyth 30 miles up the coast. The commitment to the location here and to the communities you operate in is crucial if you are going to invest and live locally. If you are not attracted to the incredible landscapes, the coastal walks, and small community or small town living, then look elsewhere for your opportunities and leave these to someone else who really wants to make a go of it.

Mainline railway station:	2 hours 30 minutes to Cardiff Central
Road access:	Main access A487 53 miles north west of Swansea 44 miles from M4
Local newspaper:	Cardigan & Tivyside Advertiser 01239 614343

Estate agents:	**Name**	**Address**	**Tel**	**Web**
	Fred Rees & Son	Castle House 42 St Mary's St Cardigan Dyfed SA43 1HA	01239 612464	www.fredrees.move.to
	Sterling Properties	20 High St Cardigan Dyfed SA43 1JJ	01239 621840	www.sterlingproperties.co.uk

Estate agents:	Name	Address	Tel	Web
	John Francis	Corner House High Street Cardigan Dyfed SA43 1HJ	01239 612080	www.johnfrancis. co.uk
Letting agents:	**Name**	**Address**	**Tel**	**Web**
	Homerent Letting Services	Preben Ferwig Cardigan Dyfed SA43 1PZ	01239 614119	No website
	Huw James Property Management	Graystones Priory St Cardigan Dyfed SA43 1BZ	01239 613775	Website currently under development

Area:	**Chelmsford, Essex**				
Category:	A				
Investor profile:	Pension, University, Business and Cash&Equity				
Population aged 15+:	90,791				
	Actual			**National Average**	
Percentage Class ABC1:	58%			44%	
Crime:	**Violence**	**Sexual**		**Burglary**	**Motor**
Per 1000 population:	6	1		2	3
Yield range:	4.8% – 10.1%				
Price ranges:	**Low £** **Hi £**	**Low £pw**	**Hi £pw**	**Low**	**Hi**
Flats & maisonettes	76,800 115,200	149	202	9.1%	10.1%
Terraced	96,000 144,000	141	190	6.9%	7.6%
Semi-detached	129,600 194,400	155	210	5.6%	6.3%
Detached	183,200 274,800	187	254	4.8%	5.3%
Percentage above the national average:	19%				
	Actual			**National Average**	
Capital growth last 12 months:	21%			18%	
Capital growth last 5 years:	81%			80%	
Large employers in the area:	M&G Group, Britvic Soft Drinks Limited, Marconi Applied Technologies, Alenia Marconi Systems Limited, Global Marine Systems Limited, Geze (UK) Ltd and Ebm Ziehl (UK) Ltd.				
Demand for letting:	**Excellent**				
Average void period:	1 week				
	Capital Growth (out of 5)		**Yield** (out of 5)	**Total** (out of 10)	
Our rating:	3		4	7	
Summary:	A great catchment area that has seen incredible growth in the past 5 years.				
Description:	Let me tell you a startling statistic – 20% of the UK's population live within 1 hour's drive from Chelmsford (I only live 15 mins away!). This makes Chelmsford a hotspot for any business. Historically it has been electronic and service sector companies locating to the town and the town has seen rapid growth in population over the last 5 years. The workforce tends to be of above average skill due to the retention of graduates from Anglia Polytechnic University students. Property prices have seen quite an increase – I remember when Chelmsford properties				

▶

	were cheaper than Harlow in Essex (10 miles closer to London) but now the reverse is true.
	There are lots of pretty new developments such as Springfields and Dukes Village that are about 3 miles from the town which prove attractive to would-be tenants.
Mainline railway station:	35 minutes to Liverpool Street, London
Road access:	Main access A12 41 miles north east of Central London 13 miles from M25
Local newspaper:	Essex Chronicle 01245 262421

Estate agents:	Name	Address	Tel	Web
	Adrians Estate Agents	16 Duke Street Chelmsford Essex CM1 1UP	01245 265303	www.adrians-property.co.uk
	Cooper Hirst	Goldlay House Parkway Chelmsford Essex CM2 2PR	01245 258141	www.cooper hirst.co.uk
	Chelmer Homes Estate Agents	132 Gloucester Avenue Chelmsford Essex CM2 9LG	01245 499188	www.chelmer homes.co.uk
	Peter Anstee & Co	65 New London Road Chelmsford Essex CM2 0ND	01245 260666	www.peter anstee.co.uk
	Owen Lyons Estate Agents	22 Duke Street Chelmsford Essex CM1 1HL	01245 256666	www.owen lyons.co.uk

Letting agents:	Name	Address	Tel	Web
	Cooper Hirst Ltd	Goldlay House 14 Parkway Chelmsford Essex CM2 7PR	01245 258141	www.cooper-hirst.co.uk
	First Choice Residential Lettings	8 Wells St Chelmsford Essex CM1 1HZ	01245 345800	www.first choicelets.co.uk

Letting agents:	Name	Address	Tel	Web
	Beresfords	10 Duke St Chelmsford Essex CM1 1HL	01245 500666	www.beresfords group.co.uk
	Your Move	6 Duke St Chemlsford Essex CM1 1HL	01245 347040	www.your-move.co.uk/ lettings
	Strutt & Parker	Coval Hall Rainsford Rd Chelmsford Essex CM1 2QF	01245 258201	www.strutt andparker.com
	Bradford & Bingley Taylor & Co	17 Duke St Chelmsford Essex CM1 1HP	01245 345454	www.bbg.co.uk

Area:	**Cleethorpes, South Humberside**				
Category:	B				
Investor profile:	Pension, Retirement, Holiday, Downshifter, Business and Cash&Equity				
Population aged 15+:	27,137				
	Actual			National Average	
Percentage Class ABC1:	48%			44%	
Crime:	Violence		Sexual	Burglary	Motor
Per 1000 population:	13		1	17	12
Yield range:	6.6% – 10.9%				

Price ranges:	Low £	Hi £	Low £pw	Hi £pw	Low	Hi
Flats & maisonettes	26,400	39,600	55	74	9.7%	10.8%
Terraced	34,400	51,600	72	97	9.8%	10.9%
Semi-detached	60,000	90,000	85	115	6.6%	7.4%
Detached	84,800	127,200	127	172	7.0%	7.8%

Percentage above the national average:	0%	
	Actual	National Average
Capital growth last 12 months:	9%	18%
Capital growth last 5 years:	33%	80%
Large employers in the area:	Frigoscandia, Christian Salvesen, large industrial areas locally at Immingham and Scunthorpe	
Demand for letting:	OK	
Average void period:	3 weeks	

	Capital Growth (out of 5)	Yield (out of 5)	Total (out of 10)
Our rating:	1	5	6

Summary:	A high yielding area, but riskier due to likely tenant demand.
Description:	All the elements you want from a historic seaside town are still alive in Cleethorpes. Three miles of beautiful sand-filled beaches, loads of traditional events and attractions and characterful accommodation. The area is next to the peaceful Lincolnshire Wolds – making Cleethorpes a great place to live, work and invest!
	If you are looking for that traditional weekend break then Cleethorpes is the popular choice. The tourism trade and its proximity to Grimsby keeps the rents high in this area hence such good yields. It's the choice of the middle class if you work in North East Lincolnshire. Cleethorpes continues to grow as a seaside resort due to the historic railway attraction dating back to 1845.

	The area is well connected. It is less than three hours to London by rail and is only a four minutes' drive to Humberside Airport. The Humber Bridge can get you to the ferry port in Hull in less than an hour and is a gateway to the area.			
Mainline railway station:	2 hours to York			
Road access:	Main access A16 & A46 36 miles north east of Lincoln 21 miles from M180			
Local newspaper:	Grimsby Evening Telegraph 01472 360360			
Estate agents:	**Name**	**Address**	**Tel**	**Web**
	David Parkinson Estate Agents	55 Grimsby Road Cleethorpes South Humberside DN35 7AF	01472 351203	No website
	Bacons	71–73 St Peters Avenue Cleethorpes South Humberside DN35 8HJ	01472 351126	www.bacons.co.uk
	Argyle Estate Agents	31 Sea View Street Cleethorpes South Humberside DN35 8EU	01472 603929	www.argyleestateagents.co.uk
	Bettles, Miles & Holland	15 Sea View Street Cleethorpes South Humberside DN35 8EU	01472 698698	www.bmhestateagents.com
Letting agents:	**Name**	**Address**	**Tel**	**Web**
	Humberstone & Partners	6 Short Street Cleethorpes South Humbershire DN35 8LZ	01472 570293	www.humberstoneproperties.com

Area:	**Colchester, Essex**				
Category:	A				
Investor profile:	Pension, Retirement, University, Downshifter, Business and Cash&Equity				
Population aged 15+:	82,121				
	Actual			**National Average**	
Percentage Class ABC1:	53%			44%	
Crime:	**Violence**	**Sexual**		**Burglary**	**Motor**
Per 1000 population:	10	1		3	3
Yield range:	4.8% – 8.6%				
Price ranges:	**Low £** **Hi £**	**Low £pw** **Hi £pw**		**Low**	**Hi**
Flats & maisonettes	51,200 76,800	85 115		7.8%	8.6%
Terraced	77,600 116,400	102 139		6.2%	6.8%
Semi-detached	93,600 140,400	131 178		6.6%	7.3%
Detached	156,000 234,000	161 218		4.8%	5.4%
Percentage above the national average:	4%				
	Actual			**National Average**	
Capital growth last 12 months:	25%			18%	
Capital growth last 4 years:	79%			74%	
Large employers in the area:	Linklater Alliance, NatWest, Allied Dunbar and AXA Direct				
Demand for letting:	Good				
Average void period:	2 weeks				
Our rating:	**Capital Growth** (out of 5) 4	**Yield** (out of 5) 4		**Total** (out of 10) **8**	
Summary:	Still providing great value properties in what is essentially a commuter town to Chelmsford and London.				
Description:	The historic town of Colchester is going to see a lot of inward investment from the government and privately, via the university, by establishing a Research Park on its Wivenhoe Park Campus. When complete it will provide a direct link between the existing University Campus buildings and the town of Colchester. Its flexible accommodation and infrastructure will suit new and growing, UK and international, knowledge and technology-based businesses that are developing and trading in innovative products and services. This will bring Colchester close behind Oxford and Cambridge for their fame in research.				

	There are around 7,000 students that attend the University of Essex and it is regularly ranked as one of the top twelve universities for research. With the arrival of the Research Park, migration of students could be low with many students staying on and building a career.
	The Colchester Business Park has successfully attracted the right mix of financial services and high tech sectors to make Colchester be seen as a premier location within the east of England. Due to this the Park is still growing, as demand exceeds supply. I predict that the working population will rise by 5% by the year 2010 and hence, growth in capital looks strong.
	With the rise of Chelmsford, Colchester is the choice of young families who want to a better quality of life because they can get a larger property with a decent garden. With salary levels within these areas being higher than average, property prices will always be sustainable in the long term.
Mainline railway station:	55 minutes to Liverpool Street, London
Road access:	Main access A12 65 miles north east of Central London 35 miles from M25
Local newspaper:	Colchester Evening Gazette 01206 506000

Estate agents:	Name	Address	Tel	Web
	Fenn Wright	146 High Street Colchester Essex CO1 1PW	01206 763388	www.fenwright. co.uk
	Gallant Richardson	5 Culver Street West Colchester Essex CO1 1JG	01206 768555	www.homesales. co.uk
	Bairstow Eves	Headgate Corner 6–10 Headgate Colchester Essex CO3 3BY	01206 768336	Website currently under development
	Desmond G Boyden	57–59 Crouch Street Colchester Essex CO3 3EY	01206 762767	Website currently under development

Estate agents:	Name	Address	Tel	Web
	Grier & Partners	The Old Shop The Street East Bergholt Colchester Essex CO7 6TF	01206 299222	Website currently under development

Letting agents:	Name	Address	Tel	Web
	William H Brown	42 St. Christopher Rd St. Johns Colchester Essex CO4 0NA	01206 765177	www.sequence home.co.uk
	Boydens	Aston House 57–59, Crouch St Colchester Essex CO3 3EY	01206 762276	www.boydens. co.uk
	Gallant Richardson	5 Culver St West Colchester Essex CO1 1JG	01206 768555	www.home- sale.co.uk
	Essex & Suffolk Lettings	The Coach House Headgate Colchester Essex CO3 3BT	01206 571111	www.essexand suffolk.co.uk

Area:	**Darlington, County Durham**					
Category:	A					
Investor profile:	Cash&Equity Investor, Business Investor					
Population aged 15+:	71,931					
	Actual			**National Average**		
Percentage Class ABC1:	44%			44%		
Crime:	Violence	Sexual		Burglary		Motor
Per 1000 population:	10	1		10		5
Yield range:	5.8% − 13.7%					
Price ranges:	Low £	Hi £	Low £pw	Hi £pw	Low	Hi
Flats & maisonettes	33,600	50,400	82	111	11.5%	12.7%
Terraced	31,200	46,800	82	111	12.3%	13.7%
Semi-detached	48,000	72,000	95	128	9.2%	10.3%
Detached	84,000	126,000	104	141	5.8%	6.4%
Percentage above the national average:	0%					
	Actual			**National Average**		
Capital growth last 12 months:	11%			18%		
Capital growth last 5 years:	30%			80%		
Large employers in the area:	Mainly tourist related small businesses and local government, i.e. schools, hospitals and councils. Few large employers locally.					
Demand for letting:	Good					
Average void period:	3 weeks					
Our rating:	**Capital Growth** (out of 5) 2		**Yield** (out of 5) 5		**Total** (out of 10) 7	
Summary:	Good yields supported by continuing redevelopment and new building. As the town becomes more attractive the demand for jobs and tenants fuels the rental market. Stick with the well maintained in neighbourhoods of the same. Great countryside on the doorstep.					
Description:	A well developed and attractive market town, that successfully blends medieval streets and modern shopping facilities, Darlington offers much to investors. The Council has created a strong local economy by placing the focus on sustainable employment. Initiatives for regeneration, employment and inward investment have stimulated development and helped to boost property values across the town. One big commercial success has been the growth of Morton Palms Business Park on a 28 acre site and potential for the creation of 1000 jobs.					

▶

Residential housing in Eastbourne and Deans offers traditional and good quality properties for cash flow landlords, whereas modern estates such as Ashbrook and Elmcroft off the Brinkburn Road provide modern housing with less maintenance and the potential for continued capital growth.

Good education facilities are one aspect of the attraction of a community to incoming tenants and the schools around Darlington have helped the inflow of people. Educational improvement rates that are faster than the national average have helped secure a place as the region's highest placed education authority in the Government's league tables.

Of particular strength are the Queen Elizabeth Sixth Form College and the College of Technology. The close proximity of the Universities of Teesside and Durham at the Stockton-on-Tees Campus, provides further opportunity for the student landlord.

Quick access to open countryside including the Pennines, the Cleveland Hills and the North York Moors National Park can provide attractions for a landlord looking to retire to the area, as well as yielding opportunities for good holiday lets across the year. Hurworth, Middleton St George, and the Staintons like many other local villages offer steady rentals.

Transportation
With a good road connection via the A66 to Stockton and Middlesbrough, as well as the A1M for easy access North or South, Darlington is well located for any business seeking a skilled workforce as well as good distribution routes. Teesside Airport is just 15 minutes away and serves as a great regional airport.

Mainline railway station:	30 minutes to Newcastle
Road access:	Main access A1(M), then A66(M) 35 miles south of Newcastle-upon-Tyne 5 miles to A1(M)
Local newspaper:	The Northern Echo 01325 381313

Estate agents:	Name	Address	Tel	Web
	J W Wood	22 Duke Street Darlington County Durham DL3 7UT	01325 485151	www.jww.co.uk
	Robinson Estate Agents	7 Duke Street Darlington County Durham DL3 7RX	01325 484440	www.robinson estateagents. co.uk

Estate agents:	Name	Address	Tel	Web
	Nick & Gordon Carver Estate Agents	14 Duke St Darlington County Durham DL3 7AA	01325 357807	www.nickcarver. co.uk
	Halifax Estate Agents	3 Deuchars Court Duke St Darlington County Durham DL3 7RU	01325 384633	www.halifax estateagency. co.uk
	Alan Ayers & Co	31 Tubwell Row Darlington County Durham DL1 1NU	01325 460584	www.alanayers. co.uk
	Stuart Edwards	28 Duke St Darlington County Durham DL3 7AQ	01325 355255	www.stuart edwardsestate agents.com
	Ann Cordey Estate Agents	13 Duke St Darlington County Durham DL3 7RX	01325 488433	Website currently under development
Letting agents:	**Name**	**Address**	**Tel**	**Web**
	Keith Pattinson	40 Duke Street Darlington County Durham DL3 7AJ	01325 364246	www.pattinson. co.uk
	Property Management North East	27 Duke St Darlington County Durham DL3 7AA	01325 382302	www.property- management- northeast.co.uk
	Countrywide Residential Lettings	25 Skinnergate Darlington County Durham DL3 7NW	01325 364578	www.right move.co.uk

Area:	**Durham, County Durham**					
Category:	A					
Investor profile:	Cash&Equity Investor, Holiday Investor, University Investor					
Population aged 15+:	38,312					
	Actual			National Average		
Percentage Class ABC1:	57%			44%		
Crime:	Violence		Sexual	Burglary		Motor
Per 1000 population:	11		1	5		4
Yield range:	6.0% − 11.4%					
Price ranges:	Low £	Hi £	Low £pw	Hi £pw	Low	Hi
Flats & maisonettes	63,200	94,800	114	155	8.5%	9.4%
Terraced	59,200	88,800	107	144	8.4%	9.4%
Semi-detached	76,000	114,000	166	225	10.3%	11.4%
Detached	133,600	200,400	172	233	6.0%	6.7%
Percentage above the national average:	0%					
	Actual			National Average		
Capital growth last 12 months:	47%			18%		
Capital growth last 5 years:	71%			80%		
Large employers in the area:	Mainly tourist related small businesses and local government, i.e. schools, hospitals and councils. Few large employers locally.					
Demand for letting:	Excellent					
Average void period:	2 weeks					
Our rating:	Capital Growth (out of 5) 3		Yield (out of 5) 4		Total (out of 10) 7	
Summary:	Fascinating town offering good to great yields. Lots to commend it as a place to focus on student lets, but equally good as a location for holiday lets given the strength of the tourist industry here.					
Description:	Bill Bryson in his book *Notes from a Small Island* wrote passionately of this place: 'I got off at Durham and fell in love with it instantly, in a serious way. Why, it's wonderful − a perfect little city. If you have never been to Durham, go there at once. Take my car. It's wonderful.' Praise indeed! And more of the same from the two of us! A beautiful place to live, work and invest, Durham has a lot of what it takes to be a 'hotspot'. A strong university town − the third oldest in					

▶

England, it also has a thriving business community, and is a major tourist attraction. This allows you to rent to students, businesses and holiday makers. In addition to this there are many who live around Durham and commute out to Newcastle, Washington or Sunderland, choosing to come home to the sense of stability and the historic environment of the town. Other areas for good lets include Chester le Street, Houghton le Spring, Sacriston and Consett.

The spread of the university between Durham and Stockton-on-Tees to the South means that properties in both towns can command decent rents because of high demand. Even though the university can accommodate more than 1,200 students on the Stockton campus there is still big demand for well managed properties from the private landlord.

Designated a World Heritage Site because of the Norman cathedral and the ancient castle, the sense of history in the town is palpable. Housing in the centre is priced accordingly and the more modern stock – with the comparably better yields – will be out of the town. The place attracts a thriving art and theatre community, with great dining, shopping and leisure facilities.

County Durham has a broad variety of landscape. Quiet roads take you to wild countryside, including some of the finest landscapes and scenery in England. Holiday lets can be busy with holidaymakers seeking a base for their cycling, riding, walking and wildlife watching breaks. Specialist agencies focussing on a specific region can get you long seasons here, especially among repeat bookers returning to the area year after year.

Transportation
The A1M or the A167 bring Newcastle within a 30 minute drive of Durham or Sunderland. The rail network serves Durham and the nearest regional airport is just 25 miles away. A steady flow of buses travels between Durham and the Stockton campus along the A177. Sunderland is quickly reached via the A690. From North Shields international ferries travel to Scandinavia, and to Germany and the Netherlands.

Mainline railway station:	20 minutes to Newcastle
Road access:	Main access route A1(M) 18 miles south of Newcastle-upon-Tyne 2 miles to M1
Local newspaper:	The North Durham Advertiser 01325 381313

Estate agents:	Name	Address	Tel	Web
	Robinson, Clough & Kearns	88 Elvet Bridge Durham DH1 3AG	0191 386 2777	www.robinson estateagents. co.uk
	Ashley Smith	67 Duke Street Darlington DL3 7SD	01325 468590	TBC

▶

Estate agents:	Name	Address	Tel	Web
	Bradley Hall	17 Old Elvet Durham DH1 3HL	0191 383 9999	www.bradley hall.co.uk
	Keith Pattinson	25 Claypath Durham DH1 1RH	0191 383 2133	www.pattinson. co.uk
	Reeds Rains Estate Agents	3a Old Elvet Durham DH1 3HL	0191 384 1222	www.reedsrains. co.uk
	Stuart Edwards Estate Agents	1–2 Blue Coat Building Clay Path Durham DH1 1RF	0191 384 8440	www.stuart edwardsestate agents.com
Letting agents:	Name	Address	Tel	Web
	Keith Pattinson	25 Claypath Durham County Durham DH1 1RH	0191 383 2133	www.pattinson. co.uk

Area:	**Edinburgh, Lothian**				
Category:	B				
Investor profile:	Cash&Equity Investor, University Investor, Business Investor				
Population aged 15+:	380,137				
	Actual			**National Average**	
Percentage Class ABC1:	57%			44%	
Crime:	**Violence**	**Sexual**		**Burglary**	**Motor**
Per 1000 population:	5	1		9	7
Yield range:	4.2% – 15.3%				
Price ranges:	**Low £** **Hi £**	**Low £pw**	**Hi £pw**	**Low**	**Hi**
Flats & maisonettes	68,657 171,273	203	274	8.3%	15.3%
Terraced	93,120 116,226	174	235	9.7%	10.5%
Semi-detached	211,410 248,060	200	271	4.9%	5.7%
Detached	248,060 273,314	201	272	4.2%	5.2%
Percentage above the national average:	51%				
	Actual			**National Average**	
Capital growth last 12 months:	21%			18%	
Capital growth last 5 years:	57%			74%	
Large employers in the area:	Lothian Health/NHS Trusts; The City of Edinburgh Council; University of Edinburgh; Bank of Scotland; Standard Life Assurance; The Scottish Office; Royal Bank of Scotland; GEC Marconi Avionics; Post Office/ Royal Mail; Scottish Widows; British Telecom; Lothian Region Transport.				
Demand for letting:	**Excellent**				
Average void period:	2 weeks				
Our rating:	**Capital Growth** (out of 5) 4	**Yield** (out of 5) 3		**Total** (out of 10) 7	
Summary:	Great opportunities in a city of diversity. Student and corporate lets alongside a buoyant tourist trade. Look for units on the edge of the redevelopment zones.				
Description:	Edinburgh is an impressive and energetic city of great contradictions and huge housing needs. Where an average figure for affluent urbanites living in city centres might be around 9% across GB, in Edinburgh this figure is a staggering 39% of the city population. Yet close by the city housing estates provide homes to more than 40,000 families deemed to be on low incomes, representing more than 20% of this urban population				

▶

where a GB average would be around 15%. 45% of households consider themselves to be professional, managerial or technically trained against a Scottish average of 23%. The biggest trend for housing is in urban flats, whether these are the purpose built tenement blocks peculiar to the city or some many thousands of conversions.

We love the energy of central Edinburgh with its fabulous restaurants, all night bars, world class hotels, and the constant bustle along the mile of shops and restaurants. The castle would be a place not to miss, but watch out also for the opportunities for housing and decent yields on the edge of town. There is steady demand for two and three month lets from tourists, but huge requirement among working professionals to find apartments from which they can travel into the centre. Flats in former industrial buildings have taken well as the growing army of professional workers within the banking, insurance and accountancy ventures seems to grow ever greater.

For students consider investing in Marchmont where there is always strong demand, but further afield for similar properties at lesser prices in neighbouring communities considered less fashionable. Leith is under-represented given its potential as a hotspot, and time will see it receiving more investors.

Other areas to look at for investment are those where a lot has been happening in line with social housing policy issues and regeneration of the city. These areas will all see strong government or council investment and initiatives for enhancement of the area and or its services. Each of these impacts on people's willingness to live in an area and should affect the likelihood of you renting well. Look at Pennywell for the longterm. Muirhouse has seen new builds by housing associations and the creation of a new public park. In West Pilton more than 200 new homes are being created with 80% of these for affordable rent. Royston and Wardieburn are at the stage where they are doing costing exercises prior to investment taking place. On the Granton Waterfront more than 6,500 homes are to be built, with perhaps 1,000 being for affordable housing needs.

Greater and better access to new opportunities in employment, housing and social services for the communities of North Edinburgh is having an impact on investment opportunities within the town. As areas are developed for the better there will always be scope for private landlords and investors to work alongside this.

Also look to the communities which feed Edinburgh with commuters each day. Many villages within a ten to fifteen mile radius can provide rich opportunities in terms of rental and refurbishment projects. Traffic in and out of the town however can be a daily challenge and anything you can get giving easier access will command you a premium rental. In line with this flats around the Scottish Parliament building or the Conference and Exhibition Centre can do well for you.

If you buy here and are not used to the system remember that your offer on a property is final and binding, so choose wisely and then stick with it. Law firms also sell property and this takes some getting used to if you are new in the Edinburgh market.

Mainline railway station:	50 minutes to Glasgow Queen Street			
Road access:	Main access M74, then M8 47 miles east of Glasgow 10 miles from M8			
Local newspaper:	Edinburgh Evening News 0131 620 8620			
Estate agents:	**Name**	**Address**	**Tel**	**Web**
	Warners	22 St Patrick Square Edinburgh Eh8 9EY	0131 662 4747	www.warnersol.com
	Valente, McCombie & Hunter	10 South Clerk St Edinburgh EH8 9JE	0131 622 2626	www.vmh.co.uk
	Neilsons	2a Picardy Place Edinburgh EH1 3JT	0131 556 5522	www.neilsons.co.uk
	Ballantynes	16 Rodney St Edinburgh EH7 4EA	0131 558 9911	Website currently under development
	Gibson Kerr & Co	46 India St Edinburgh EH3 6HJ	0131 225 7558	Website currently under development
	Rettie & Co	1–3 India St Edinburgh EH3 6HA	0131 220 4160	Website currently under development
	Fisher Wilson	137a George St Edinburgh EH2 4JY	0131 220 3220	Website currently under development
	The Property Shop	24 St Stephens St Edinburgh EH3 5AL	0131 226 1070	www.thepropertyshop-edinburgh.com
	James Gibb	4 Atholl Place Edinburgh EH3 8HT	0131 229 3481	Website currently under development
Letting agents:	**Name**	**Address**	**Tel**	**Web**
	Central Letting Ltd	7 Cumberland St Edinburgh Midlothian EH3 8HT	0131 622 5000	www.centralletting.co.uk
	Ryden Lettings	100 Hanover St Edinburgh Midlothian EH2 1DR	0131 226 2545	www.rydenlettings.co.uk

Letting agents:	Name	Address	Tel	Web
	Braemore Property Management	Brae House 53 Dundas St Edinburgh Midlothian EH3 6RS	0131 624 6666	www.braemore. co.uk
	Dove Davies & Partners	9–11 Atholl Place Edinburgh Midlothian EH3 8HP	0131 228 3999	www.dovedavies. com
	Let It	5 Dundonald St Edinburgh Midlothian EH3 6RX	0131 623 0006	www.let-it.co.uk
	D R M Residential Property Letting	3 Coniston Place Edinburgh Midlothian EH10 6AF	0131 466 4661	www.drm-residential.co.uk
	Countrywide Residential Lettings	3 North West Circus Place Edinburgh EH3 6ST	0131 226 7407	sales@ edinburgh.cwrl. co.uk

Area:	**Epping, Essex**					
Category:	C					
Investor profile:	Pension, Retirement and Cash&Equity					
Population aged 15+:	18,198					
	Actual			**National Average**		
Percentage Class ABC1:	65%			44%		
Crime:	Violence		Sexual	Burglary		Motor
Per 1000 population:	6		1	6		5
Yield range:	4.8% – 8.6%					
Price ranges:	Low £	Hi £	Low £pw	Hi £pw	Low	Hi
Flats & maisonettes	95,200	142,800	157	212	7.7%	8.6%
Terraced	123,200	184,800	187	253	7.1%	7.9%
Semi-detached	184,000	276,000	188	255	4.8%	5.3%
Detached	267,200	400,800	293	396	3.0%	5.3%
Percentage above the national average:	79%					
	Actual			**National Average**		
Capital growth last 12 months:	16%			18%		
Capital growth last 4 years:	84%			74%		
Large employers in the area:	Mainly tourist related small businesses and local government, i.e. schools, hospitals and councils. Few large employers locally.					
Demand for letting:	Excellent					
Average void period:	1 week					
	Capital Growth (out of 5)		**Yield** (out of 5)		**Total** (out of 10)	
Our rating:	5		2		7	
Summary:	Has a tube station and provides great country living thus being very desirable to certain city workers who work in London but desire a calmer home life.					
Description:	Epping, part of the Epping Forest District, is at the north-eastern end of the Central Line for the London Underground, and is the only hotspot I have chosen that is on the tube. Other commuter towns in the Epping Forest District are Chigwell, Buckhurst Hill and Loughton which are all on the Central Line but have all seen astronomical property price increases – Loughton hit the front page of the Daily Express with a 75% increase in prices in 3 months!					

	Epping has seen big increases in prices over the last 2 years, but not as extreme as its other neighbouring commuter areas. Personally, I find Epping more pleasant than the others, as it does not have that London feel. It has a quaint but resourceful high street, enough restaurants, bars & pubs that do not over crowd the area, it's only 4 miles from a major town, Harlow, and it's all set within the picturesque and famous Epping Forest.
	There are many new development apartments that have been built in the last 10 years, mainly around the station, and there are still more being built around the station and spilling on to the high street.
	This part of Essex, Epping Forest is a hit with some of the London football club professional players which can only act as good PR for the area.
Mainline railway station:	30 minutes to Liverpool Street, London
Road access:	Main access M25 & M11 21 miles north east of Central London 2 miles from M11/M25
Local newspaper:	Redbridge & West Essex Guardian 0208 498 3400

Estate agents:	**Name**	**Address**	**Tel**	**Web**
	Bairstow Eves West	48 High Street Epping Essex CM16 4AE	01992 560520	www.rightmove. co.uk
	Millers Estate Agents	65 High Street Epping Essex CM16 4BA	01992 560555	Website currently under development
	Hetheringtons Countrywide	4 Forest Drive Theydon Bois Epping Essex CM16 7EY	01992 815314	www.rightmove. co.uk
	James Sear Estate Agents	311 High Street Epping Essex CM16 4DA	01992 560056	www.jamessear. co.uk
	Nicholsons	3 Station Road Epping Essex CM16 4HA	01992 572551	www.fish4 homes.co.uk

Letting agents:	**Name**	**Address**	**Tel**	**Web**
	McKinley Residential	2 Slade End Theydon Bois Epping Essex CM16 7EP	01992 619999	Website currently under development

Area:	**Exeter, Devon**				
Category:	C				
Investor profile:	Retirement Investor, Holiday Investor, University Investor, Business Investor				
Population aged 15+:	92,544				
	Actual			**National Average**	
Percentage Class ABC1:	52%			44%	
Crime:	**Violence**	**Sexual**		**Burglary**	**Motor**
Per 1000 population:	10	1		7	3
Yield range:	2.4% – 5.3%				

Price ranges:	Low £	Hi £	Low £pw	Hi £pw	Low	Hi
Flats & maisonettes	76,800	115,200	78	105	4.7%	5.3%
Terraced	115,200	172,800	76	103	3.1%	3.4%
Semi-detached	124,000	186,000	97	132	3.7%	4.1%
Detached	199,200	298,800	102	139	2.4%	2.7%

Percentage above the national average:	0%	
	Actual	**National Average**
Capital growth last 12 months:	28%	18%
Capital growth last 4 years:	218%	74%
Large employers in the area:	Bank of England, The Met Office, CIT Publications, DEFRA, the National Federation of Builders and the Devon Health Authority.	
Demand for letting:	Good	
Average void period:	2 weeks	

	Capital Growth (out of 5)	**Yield** (out of 5)	**Total** (out of 10)
Our rating:	3	2	5

Summary:	If you are investing long-term then Exeter can supply the potential for growth of equity. Plenty of accommodation means yields are reasonable without being special. However, this is a very good lifestyle city where regular income will go a long way.
Description:	Centrally located in the SouthWest between Bristol and Truro lies this busy and dynamic university town. Only a few miles in any direction from the countryside of rural Devon, and with the leisure and sporting facilities of a larger city, Exeter has an appeal for various types of tenant and offers much scope for the landlord. Retirees can establish themselves here, along with holidaymakers, students and working households.

The enhancement of communication in recent years has allowed many individuals as well as large organisations to look at the potential for better lifestyle by moving away from the South east of England. Exeter has benefited from this trend and attracted some big names to the local economy and region. Typical of this movement are The Met Office and The Bank of England. Other major employers are CIT Publications, DEFRA, the National Federation of Builders and the Devon Health Authority.

There is a high standard of housing across the city. Of the 40,000 homes around 6,000 are owned and managed by the council. The largest single group of tenants are the students at the university, where an experienced accommodation team at the university deals with private sector landlords as well as with their own stock. More than 4,000 students can be housed within either the self-catering accommodation or the halls of residence owned by the university. This still leaves a huge opportunity for the landlord who provides decent quality property.

For the highly qualified workforce at both administrative and management levels, work is plentiful on the many business parks and city centre office units. This population creates an ever strong demand for rentals as the city council work to create greater technology networks and links for the business community. The excellent leisure and shopping facilities of the town mean that for holiday lets in the surrounding area steady returns can be made from high occupancy of cottages, small houses, village homes available through specialised letting agents. Dartmoor National Park is just a few miles to the SouthWest and the open sea available from the River Exe estuary as you pass Exmouth.

The dualling of many of the local roads has enhanced values in commuter villages within perhaps twenty minutes of the town, and one of the big attractions of Exeter as the 'capital' of the South West is that your tenants can work in a national organisation in the city and only a short drive away be living in a rural location.

Transportation
Easily reached via the M5 motorway Taunton is well served by the rail network. London is less than two hours by train. The town has a good regional airport just three miles from the city.

Mainline railway station:	60–70 minutes to Plymouth
Road access:	Main access M5 42 miles north east of Plymouth 2 miles from M5
Local newspaper:	Exeter Express & Echo 01392 442 211

Estate agents:	Name	Address	Tel	Web
	Turner Locker & Co	Southernhay Lodge 1a Barnfield Crescent Exeter Devon EX1 1QT	01392 201202	www.turner-locker.co.uk
	Force & Sons	18 Sidwell St Exeter Devon EX4 6NR	01392 205040	www.teamprop.co.uk
	Samuels Estate Agents	38 Longbrook St Exeter Devon EX4 6AE	01392 494999	www.samuels-estate-agents.co.uk
	Cooksleys	86 South St Exeter Devon EX1 1EQ	01392 202220	www.teamprop.co.uk
	Rendells	62 South St Exeter Devon EX1 1EE	01392 276404	www.rendells.co.uk
	Redferns Estate Agents	8 Fore St Topsham Exeter Devon EX3 0HF	01392 875126	www.redferns.net
	Fulfords Estate Agents	21 Cowick St Exeter Devon EX4 1AL	01392 411255	www.fulfords.co.uk
Letting agents:	**Name**	**Address**	**Tel**	**Web**
	Stratton Creber	12–13 South St Exeter Devon EX1 1DZ	01392 498336	www.bbg.co.uk
	Strutt & Parker	24 Southernhay West Exeter Devon EX1 1PR	01392 215631	www.struttandparker.com
	Fulfords Estate Agents	21 Cowick St Exeter Devon EX4 1AL	01392 270105	www.fulfords.co.uk

Area:	**Fowey, Cornwall**					
Category:	B					
Investor profile:	Retirement and Holiday Lettings (including all-year-round).					
Population aged 15+:	3,695					
	Actual			National Average		
Percentage Class ABC1:	57%			44%		
Crime:	Violence		Sexual	Burglary		Motor
Per 1000 population:	7		1	4		3
Yield range:	3.5% – 6.6%					
Price ranges:	Low £	Hi £	Low £pw	Hi £pw	Low	Hi
Flats & maisonettes	61,600	92,400	78	105	5.9%	6.6%
Terraced	76,800	115,200	87	118	5.3%	5.9%
Semi-detached	95,200	142,800	92	125	4.6%	5.0%
Detached	150,400	225,600	113	152	3.5%	3.9%
Percentage above the national average:	20%					
	Actual			National Average		
Capital growth last 12 months:	6%			18%		
Capital growth last 4 years:	84%			74%		
Large employers in the area:	Mainly tourist related small businesses and local government, i.e. schools, hospitals and councils. Few large employers locally.					
Demand for letting:	OK					
Average void period:	5 weeks					
	Capital Growth (out of 5)		Yield (out of 5)		Total (out of 10)	
Our rating:	4		3		7	
Summary:	Pure escapism and lifestyle offered by a village that becomes a town each year. Holiday lets may offer the real opportunity given the distance to large employers from here. Keep one for yourself!					
Description:	On the Southern Cornish coast Fowey holds a special place in the hearts of many visitors. With its reputation boosted by the writings of Daphne du Maurier and others, the town has a distinctive identity with its narrow and steep streets and houses hewn of granite. Clever and practical planning rules have allowed it to be largely unharmed by the advances of technology and urban development. Even today you can see why the place was a 14th century naval seaport and later became a favoured anchorage of pirates with the natural protected harbour afforded by the river Fowey.					

There is a primary and a comprehensive school serving the town, as well as a broad range of high quality shops, bars, seafood restaurants and antique shops. There are also several good golf courses within just a few miles and a new leisure centre in the town. Retiring here might be possible but a community outside the town itself would offer a greater consistency of neighbours since Fowey changes its character so much in the summer months. Look to St Austell, Lostwithiel, Looe, Liskeard, Truro and Falmouth if you want a more active town all year round.

From June to September this community of just 4,000 becomes a heaving town with no available accommodation here, or in surrounding villages. August heralds the Royal Regatta and fulltime and weekend sailors all come out from their cover to take part or to observe. Walking in the area is excellent with the 26-mile Saint's Way linking Fowey and Padstow together. Fowey is also an excellent stopping off point for those walking the breathtaking 500-mile South West Way as its follows the coastline from Dorset to North Somerset. The Eden Project and the Lost Gardens of Heligan also attract high visitor numbers to the area and put pressure on rental accommodation throughout the year. Talk to specialist letting agencies for Southern Cornish property and consider whether you want high rents for the holiday season, or good rents all year round aiming at a broader group of visitors.

A factor to consider is that Cornwell is to receive the largest increase of new households for any county over the next twenty years. This is placing upward pressure on prices and also ensuring that good quality rental accommodation can be let quickly and for good terms. The capital growth score here is higher than the % given for the simple reason that few lucky enough to own a house here wish to sell, giving slight distortion to the Land Registry figures.

Transportation
The railway station at Par is just three miles away giving access to Plymouth, Truro and London. Exeter is the nearest regional airport.

Mainline railway station:	55 minutes to Plymouth
Road access:	Main access A390, then 35 miles west of Plymouth 70 miles from M5
Local newspaper:	Cornish Guardian 01208 781338

Estate agents:	Name	Address	Tel	Web
	Fowey River	13 Fore St Fowey Cornwall PL23 1AH	01726 833000	www.foweyriver. co.uk
	May, Whetter & Grose Ltd	Estuary House Fore St Fowey Cornwall PL23 1AH	01726 832299	www.may whetter.co.uk

Letting agents:	Name	Address	Tel	Web
	Residential Property Management	2 Market Hill St Austell Cornwall PL25 5QA	01726 64012	www.rpmletting. co.uk
	Stratton Creber	Estate House 1 Market St St Austell Cornwall PL25 4BB	01726 71500	www.bbg.co.uk
	Lewis & Co Property Management	9–10 Market St St Austell Cornwall PL25 4BB	01726 75944	

Area:	**Frome, Somerset and Avon**					
Category:	A					
Investor profile:	Cash&Equity Investor, Holiday Investor, Downshifter Investor					
Population aged 15+:	23,194					
	Actual			**National Average**		
Percentage Class ABC1:	45%			44%		
Crime:	**Violence**		**Sexual**	**Burglary**		**Motor**
Per 1000 population:	9		1	6		3
Yield range:	5.4% – 10.1%					
Price ranges:	Low £	Hi £	Low £pw	Hi £pw	Low	Hi
Flats & maisonettes	53,600	80,400	81	110	9.2%	10.1%
Terraced	88,800	133,200	87	118	8.7%	9.6%
Semi-detached	92,800	139,200	97	132	7.0%	7.7%
Detached	136,000	204,000	112	151	5.4%	6.0%
Percentage above the national average:	0%					
	Actual			**National Average**		
Capital growth last 12 months:	21%			18%		
Capital growth last 4 years:	122%			74%		
Large employers in the area:	Mainly tourist related small businesses and local government, i.e. schools, hospitals and councils. Few large employers locally.					
Demand for letting:	Good					
Average void period:	3 weeks					
Our rating:	**Capital Growth** (out of 5) 4		**Yield** (out of 5) 4	**Total** (out of 10) **8**		
Summary:	Lively and welcoming market town, with good options for both resident investor and distant landlord. Popular location with tenants. Good leisure and social facilities. Decent yields and excellent capital growth potential.					
Description:	The largest of the Mendip towns, Frome rightly enjoys its reputation for arts and crafts, textiles and antiques. With large numbers of attractive listed buildings, steep streets that wind and bend through the town, and regular market days, this is a town worthy of serious consideration by people seeking a lifestyle location as well as investment for rental. From a personal perspective Frome provides a relaxed environment for family living, and is close to major work centres such as Bristol and Bath.					

| | Recent housing developments have brought new residents and served to attract national retailers to the town without taking away from the many small specialist shops in the historic centre. The appeal of this place to commuters is obvious, giving fast access to the road networks and yet with the open countryside just minutes away. For those seeking a retirement location there is much to commend it. For the portfolio investor looking for continued cashflow and some good capital growth, there are many opportunities here.

Initiatives supported locally for the regeneration of Frome have been well received as have those for Whatley, Holcombe, Mells and Chantry in the more rural area. Several buildings that were previously derelict have seen a new lease of life after development work.

If you love markets, you'll love Frome! Every day of the week has something different. Farmers' Markets, Indoor Markets in the Cheese & Grain Community Centre, the Monday Flea Market, Tuesday Arts & Crafts, Wednesday Antiques & Collectors, Thursday the W.I., etc! |
|---|---|
| **Mainline railway station:** | One hour to Bristol Temple Meads |
| **Road access:** | Main access A37, then A361 or A36
22 miles south east of Bristol
33 miles from M5 |
| **Local newspaper:** | Bath Times 01225 322322 |

Estate agents:	Name	Address	Tel	Web
	Cooper & Tanner	6 The Bridge Frome Somerset BA11 1AR	01373 455060	www.prime location.com
	The House Shop	2 Catherine Hill Frome Somerset BA11 1BY	01373 471061	www.thehouse shop.info
	Rogers & Govier	24 Bath St Frome Somerset BA11 1DJ	01373 454335	www.rogersand govier.net
	Allen & Harris	5 The Bridge Frome Somerset BA11 1AR	01373 462999	www.rightmove. co.uk
	Simon Heal Estate Agents	12 Market Place Frome Somerset BA11 1AB	01373 454454	www.simonheal. com

Estate agents:	Name	Address	Tel	Web
	Taylors Estate Agents	16 North Parade Frome Somerset BA11 1AU	01373 462045	www.rightmove. co.uk
Letting agents:	**Name**	**Address**	**Tel**	**Web**
	Swallows Property Letting Agency	Turnpike House Bridge Street Frome Somerset BA11 1BB	01373 463002	Website currently under development

Area:	**Goole, North Humberside**					
Category:	A					
Investor profile:	Cash&Equity Investor, Business Investor					
Population aged 15+:	19,736					
	Actual			**National Average**		
Percentage Class ABC1:	42%			44%		
Crime:	**Violence**		**Sexual**	**Burglary**		**Motor**
Per 1000 population:	7		1	5		3
Yield range:	3.2% – 8.0%					
Price ranges:	Low £ Hi £		Low £pw	Hi £pw	Low	Hi
Flats & maisonettes	28,800 43,200		39	54	6.5%	7.0%
Terraced	32,000 48,000		49	66	7.2%	8.0%
Semi-detached	53,600 80,400		56	77	5.0%	5.4%
Detached	92,800 139,200		62	85	3.2%	3.5%
Percentage above the national average:	0%					
	Actual			**National Average**		
Capital growth last 12 months:	7%			18%		
Capital growth last 4 years:	26%			74%		
Large employers in the area:	Mainly tourist related small businesses and local government, i.e. schools, hospitals and councils. Few large employers locally.					
Demand for letting:	Good					
Average void period:	3 weeks					
	Capital Growth (out of 5)		**Yield** (out of 5)		**Total** (out of 10)	
Our rating:	2		3		5	
Summary:	Largely ignored by long-term investors, Goole sees decent yields on some tired housing stock, yet is so close to the M62 that you can be there quickly to explore and your tenants can commute to good jobs in Leeds, Doncaster and Sheffield. Good town centre and a strong sense of community.					
Description:	Referred to fondly as the 'Port in Green Fields' or even as Sleepy Hollow, Goole is Britain's most inland port, hugely busy with shipping links directly to mainland Europe and beyond. The main imports handled here are timber, cars and grain that then have to connect with the motorways and the rail network. As a distribution location Goole may be tremendous. As a residential investment spot it also does very well.					

Still a place where you can pick up clean and tidy property for below £35,000 with little or no work to be done to it, Goole rightly deserves the Hotspot label, providing good yields as well as some excellent scope for capital over the longer term. Not surprisingly this yield comes from some very traditional redbrick terraced stock.

Other more recent developments on the edge of town and in villages such as Airmyn, Rawcliffe and Drax have been welcomed and can provide decent yields. Slightly further afield Holmes upon Spalding Moor for village living, Portington, Knedlington, Asselby and Newsholme all provide good potential for reasonable rents and better capital growth. Howden merits a visit given that it shares the same fast access to the motorway for Leeds, Hull and Doncaster commuters.

If you want to make a flying visit then Humberside Airport and Leeds Bradford Airport are both within an hour by car.

The town has attracted plenty of funding for enhancement initiatives, to create new jobs through the attraction of new businesses to the area and the East Riding of Yorkshire offers good benefits to companies relocating to the area. As you look at housing here consider the appeal it will have to a wide variety of potential tenants. While there is much here to let easily at the lower section of the market, there will also be demand for better quality property that may earn you better cashflow, albeit at a slightly lesser margin after your investment has been accounted for.

The renewed town centre and its pedestrianised areas have improved the shopping and leisure opportunities for tenants and the traffic system is much improved as a result.

Mainline railway station:	90 minutes to Leeds
Road access:	Main access A1(M), then M18, then M62 35 miles east of Leeds 1 mile from M62
Local newspaper:	Evening Press 01904 653 051

Estate agents:	Name	Address	Tel	Web
	Reeds Rains Estate Agents	67–69 Pasture Road Goole North Humberside DN14 6BP	01405 761475	www.reedsrains.co.uk
	Clegg & Son	68 Aire St Goole North Humberside DN14 5QE	01405 763140	Website currently under development

Estate agents:	Name	Address	Tel	Web
	Neville E Townend	4 Belgravia Goole North Humberside DN14 5BU	01405 762557	www.neville townend.co.uk
	Halifax Estate Agents	11 Pasture Road Goole North Humberside DN14 6BP	01405 765068	www.halifax estateagency. co.uk
	Screetons	79 Boothferry Road Goole North Humberside DN14 6BB	01405 765265	www.screetons. co.uk
Letting agents:	Name	Address	Tel	Web
	Link Agency	27 Pasture Road Goole North Humberside DN14 6BP	01405 768401	www.linkagency. co.uk
	Surelet	53 Pasture Road Goole North Humberside DN14 6BP	01405 766482	Website currently under development

Area:	**Gosport, Hampshire**					
Category:	A					
Investor profile:	Cash&Equity Investor, Business Investor					
Population aged 15+:	36,028					

	Actual			National Average		
Percentage Class ABC1:	51%			44%		

Crime:	Violence		Sexual	Burglary		Motor
Per 1000 population:	11		1	6		3

Yield range:	3.7% – 9.7%					

Price ranges:	Low £	Hi £	Low £pw	Hi £pw	Low	Hi
Flats & maisonettes	60,800	91,200	108	147	8.4%	9.2%
Terraced	69,600	104,400	130	177	8.8%	9.7%
Semi-detached	84,800	127,200	107	144	5.9%	6.6%
Detached	145,600	218,400	156	211	3.7%	5.6%

Percentage above the national average:	0%					

	Actual			National Average		
Capital growth last 12 months:	37%			18%		
Capital growth last 4 years:	121%			74%		

Large employers in the area:	Mainly tourist related small businesses and local government, i.e. schools, hospitals and councils. Few large employers locally.					
Demand for letting:	Good					
Average void period:	2 weeks					

	Capital Growth (out of 5)	Yield (out of 5)	Total (out of 10)
Our rating:	4	3	7

Summary:	Close to Portsmouth, yet more an extension of Southampton suburbs, given the natural water break between Gosport and 'Pompey'. Traditionally huge naval housing area, but now with lots of good newbuilds including sea view and marina type development. The yields are still on the older red brick stock which needs some exploration to find the ones you want for your portfolio.
Description:	With some potential for higher growth over the next four to five years once the tram system is developed, funded and launched, Gosport has already enjoyed decent returns recently.
	The A37 running from the harbour side up to Fareham carries the bulk of the traffic but the road can be slow and unreliable. The enhancements

▶

	to Portsmouth Harbour and the reclaiming of the former naval dockyard and facilities into private dwellings has seen great demand almost regardless of pricing as people pay to live near the water.
	Former local authority housing can be an exception to the pricing, yet still provides plenty of space for your money and the views from the higher floors of some blocks can be quite spectacular especially if they provide views over the Solent and out to the Isle of Wight.
	Lee on the Solent and Stubbington can also provide decent rent roll returns especially if you can acquire an older property requiring some small modernisations. From here most tenants focus on work in Southampton.
	For the better yields, stay small, with flats and terraced or ex-local authority. For capital growth these can be decent. As the tram link with Portsmouth is built the pricing will climb to match the accessibility of jobs. Currently people have to drive to Southampton or Portsmouth but neither of these journeys is straightforward or predictable. The new South Hampshire Rapid Transport system promises to run from Fareham town centre and along the former railway line down to Forton Field in Gosport. From here the tram will turn into North Cross Street and then to South Street. Here's the best bit – the tram will then enter a new tunnel system and travel under Portsmouth Harbour to emerge on the other side and connect with the mainline rail station! If this deal really does get the go ahead – as seems to be the case – it opens up all sorts of possibilities for living and working in or around Gosport.
Mainline railway station:	Southampton. 1 hour 40 minutes to London Waterloo
Road access:	Main access route M27 17 miles south east of Southampton miles from M27
Local newspaper:	Portsmouth News 023 9266 4488

Estate agents:	Name	Address	Tel	Web
	Dimon Estate Agents	6 Stokesway Stoke Road Gosport Hampshire PO12 1PE	023 9258 7521	www.dimon-estate-agents.co.uk
	Fox Property	10 High Street Gosport Hampshire PO12 1BX	023 9250 3733	www.rightmove.co.uk
	Eckersley White	48 Stoke Road Gosport Hampshire PO12 1HX	023 9251 1515	www.teamprop.co.uk

▶

Estate agents:	Name	Address	Tel	Web
	Saltmarsh Estate Agents	30 High Street Gosport Hampshire PO12 1DF	023 9251 3514	www.saltmarsh. co.uk
	Blakes	126 High Street Gosport Hampshire PO12 1DU	023 9260 2155	www.blakes estateagents. com
	Wyatts	123 High Street Gosport Hampshire PO12 1DU	023 9258 2245	Website currently under development
	Buchanan & Goodwin	46 Stoke Road Gosport Hampshire PO12 1HX	023 9252 4911	www.buchanan and goodwin. co.uk
Letting agents:	Name	Address	Tel	Web
	Leaders Executive Homes	14 North Cross St Gosport Hampshire PO12 1BE	023 9258 5577	www.executive-homes.com
	Beals Independent Letting Agents	119 High St Gosport Hampshire PO12 1DU	023 9258 9933	www.beals.co.uk

Area:	**Grantham, Lincolnshire**				
Category:	B				
Investor profile:	Pension, Retirement, Downshifter, Business and Cash&Equity				
Population aged 15+:	33,179				

	Actual			National Average	
Percentage Class ABC1:	45%			44%	

Crime:	Violence	Sexual	Burglary	Motor
Per 1000 population:	8	1	7	4

Yield range:	4.1% – 12.4%					
Price ranges:	Low £	Hi £	Low £pw	Hi £pw	Low	Hi
Flats & maisonettes	33,600	50,400	80	109	11.2%	12.4%
Terraced	45,600	68,400	85	115	8.7%	9.7%
Semi-detached	63,200	94,800	106	143	7.8%	8.7%
Detached	132,000	198,000	115	156	4.1%	4.5%

Percentage above the national average:	0%	
	Actual	National Average
Capital growth last 12 months:	25%	18%
Capital growth last 5 years:	78%	80%

Large employers in the area:	Park Air Electronics Ltd, Padleys, and Wordsworth Holdings
Demand for letting:	Good
Average void period:	2 weeks

	Capital Growth (out of 5)	Yield (out of 5)	Total (out of 10)
Our rating:	3	4	7

Summary:	A thriving economy that looks to continue with properties still available at good yields.
Description:	Grantham has had long associations with the engineering industry and the manufacturing economy continues to grow and diversify. Recent growth has included firms based on new technology, now capable of producing an increasingly diverse range of end products including food, timber, plastics and textile products. The availability of sites and premises in urban and rural locations has helped local firms to expand and has encouraged new companies to relocate in this part of Lincolnshire. If companies carry on locating to Grantham at the current rate, then property prices can only go up.

	The service sector has also grown rapidly in recent years with increases in sectors such as hotel and catering and financial services. Unemployment is lower than the UK average and is the 2nd lowest for the district.
	Grantham serves the four main towns in the district when it comes to shopping and there have been a number of high quality retail schemes developed, the most recent being a major high quality indoor shopping centre, St Peters Place. The main towns within the district boast major High Street names such as Marks & Spencer, Body Shop, Woolworths and Boots.
Mainline railway station:	30 minutes to Nottingham Central Station
Road access:	Main access routes A1 and A52 29 miles east of Nottingham 30 miles to M1
Local newspaper:	Grantham Journal 01476 562291

Estate agents:	**Name**	**Address**	**Tel**	**Web**
	Halifax Estate Agents	23 Watergate Grantham Lincolnshire NG31 6NS	01476 591414	www.rightmove. co.uk
	Humberts	14 Finkin Street Grantham Lincolnshire NG31 6QZ	01476 576133	www.humberts. co.uk
	Newton & Derry	68 High Street Grantham Lincolnshire NG31 6NR	01476 591900	www.newton derry.co.uk

Letting agents:	**Name**	**Address**	**Tel**	**Web**
	Humberts Hill & Hill	13, Finkin St Grantham Lincolnshire NG31 6QZ	01476 565626	www.hillprop. co.uk
	Knights Property Management	13, Castlegate Grantham Lincolnshire NG31 6SE	01476 401555	www.knights property.com
	Belvoir Property Management	The Old Court House 60a London Rd Grantham Lincolnshire NG31 6HR	01476 584900	www.belvoir group.com

Area:	**Great Yarmouth, Norfolk**					
Category:	B					
Investor profile:	Pension, Retirement, Holiday, Downshifter, Business and Cash&Equity					
Population aged 15+:	45,752					
	Actual			**National Average**		
Percentage Class ABC1:	36%			44%		
Crime:	**Violence**		**Sexual**	**Burglary**		**Motor**
Per 1000 population:	14		1	7		3
Yield range:	6.1% – 12.7%					
Price ranges:	**Low £**	**Hi £**	**Low £pw**	**Hi £pw**	**Low**	**Hi**
Flats & maisonettes	32,000	48,000	78	105	11.4%	12.7%
Terraced	57,600	86,400	87	118	7.1%	7.9%
Semi-detached	72,000	108,000	127	182	8.8%	9.2%
Detached	119,200	178,800	155	210	6.1%	6.8%
Percentage above the national average:	0%					
	Actual			**National Average**		
Capital growth last 12 months:	25%			18%		
Capital growth last 4 years:	71%			74%		
Large employers in the area:	Mainly tourist related small businesses and local government, i.e. schools, hospitals and councils. Few large employers locally.					
Demand for letting:	Excellent					
Average void period:	1 week					
Our rating:	**Capital Growth** (out of 5) 2		**Yield** (out of 5) 5	**Total** (out of 10) 7		
Summary:	An excellent high yielding town but be careful of the off-season periods.					
Description:	Great Yarmouth itself is a medium-sized port and industrial centre as well as a major seaside resort near to coastal and marshland areas that are of national significance for their environmental interest as well as recreation. The tourism industry is worth nearly £400m. 13 million people stayed in the borough overnight and the tourist industry for the area employs 8,000 people full- or part-time. Unemployment levels in the area fluctuate with the seasons and are at their lowest during the summer months. The level of unemployment (claimant count) for the Great Yarmouth Travel to Work Area in October 2002 was 4.8%, when for Great Britain as a whole the average was					

▶

	3.0%. Unemployment is highest in the inner urban areas during the winter months when it reaches about 20%. About 31% of employees in Great Yarmouth work part-time.
	Great Yarmouth has Assisted Area Status and more than £2.84 million of grant aid has been offered to nearly 65 local companies. The port of Great Yarmouth provides the main supply base for the offshore gas industry in the southern North Sea.
	Electronics, food packaging, off-shore related businesses and other service industries provide the major sources of employment in the Great Yarmouth Travel to Work Area. In the rural areas, agriculture now employs about 2% of the total workforce.
Mainline railway station:	2 hours 35 minutes to Liverpool Street, London (change at Norwich)
Road access:	Main access A47 20 miles of Norwich 87 miles from M11
Local newspaper:	Great Yarmouth Mercury 01603 628311

Estate agents:	**Name**	**Address**	**Tel**	**Web**
	Aldreds	116a high St Gorleston Great Yarmouth Norfolk NR31 6RE	01493 664600	www.home-sale.co.uk
	Larkes Estate Agents	Unit 2 17–18 Broad Row Howard Street North Great Yarmouth Norfolk NR30 1HT	01493 330299	www.larkes.co.uk
	Ian Sinclair	3 Hall Quay Great Yarmouth Norfolk NR30 1HX	01493 331144	Website currently under development
	Norfolk Estate Agents	28 King Street Great Yarmouth Norfolk NR30 2NZ	01493 853444	www.norfolkestateagents.com
	Charles Bycroft & Co	14 Regent Street Great Yarmouth Norfolk NR30 1RN	01493 844484	www.charlesbycroft.co.uk

Letting agents:	**Name**	**Address**	**Tel**	**Web**
	Howards Chartered Surveyors	31 Hall Plain Great Yarmouth Norfolk NR30 2QD	01493 331435	www.howards.co.uk

Area:	**Guildford, Surrey**						
Category:	C						
Investor profile:	Pension, Retirement, University and Cash&Equity						
Population aged 15+:	48,135						
	Actual				National Average		
Percentage Class ABC1:	64%				44%		
Crime:	Violence		Sexual		Burglary		Motor
Per 1000 population:	7		1		3		4
Yield range:	5.0% – 8.1%						
Price ranges:	Low £	Hi £	Low £pw	Hi £pw	Low		Hi
Flats & maisonettes	124,800	187,200	195	264	7.3%		8.1%
Terraced	151,200	226,800	170	230	5.3%		5.8%
Semi-detached	196,000	294,000	225	304	5.4%		6.0%
Detached	341,600	512,400	361	488	5.0%		5.5%
Percentage above the national average:	88%						
	Actual				National Average		
Capital growth last 12 months:	17%				18%		
Capital growth last 4 years:	83%				74%		
Large employers in the area:	Avaya, BOC Ltd, Vision Engineering, Kobe Steel and the Smith Group Criterion Software, Bullfrog, Lionhead Studios, Big Blue Box Dogfish Entertainments, Cleansorb, Disperse Technologies plc, ANGLE Technology, DevCo Pharmaceuticals						
Demand for letting:	Good						
Average void period:	2 weeks						
	Capital Growth (out of 5)		Yield (out of 5)			Total (out of 10)	
Our rating:	4		3			7	
Summary:	An affluent town in Surrey that offers scope for good capital growth.						
Description:	With its roots in Anglo-Saxon England, Guildford's history goes all the way back to the 5th Century and this can be clearly seen from the beautiful buildings that adorn the town. It's reasonably close to London yet 70% of the borough lies within the green belt and some parts are officially recognised as Areas of Outstanding Natural Beauty. All this only 40 minutes away from Gatwick and Heathrow. The University of Surrey occupys a prominent place within Guildford and together with the Research Park brings in £450m to the local						

economy every year and the university's hi-tech expertise plays a big role in the national economy. The Park employs around 3,000 people.

In 1997 the town won the British Council of Shopping Centres' Environment Award and came in the top 20 out of 1,100 shopping centres for retail facilities judged by Experian. This makes Guildford number 1 for shopping in the whole of Surrey and in the top 3 in the South East of England.

75% of the town's employees are in the service sector and 95% of businesses employ fewer than 50 employees. This would mean that a large proportion of the town's population would be working for a small company in the services sector thus making the community a tight knit one. Farming is also an essential part of the local economy and there is a market once a month which is now a tourist attraction.

Unemployment is extremely low at 0.7% and average annual income is above average at £23,000 – this has got to be a good town!

Mainline railway station:	40 minutes London Waterloo
Road access:	Main access A3 38 miles south west of Central London 8 miles from M25
Local newspaper:	Surrey Advertiser 01483 508700

Estate agents:	Name	Address	Tel	Web
	Clarke Gammon	45 High Street Guildford Surrey GU1 3ER	01483 880900	www.clarke gammon.co.uk
	Seymours Estate Agents	249 High Street Guildford Surrey GU1 3BJ	01483 457722	www.seymour- estate-agents. co.uk
	Burns & Webber	The Clock House 2 London Road Guildford Surrey GU1 2AF	01483 440800	www.burnsand webber.com
	Curchods	4 London Road Guildford Surrey GU1 2AF	01483 458800	www.churchods. com
	Meldrum Salter Edgley	254 High Street Guildford Surrey GU1 3JG	01483 535533	www.mse property.co.uk

▶

Letting agents:	Name	Address	Tel	Web
	FPD Savills plc	8 Quarry St Guildford Surrey GU1 3UY	01483 796830	www.fpdsavills.co.uk
	Seymours Letting & Management Services	249 Quarry St Guildford Surrey GU1 3BJ	01483 457722	www.seymours-letting.co.uk
	Principal	2 The Mount Guildford Surrey GU2 4HN	01483 455990	www.principal.uk.com
	Hamptons International	8 Chertsey St Guildford Surrey GU1 4HD	01483 577577	www.hamptons.co.uk
	Townends Guildford	5 Epsom Rd Guildford Surrey GU1 3JT	01483 505535	www.townends.co.uk
	Castlekeys	250 High Street Guildord Surrey GU1 3JG	01483 301919	No web site
	Countrywide Residential Lettings	4–8 Epsom Rd Guildford Surrey GU1 3JN	01483 535321	www.rightmove.co.uk

Area:	**Harrogate, North Yorkshire**					
Category:	C					
Investor profile:	Capital Growth, Corporate Lets and Retirement					
Population aged 15+:	60,676					
	Actual			**National Average**		
Percentage Class ABC1:	60%			44%		
Crime:	**Violence**	**Sexual**		**Burglary**		**Motor**
Per 1000 population:	8	1		5		3
Yield range:	3.2% – 7.2%					
Price ranges:	Low £	Hi £	Low £pw	Hi £pw	Low	Hi
Flats & maisonettes	83,200	124,800	92	125	5.2%	5.8%
Terraced	79,200	118,800	110	149	6.5%	7.2%
Semi-detached	106,400	159,600	122	165	5.4%	6.0%
Detached	193,600	290,400	131	178	3.2%	3.5%
Percentage above the national average:	13%					
	Actual			**National Average**		
Capital growth last 12 months:	23%			18%		
Capital growth last 4 years:	72%			74%		
Large employers in the area:	Mainly tourist related small businesses and local government, i.e. schools, hospitals and councils. Few large employers locally.					
Demand for letting:	Good					
Average void period:	2 weeks					
	Capital Growth (out of 5)		**Yield** (out of 5)		**Total** (out of 10)	
Our rating:	5		3		8	
Summary:	Statistics don't tell you everything! Harrogate is always in a league of its own for property demand and rentals can be strong all year round. Stick with normal lets rather than go the way of conference lets, or you will end up with a B & B! Old money town, where your money in bricks and mortar here is perhaps as safe as money ever can be. Still lots of ex-local authority stock that offers best yields.					
Description:	Harrogate is a jewel in the crown of the North, rightly regarded by local people as 'the big park with a town'. Surrounded by acres of public parkland including The Stray and Valley Gardens, the town centre shopping opportunities that you would normally find in a town of 153,000 people. Harrogate banks are reputed to enjoy deposits second only to those of Kensington & Chelsea.					

▶

Strong rental market here to the recently retired and affluent as they spend six months looking for a property in or around the town. Harrogate enjoys several of the best state schools in the country and a very buoyant housing market where sealed bids are frequent. Also, opportunity for corporate rentals to senior executives who have moved to work in the Leeds finance district but choose a more sedate life for their own families. Many of the top-drawer agents have an office in the town, offering both town and country properties to their clientele.

Just 10 miles from central Leeds, 20 miles from the Yorkshire Dales and 15 miles from the ancient walled city of York, Harrogate commands a splendid living or investing opportunity.

Investors here will find good capital appreciation and strong maintenance of value. Tenants can commute to Leeds by various local train stations, or drive to Leeds and York for work. A busy conference and exhibition industry means Harrogate enjoys tremendous numbers of restaurants and wine bars as well as the famous Betty's Tea Rooms owned and operated by Taylors of Harrogate.

In addition to the usual rental requirements, the local RAF Menworth Hill base is occupied by USAF staff with their families paying top notch money for three and four bedroom properties in the surrounding villages of Birstwith, Kettlesing and Hampsthwaite. Also look to Knaresborough, Wetherby and Collingham as good for capital growth, with the first two offering decent yields for Cashflow investors.

There is no college or university requirement for accommodation, but good rentals can be achieved at the mid to upper levels of the market, always underwritten by Harrogate's strong capital appreciation.

Transportation
Good road links with A1, M1, M62 Leeds-Bradford airport expansion plans will boost house prices to the South West of Harrogate. Increasingly more people commuting to Teeside and the North East via the A1 and A19 routes.

Mainline railway station:	35 minutes to Leeds
Road access:	Main access A1, then A59 15 miles north of Leeds 5 miles from A1
Local newspaper:	Yorkshire Evening Post 0113 243 2701

Estate agents:	Name	Address	Tel	Web
	Hunters the Estate Agent	15 Princes Street Harrogate North Yorkshire HG1 1NG	01423 536222	www.hunters net.co.uk

Estate agents:	Name	Address	Tel	Web
	Taylor Ellington	30 High Street St Pateley Bridge Harrogate North Yorkshire HG3 5JU	01423 712461	Website currently under development
	Strutt & Parker	Princes House 13 Princes Square Harrogate North Yorkshire HG1 1LW	01423 561274	www.struttand parker.com
	Beadnall Copley	8 Albert St Harrogate North Yorkshire HG1 1JG	01423 503500	www.beadnall copley.com
	Simon Dunn	4 St Ronans Road Harrogate North Yorkshire HG2 8LE	01423 885758	www.simondunn. co.uk
	Nicholls Tyreman	9 Albert Street Harrogate North Yorkshire HG1 1JX	01423 503076	www.nicholls-tyreman.co.uk
Letting agents:	Name	Address	Tel	Web
	Strutt & Parker	Princes House 13 Princes Square Harrogate North Yorkshire HG1 1LW	01423 561274	www.struttand parker.com
	William H Brown	4 Albert St Harrogate North Yorkshire HG1 1JL	01423 526956	www.sequence home.co.uk
	Carter Jonas	Regent House 13–15 Albert St Harrogate North Yorkshire HG1 1JX	01423 523423	www.carter jonas.co.uk
	Feather Smailes & Scales	8 Raglan St Harrogate North Yorkshire HG1 1LJ	01423 529552	www.fss4 property.co.uk

Area:	**Hull, North Humberside**					
Category:	B					
Investor profile:	Cash&Equity Investor, University Investor, Business Investor					
Population aged 15+:	278,300					
	Actual			**National Average**		
Percentage Class ABC1:	42%			44%		
Crime:	**Violence**	**Sexual**		**Burglary**	**Motor**	
Per 1000 population:	15	1		19	11	
Yield range:	3.5% – 8.1%					
Price ranges:	Low £	Hi £	Low £pw	Hi £pw	Low	Hi
Flats & maisonettes	29,600	66,600	46	63	4.9%	8.1%
Terraced	35,200	52,800	53	72	7.1%	7.8%
Semi-detached	56,000	84,000	60	81	5.0%	5.6%
Detached	88,000	132,000	66	89	3.5%	3.9%
Percentage above the national average:	0%					
	Actual			**National Average**		
Capital growth last 12 months:	17%			18%		
Capital growth last 5 years:	38%			80%		
Large employers in the area:	Sumitomo; Smith & Nephew; BAE, and BP.					
Demand for letting:	Good					
Average void period:	2 weeks					
	Capital Growth (out of 5)		**Yield** (out of 5)		**Total** (out of 10)	
Our rating:	3		3		6	
Summary:	Huge amount of housing stock, much of it already tired and requiring replacement. Apparently good yields can mask other troubles. Look to the more recent builds, or to the more substantial older properties. The further west the better. The harbour and dockside offer some decent capital opportunity as well as strong rents for mid week corporate tenants in this town that is working hard on a renewal plan.					
Description:	A city rich in contrasts and offering great opportunities at several levels on the investment curve. While Hull offers many properties at prices below £30,000 it also has the attractions of the beautiful town of Beverley just to the North, as well as the prosperous neighbourhoods of Kirk Ella and Willerby. The harbour front and the redeveloped quays					

▶

offer quality upmarket lets to the midweek business tenant and second homes to the weekend sailor. Some difficult property around the north east borders of the town require? Just outside the town the countryside opens up to small market towns and rural communities, yet the city centre night life is vibrant and hotels, restaurants and café bars are doing a strong trade.

In business too, the city is building on its strengths and then turning them around. Technology arks have developed on the site of former heavy industry premises. E-commerce and technology businesses are tenanting the many business parks attracted to the town. The deep waters of the Humber river mean that Hull hosts some of the biggest ferries in the world, operating between Scandinavia and Northern Europe and the International Ferry Terminal.

Regeneration with firm financial backing from regional and national government is seeing changes to community projects, social housing stock enhancements, and support for small businesses.

The market towns of Pocklington, Market Weighton, and Driffield all offer scope for small community living and the lifestyle benefits this brings. Rental yields in these towns are reasonable while equity growth here and in the more affluent suburbs of Hull have been strong over the past two years. Villages to the West of Beverley such as Cherry Burton, Bishop Burton and Walkington can provide steady rentals. With easy access to the A63 and M62 Welton, Everthorpe and North Cave are attractive to tenants wanting an easy commute.

High yields on traditional terraced housing are good, where the equity growth is less of an issue. Early phases of the Marina developments have seen strong capital appreciation with subsequent phases likely to experience the same.

Holiday lets can be good given the closeness of the Yorkshire Wolds and also the scope for seaside properties in places along the coast. Look to Withernsea, Patrington, Hornsea and Bridlington for some steady holiday lets.

Transportation
York and Doncaster are both within a one hour drive. The A63 dual carriageway offers fast access West to the 62, M18, and A1M. From here the M1 connects quickly to South Yorkshire and the East Midlands. Train services to Doncaster and Leeds make daily commuting a realistic option.

Mainline railway station:	One hour to Leeds
Road access:	Main access A1, then M62 61 miles east of Leeds 16 miles from M62
Local newspaper:	Hull Daily Mail 01482 327111

Estate agents:	Name	Address	Tel	Web
	Larads	26 Princes Dock St Hull North Humberside HU1 2JX	01482 223300	www.larads.com
	Halifax Estate Agents	Queen Victoria House Alfred Gelder St Hull North Humberside HU1 2AW	01482 228400	www.rightmove.com
	Blue Bell Estate Agents	623 Spring Bank West Hull North Humberside HU3 6LD	01482 333162	Website currently under development
	Mark Stephenson	The Square 1 Kingston Road Willerby Hull North Humberside HU10 6AD	01482 654959	www.mark stephenson.co.uk
	Todds Estate Agents	198 Willberby Rd Hull North Humberside HU5 5JW	01482 562195	www.todds estates.co.uk
	Whitaker & Thompson	366 Holderness Rd Hull North Humberside HU9 3DL	01482 790970	www.whitaker thompson.co.uk
	Larards	518 Holderness Rd Hull North Humberside HU9 3DT	01482 787555	www.larads.co.uk
	Quick & Clarke	The Square Willerby Hull North Humberside HU10 7UA	01482 651155	www.quickclarke.co.uk

▶

Letting agents:	Name	Address	Tel	Web
	Specialist Lettings & Management	61 Market Place Lowgate Hull East Yorkshire HU1 1RQ	01482 328068	ww.speclets. co.uk
	J K T Property Management	5 Church Rd Warne Hull North Humberside HU7 5XJ	01482 822230	Website currently under development
	Belvoir Lettings	227 Hull Rd Analby Common Hull North Humberside HU4 7RY	01482 501644	Website currently under development
	Accommodation Centre	70 Spring Bank Hull North Humberside HU3 1AB	01482 326742	Website currently under development
	Maltings Property Management	32 Beverley Rd Hull North Humberside HU3 1YE	01482 580608	Website currently under development
	Davis Graham Partnership	939 Spring Bank West Hull North Humberside HU5 5BE	01482 569912	Website currently under development

Area:	**Ipswich, Suffolk**					
Category:	A					
Investor profile:	Pension, Retirement, University, Business and Cash&Equity					
Population aged 15+:	100,126					
	Actual			**National Average**		
Percentage Class ABC1:	42%			44%		
Crime:	**Violence**	**Sexual**		**Burglary**		**Motor**
Per 1000 population:	18	1		6		5
Yield range:	4.5% – 9.3%					
Price ranges:	Low £	Hi £	Low £pw	Hi £pw	Low	Hi
Flats & maisonettes	46,400	69,600	83	112	8.4%	9.3%
Terraced	56,800	85,200	97	132	8.1%	8.9%
Semi-detached	83,200	124,800	124	167	7.0%	7.8%
Detached	156,000	234,000	150	203	4.5%	5.0%
Percentage above the national average:	0%					
	Actual			**National Average**		
Capital growth last 12 months:	13%			18%		
Capital growth last 4 years:	95%			74%		
Large employers in the area:	Ipswich Hospital, Royal & Sun Alliance, AXA Insurance, BTexact technologies, Corning Research, UCL, Textron Turfcare, CompAir UK Ltd, Celestion International, Bull Electric, Crane, Cerro (MB) and Manganese Bronze Components Ltd					
Demand for letting:	Good					
Average void period:	2 weeks					
	Capital Growth (out of 5)		**Yield** (out of 5)		**Total** (out of 10)	
Our rating:	3		4		7	
Summary:	Great yields and good communications.					
Description:	Ipswich is the closest city for nearly half a million people, which makes it a major city when talking within catchment terms. Unemployment is lower than the average and there are two hi-tech business parks – IP City & Adastral Park, both rapidly expanding, providing further jobs. There has been a trend of call centres locating to Ipswich by some of the large financial and insurance companies which further keeps the unemployment rate down.					

	Ipswich is in a prime location on the trans-European Transport Network, connecting the UK and the Benelux countries. These routes constantly improve and are heavily invested in to enhance their key role in the European Union – which we will see pay off in later years.
	A £20 million investment has been made for the Cardinal Park leisure development incorporating an 11-screen UGC cinema complex, Brannigan's Music Bar, night-club, casino and restaurants, all just five minutes' walk from the town centre and the historic waterfront. Since 1999 over £4m has been guaranteed from the Single Regeneration Budget and from the English Partnerships for residential and business development.
Mainline railway station:	One hour 15 minutes to Liverpool Street, London
Road access:	Main access routes A14 & A12 82 miles north east of Central London 50 miles to M25 & M11
Local newspaper:	Ipswich Evening Star 01473 230023

Estate agents:	Name	Address	Tel	Web
	David Brown & Co	8–10 Falcon Street Ipswich Suffolk IP1 1SL	01473 222266	Website currently under development
	Woodcock & Son	16 Arcade Street Ipswich Suffolk IP1 1EP	01473 233355	www.woodcock andson.co.uk
	Colin Gerling & Co	19a–21 Great Colman Street Ipswich Suffolk IP4 2AN	01473 252555	Website currently under development
	Frost & Partners	76 High Street Hadleigh Ipswich Suffolk IP7 5EF	01473 823456	www.frostand partners.co.uk
	Fenn Wright	1 Buttermarket Ipswich Suffolk IP1 1BA	01473 232700	www.fenn wright.co.uk
	Goddard & Co	12 Old Foundry Road Ipswich Suffolk IP4 2AS	01473 254676	goddard@ipsw 80.freeserve. co.uk

Estate agents:	Name	Address	Tel	Web
	William H Brown	25 Queen Street Ipswich Suffolk IP1 1SW	01473 226101	www.sequence home.co.uk

Letting agents:	Name	Address	Tel	Web
	Goddard & Co Rentals	Old Foundry Rd Ipswich Suffolk IP4 2AS	01473 216412	goddard@ipsw 80.freeserve. co.uk
	Strutt & Parker	4 Upper King St Norwich Norfolk NR3 1HA	01473 214841	www.struttand parker.com
	J S M Property	36–38 Queen St Ipswich Suffolk IP1 1SS	01473 214441	www.jsm property.com
	Seatons	4 Great Colman St Ipswich Suffolk IP4 2AD	01473 289444	www.seatons. com
	Pennington Chartered Surveyors	10 Crown St Ipswich Suffolk IP1 3LD	01473 214343	www.penning ton-online.co.uk

Area:	**Isle of Wight**					
Category:	A					
Investor profile:	Pension, Holiday, Retirement, Downshifter					
Population aged 15+:	108,546					
	Actual			**National Average**		
Percentage Class ABC1:	57%			44%		
Crime:	**Violence**		**Sexual**	**Burglary**		**Motor**
Per 1000 population:	10		1	4		2
Yield range:	5.0% – 9.9%					
Price ranges:	**Low £**	**Hi £**	**Low £pw**	**Hi £pw**	**Low**	**Hi**
Flats & maisonettes	54,400	81,600	103	140	9.0%	9.9%
Terraced	72,800	109,200	107	144	6.9%	7.6%
Semi-detached	91,200	136,800	127	172	6.5%	7.2%
Detached	141,600	212,400	151	204	5.0%	5.5%
Percentage above the national average:	0%					
	Actual			**National Average**		
Capital growth last 12 months:	21%			18%		
Capital growth last 5 years:	111%			80%		
Large employers in the area:	Mainly tourist related small businesses and local government, i.e. schools, hospitals and councils. Few large employers locally.					
Demand for letting:	Good					
Average void period:	4 weeks					
	Capital Growth (out of 5)		**Yield** (out of 5)		**Total** (out of 10)	
Our rating:	4		4		**8**	
Summary:	Since a cycling holiday here as a teenager and a round-the-island walk when I was at Portsmouth for my degree, the island has held my imagination. It has some of the most beautiful scenery and villages in the whole of the UK, with a temperate climate that can become a wild storm without warning. For tenants who have always lived here, or for holiday makers seeking a relaxing break the investment you make can be a good one in terms of both yield and capital. Like Portsmouth mentioned elsewhere, because this is an island there will always be a premium for rental accommodation because they can only build so much.					
Description:	For a piece of land that otherwise would be considered small there is a huge amount going on in this island. Whether it is the strength of the					

tourist industry and the associated events and competitions which attract people to the place, or whether it is the possibilities that Wight offers to relocating small businesses, you should take a good look at this. Especially so if you consider yourself a downshifter or lifestyle investor.

One of the most beautiful parts of the UK, the Isle sits like a diamond on its side in the Solent, with a strong minded community of long-term residents and incomers from recent years. The pricing of property here is significantly less than it would be across the water in Hampshire or Dorset and comes with arguably fewer hassles. On the other hand spending so much time on the island can also get to you until you are used to it. Having some investments on the mainland that produce good rents would allow for a very good lifestyle on less money than you would manage on across the water.

There is a great coastal footpath where you can't get lost. You just keep the sea on one side until you get back to where you started from! I walked it with a group of friends one weekend and it was great. Vast areas of the island are designated Areas of Outstanding Natural Beauty and rightly so. Great beaches, towering cliffs, and traditional seaside towns within just a few minutes' drive of isolated rural villages or small towns. With such diversity comes a diversity of rental investments. In Shanklin or Ryde for example, you can buy decent holiday apartments that will have high summer usage, very close to good two- and three-bed properties that will rent out on the usual AST contracts to busy working families. In Newport or Cowes you can get hold of good small office units as well as the residential opportunities. Across the island, and certainly on the southern coast you can buy great quality village properties that will command high prices for the summer season, and which the same families may rent from you for years on the basis of the same week every year.

If you are going to live here as well as invest here then get to enjoy the history and attractions of the island such as the Roman Villas at Brading and Newport, Carisbrooke Castle, and Osborne House. Look at Ventnor for good capital appreciation and some decent rent. But also look to smaller places like Carisbrooke, Niton, and Chale.

Around 20% of the island's people are employed in the tourist industry somehow and as much as 24% of GDP here is from that very same industry. Sailing events such as Skandia Cowes Week, and the Little Britain Challenge Cup attract many new people each year, as do the ballooning, cycling and walking festivals or events held on the island each year.

Regeneration projects to boost the standards of some housing, or to benefit the shopping districts have been implemented with some success recently. Take a look at East Cowes, Ryde and Ventnor to find out more about the potential for higher yields.

Mainline railway station:	n/a – sea ferry or small plane to and from UK mainland
Road access:	Main access M27, then ferry 13 miles south of Southampton
Local newspaper:	Isle of Wight County Press 01983 521333

Estate agents:	Name	Address	Tel	Web
	Kingston & Grist	The Square Yarmouth IoW PO41 0NP	01983 761005	www.kingston andgrist.co.uk
	The Wright Estate Agency	140 High St Newport IoW PO30 1TY	01983 822122	www.wright-iw. co.uk
	The Solent Estate Agents	40 High Street Shanklin IoW PO37 6JN	0800 0935919	Website currently under development
	Keith Rogers	11 St Thomas Square Newport IoW PO30 1SN	01983 821020	www.creasey-biles-king.co.uk
	Marvins	5–7 Carisbrooke Rd Newport IoW PO30 1BJ	01983 533633	www.marvins. co.uk
	K J Daniells Estate Agents	7 High St Shanklin IoW PO37 6JZ	01983 868686	www.rightmove. co.uk
	Deacons Estate Agents	37 Union St Ryde IoW PO33 2LE	01983 812000	Website currently under development
	The Real Estate Agents	5 Cross St Ryde IoW PO33 2AA	01983 810101	www.thereal-estateagents. co.uk
Letting agents:	Name	Address	Tel	Web
	Marvins Rentals	41a High St Cowes IoW PO31 7RS	01983 282424	www.marvins. co.uk
	Quay Management	283 Park Rd Cowes IoW PO31 7NQ	01983 291369	Website currently under development
	Arthur Wheeler	46 Regent St Shanklin IoW PO37 7AA	01983 862653	www.arthur-wheeler.co.uk

Area:	**Kendal, Cumbria**				
Category	C				
Investor profile	Holiday, Retirement, Downshifter				
Population aged 15+:	23,854				
	Actual			**National Average**	
Percentage Class ABC1:	45%			44%	
Crime:	**Violence**	**Sexual**		**Burglary**	**Motor**
Per 1000 population:	6	1		2	1
Yield range:	3.7% – 6.7%				
Price ranges:	**Low £** **Hi £**	**Low £pw** **Hi £pw**		**Low**	**Hi**
Flats & maisonettes	59,200 88,800	65 88		5.1%	5.7%
Terraced	76,800 115,200	78 105		5.3%	6.1%
Semi-detached	90,400 135,600	117 158		6.1%	6.7%
Detached	154,400 231,600	120 163		3.7%	4.0%
Percentage above the national average:	68%				
	Actual			**National Average**	
Capital growth last 12 months:	29%			18%	
Capital growth last 4 years:	202%			74%	
Large employers in the area:	Farley Health Products, Furmanite, Gilbert Gilker & Gordon, Lowe Alpine, K Village, North Lakeland Healthcare Trust, Jennings Brothers, Nestle Co Ltd, McVities Group, British Gypsum, Sealy UK, Rexam, BNF, Glaxo Wellcome, Goodacre Carpets.				
Demand for letting:	Good				
Average void period:	2 weeks				
	Capital Growth (out of 5)	**Yield** (out of 5)		**Total** (out of 10)	
Our rating:	4	3		7	
Summary:	Crowded in the summer and all yours in the winter Kendal can provide you with tenants of broad variety. Holiday lets on the outskirts are strong, with weekend rentals solidly throughout the year. Look to some of the housing estates with stock less than ten years old, as well as to small flats in town. Can also represent a lifestyle move for yourself, releasing equity elsewhere for high yields that support a life in the Lake District and all the benefits it brings.				
Description:	If you love the countryside, have a sense of adventure, and yet want to be part of a community, then drop everything and make the move to				

Kendal. Surrounded by mountains and within easy access to the whole of the Lake District, Kendal can be a place for downshifting, retiring, or starting a new business.

Each autumn the town plays host to the prestigious Mountain Festivals where the world of climbing meets up for one giant celebration. The town is heaving with events – films, lectures, seminars and general entertainment. In the winter the mountains offer dangerous company and even in the spring unexpected changes in weather can affect the local countryside. But this backdrop of the countryside has only strengthened the demand for housing. Getting on the ladder locally can be slow and difficult as prices in the area have been fuelled by the demand for second homes within the Lake District National Park.

The busy southern gateway to the Lakes, Kendal is the stopping off point for walkers, climbers, romantic weekenders and anyone seeking to reach the Lakes from the M6. As such it is better to live slightly out of town or off one of the lesser routes into the centre if you have to. Traffic most weekends and throughout the summer can be unbearable. If you are passing though or merely holidaying in the area you can perhaps put up with it. However, this is a real problem if you intend to move into the town on a more permanent basis.

Investment opportunities vary from country holiday properties commanding year-round demand in Britain's first National Park, to trendy modern apartments with urban views. For family homes do consider staying just on the outskirts given the traffic congestion and the impact of this on the school run, but also look at the beautiful townhouses closer in.

Investment opportunities vary from country holiday properties commanding year round demand in Britain's first National Park, to trendy modern apartments with urban views. For family homes do consider staying just on the outskirts given the traffic congestion and the impact of this on the school run, but also look at the beautiful townhouses closer in. Nicknamed the 'auld grey town' because of the local stone, Kendal is a busy and prosperous place. Looking after its own urban and rural communities, it also has to cater for the demands of visiting tourists across the whole year and so provides good shopping, with great restaurants and hotels. You can stay busy with the craft shops, art galleries and museums.

Cumbria County Council works very closely with other agencies to develop business opportunities and regeneration across the county. The greater the amount of business support in the area, the easier it can be for new households to move into the area. If you can do a lot via email and telephone then the lifestyle attractions of being able to base yourself in Kendal or the surrounding villages are very high.

Getting into the wider area is easy. Coaches run from London (Victoria) to Kendal, Ulverston, Ambleside, Barrow and Windermere. Local rail stations are Lancaster and Oxenholme, with connections Kendal and Windermere. In addition to this the beautiful and historic Settle to Carlisle Railway line runs through the east of the area with stations at Dent and Garsdale. Manchester Airport has its own rail station with direct services to Windermere and Barrow-in Furness.

Mainline railway station:	2 hours to Liverpool Lime Street			
Road access:	Main access route M6, then A684 54 miles north or Blackpool 8 miles from M6			
Local newspaper:	Westmorland Gazette 01539 720555			
Estate agents:	**Name**	**Address**	**Tel**	**Web**
	Michael C L Hodgson	10 Highgate Kendal Cumbria LA9 4SX	01539 721375	www.michael-hodgson.co.uk
	Arnold Greenwood	8–10 Highgate Kendal Cumbria LA9 4SX	01539 733383	www.arnold greenwood.co.uk
	Cumberland Estate Agents	12 Finkle Street Kendal Cumbria LA9 4AB	01539 738006	www.cumberian.co.uk
	Hackney & Leigh	100 Stricklandgate Kendal Cumbria LA9 4PU	01539 729711	www.hackey-leigh.co.uk
	Poole Townsend	2 Market Place Kendal Cumbria LA9 4TN	01539 734455	www.poole town.co.uk
	Milne Moser	100 Highgate Kendal Cumbria LA9 4HE	01539 725582	www.milnemoser.co.uk
Letting agents:	**Name**	**Address**	**Tel**	**Web**
	Open Door Properties	134 Stricklandgate Kendal Cumbria LA9 4QG	01539 731478	www.lakes property.co.uk
	Turner Scott Property	53 Highgate Kendal Cumbria LA9 4ED	01539 736999	

Area:	**Kettering, Northamptonshire**					
Category:	A					
Investor profile:	Pension, Business and Cash&Equity					
Population aged 15+:	48,787					
	Actual			**National Average**		
Percentage Class ABC1:	45%			44%		
Crime:	**Violence**		**Sexual**	**Burglary**		**Motor**
Per 1000 population:	8		1	1		5
Yield range:	9.6% – 14.0%					
Price ranges:	Low £	Hi £	Low £pw	Hi £pw	Low	Hi
Flats & maisonettes	40,800	61,200	86	117	10.0%	11.0%
Terraced	49,600	74,400	102	138	9.6%	10.7%
Semi-detached	71,200	106,800	191	258	12.6%	14.0%
Detached	106,400	159,600	250	339	11.0%	12.2%
Percentage above the national average:	0%					
	Actual			**National Average**		
Capital growth last 12 months:	25%			18%		
Capital growth last 4 years:	75%			74%		
Large employers in the area:	Kettering General Hospital, Weetabix					
Demand for letting:	**Excellent**					
Average void period:	1 week					
	Capital Growth (out of 5)		**Yield** (out of 5)		**Total** (out of 10)	
Our rating:	4		4		**8**	
Summary:	An expanding town with excellent tenant demand.					
Description:	The East Midlands have seen some of the biggest increases in prices in the last 24 months – and about time too! Property was far too cheap back then and I still feel it is now; even though not as cheap as before, bargains can still be had.					
	There is a real shortage of single room occupancy for a reason that I am not too sure about. I was considering buying a 5 bedroomed house and converting it into a House in Multiple Occupancy (HMO) with 7 letting rooms and I was assured that I would let the whole house out within 2 days. I eventually lost the property (probably to another investor!) but was then never able to find another suitable property with the right					

	number of bedrooms – but that does not mean there are not suitable properties out there.
	Kettering's location is bang in the middle of England – some say it is in the heart of England – and the Council are aware of this and have started to prepare for Kettering's involvement with the rest of Europe. Three business parks have been granted approval for expansion which will further increase the number of people employed in or locating to the area. Unemployment is incredibly low at 2.3% and this, coupled with the fact that nearly 90% of Kettering's businesses made a profit (6th highest in UK), makes it no surprise that the local economy has beaten the UK's average for GDP growth.
Mainline railway station:	One hour to St Pancras, London
Road access:	Main access A14 55 miles east of Birmingham 22 miles from M1/M6
Local newspaper:	Northants Evening Telegraph 01536 506100

Estate agents:	Name	Address	Tel	Web
	Parkhouse & Partners	2 Gold Street Kettering Northamptonshire NN16 8JA	01536 517003	www.property-platform.com
	William H Brown	28 Gold Street Kettering Northamptonshire NN16 8JE	01536 518555	Website currently under development
	Simon Musto Estate Agents	9 Piccadilly Buildings Sheep Street Kettering Northamptonshire NN16 0AN	01536 512155	Website currently under development
	Pattison Lane Estate Agents	60–70 Gold Street Kettering Northamptonshire NN16 8JB	01536 524425	www.pattison lane.co.uk

Letting agents:	Name	Address	Tel	Web
	William H Brown	28 Gold Street Kettering Northants NN16 8JE	01536 518555	www.sequence home.co.uk
	Ashby Lowery Residential	7 Bridge Street Northampton NN1 1NH	01604 603333	www.ashby-lowery.co.uk

Area:	**King's Lynn, Norfolk**					
Category:	A					
Investor profile:	Pension, Retirement, Business and Cash&Equity					
Population aged 15+:	31,041					
	Actual			**National Average**		
Percentage Class ABC1:	41%			44%		
Crime:	**Violence**		**Sexual**	**Burglary**		**Motor**
Per 1000 population:	7		1	5		3
Yield range:	6.4% – 9.5%					
Price ranges:	Low £	Hi £	Low £pw	Hi £pw	Low	Hi
Flats & maisonettes	44,000	66,000	80	109	8.6%	9.5%
Terraced	60,000	90,000	85	116	6.7%	7.4%
Semi-detached	72,000	108,000	97	132	6.4%	7.0%
Detached	121,600	182,400	209	284	8.1%	9.0%
Percentage above the national average:	0%					
	Actual			**National Average**		
Capital growth last 12 months:	20%			18%		
Capital growth last 5 years:	88%			80%		
Large employers in the area:	Biddles (Bookbinders) Ltd, CPC King's Lynn Ltd., Sanford UK Ltd., Tollit & Harvey Ltd.					
Demand for letting:	Good					
Average void period:	2 weeks					
Our rating:	**Capital Growth** (out of 5) 5		**Yield** (out of 5) 5	**Total** (out of 10) **10**		
Summary:	This place has it all for any serious property investor.					
Description:	King's Lynn's population is set to grow by over 10% by 2011 and it is part of the Eastern Region which is the fastest growing region in the UK. It is at the intersection of the A10, A17 & A47, the 3 main routes to the Midlands, East Anglia and The South. The A47 is part of the EU designated Trans European Road Network. Kings Lynn is close to the coast and is the gateway to Northern Europe and Scandinavia. It is also close to Norwich Airport.					
	King's Lynn has a wide range of historic buildings and architecture hinting at its nautical and fishing industries. This area is a key service					

▶

<table>
<tr><td></td><td>centre serving West Norfolk and parts of Lincolnshire and Cambridgeshire. Its town centre has not only a great range of quaint little shops but has a touristy feel to it, where there are visitor attractions, museums and a well supported market three days a week. Shopping facilities include a wide range of national chains as well and there is loads of parking within the town, as well as regular bus and train services. This all makes Kings Lynn a great place to live and people who live here tend not to leave.

As you can see, the property prices are a lot cheaper than the national average, which means that the yields are fantastic but also, due to the population increase predictions the prospect for capital growth is fantastic too.</td></tr>
</table>

Mainline railway station:	$1\frac{1}{2}$ hours to London Kings Cross
Road access:	Main access A17, A47 83 miles east of Nottingham 44 miles from M11 78 miles from M1/M69
Local newspaper:	Lynn News 01553 761188

Estate agents:	Name	Address	Tel	Web
	The Property Bureau	50 King Street King's Lynn Norfolk PE30 1ES	01553 777878	www.theproperty bureau.com
	Fisher Associates	1 Hall Orchards Middleton King's Lynn Norfolk PE32 1RY	01553 844070	www.norfolk homesearch. co.uk
	Sowerbys	Market Place Burnham Market King's Lynn Norfolk PE31 8HD	01328 730340	www.sowerbys. com
	Brittons Estate Agents	21 Norfolk Street King's Lynn Norfolk PE30 1AN	01553 692828	www.brittons.net
	Bedford Estate Agents	The Bower House Market Place Burnham Market King's Lynn Norfolk PE31 8HF	01328 730500	www.bedfords. co.uk

Letting agents:	Name	Address	Tel	Web
	Bradford & Bingley Letting Agents Charles Hawkins	23, Tuesday Market Place King's Lynn Norfolk PE30 1JR	01553 773077	www.bbg.co.uk
	Rounce & Evans Property Management	3, Jubilee Court Dersingham King's Lynn Norfolk PE31 6HH	01485 541843	www.rounce andevans.co.uk

Area:	**Leamington Spa**					
Category:	B					
Investor profile:	Cash & Equity, Retirement					
Population aged 15+:	52,072					
	Actual			**National Average**		
Percentage Class ABC1:	51%			44%		
Crime:	**Violence**		**Sexual**	**Burglary**		**Motor**
Per 1000 population:	10		1	6		3
Yield range:	3.5% – 8.6%					
Price ranges:	Low £	Hi £	Low £pw	Hi £pw	Low	Hi
Flats & maisonettes	66,400	99,600	110	149	7.8%	8.6%
Terraced	105,600	158,400	112	151	4.6%	5.5%
Semi-detached	119,200	178,800	124	167	4.9%	5.4%
Detached	172,800	259,200	127	172	3.5%	3.8%
Percentage above the national average:	60%					
	Actual			**National Average**		
Capital growth last 12 months:	88%			18%		
Capital growth last 5 years:	144%			74%		
Large employers in the area:	University of Warwick, NFU Mutual, Premier Automotive, Woodwards Department Store, Stoneleigh Agricultural College, Jaguar, Peugeot, Ford, Land Rover, Coventry Airport, Warwickshire County Council, Solihull Council, Warwick Castele.					
Demand for letting:	Good					
Average void period:	3 weeks					
Our rating:	**Capital Growth** (out of 5) 5		**Yield** (out of 5) 3		**Total** (out of 10) 8	
Summary:	If you can afford to get something here for your portfolio then consider it hard. This is a prosperous community that likes to shop and enjoys a good lifestyle. To get the best yields you have to be at one end of the spectrum or the other, preferably the lower to avoid tying up too much cash given existing pricing.					
Description:	It should come as no surprise that you can pamper yourself in a Spa town. However, Leamington has a stronger supply of lifestyle boutiques and retailers than other towns locally making it a busy shopping location without having been damaged by over development, or ignored					

▶

in favour of out-of-town retail sites. For professional service too the town is well served, making it an attractive location for new businesses requiring office accommodation and workspace.

The surrounding area is predominantly agricultural green-belt land and many attractive and expensive villages dot the outskirts of the town. Close by are the headquarters of the Royal Agricultural Society and the Royal Showground at Stoneleigh. Warwick with its beautiful small streets and the Castle, attract visitors all year round, as does Stratford upon Avon just 12 miles away. Easy and quick access to the Cotswolds from here makes the area a popular location for visitors seeking a two or three month UK base and boosts the potential for the letting of houses with parking. Within the town there is a higher than normal proportion of apartments. The University of Warwick nearby also creates student rental opportunities. The Business School there and its MBA programme can be a source of mature tenants taking a study year out from their corporate work. Good state and public schools also serve to attract potential tenants to the area.

The much discussed Rugby Airport that has been intended to take traffic away from Birmingham as well as Coventry and release pressure on development land there, continues to cause strong debate locally. Villages most at threat from construction plans and then from air traffic noise include Church Lawford, Long Lawford, Kings Newnham and Fenny Compton. Others potentially badly affected by the airport are Stretton, Marbury, Kineton, Marton and Princethorpe. From a future perspective however, it is standard for house prices to increase once an airport has been built, adding strongly to values where commuting for senior executives can be made easier.

Transportation
Sitting between the A46 and the M40 Leamington and neighbouring Warwick have both seen a rise in demand from commuters seeking a decent town and facilities, yet within easy access by road of the rest of the country. The closest existing major airport is Birmingham International just 40 minutes away. Rail access to London and Birmingham is easy and fast.

Mainline railway station:	35 minutes to Birmingham New Street
Road access:	Main access M40, then A46 35miles south east of Birmingham 4 miles from M40
Local newspaper:	Leamington Spa Review 01926 457777

Estate agents:	Name	Address	Tel	Web
	Dixons the Estate Agents	45 Warwick St Leamington Spa Warwickshire CV32 5JX	01926 451411	www.rightmove.co.uk

Estate agents:	Name	Address	Tel	Web
	Halifax Estate Agents	5 Euston Place Leamington Spa Warwickshire CV32 4LH	01926 311431	www.halifax estateagency. co.uk
	Peter Bromwich & Co	Somerset House Clarendon Place Leamington Spa Warwickshire CV32 5QN	01926 881144	www.bromwich. co.uk
	Connell Estate Agents	708 Euston Place Leamington Spa Warwickshire CV32 4LN	01926 881441	www.connells. co.uk
	Wiglesworth & Co	14 Euston Place Leamington Spa Warwickshire CV32 4LY	01926 888998	www.wigles worth.co.uk
Letting agents:	**Name**	**Address**	**Tel**	**Web**
	Locke & England		01926 330435	www.bbg.co.uk
	Crabb Curtis Property Services		01926 888844	www.crabb curtis.co.uk

Area:	**Leeds, Yorkshire**					
Category:	A					
Investor profile:	Cash & Equity, Pension, University					
Population aged 15+:	376,422					
	Actual			**National Average**		
Percentage Class ABC1:	45%			44%		
Crime:	**Violence**		**Sexual**	**Burglary**		**Motor**
Per 1000 population:	9		1	22		13
Yield range:	9.1% – 15.2%					

Price ranges:	Low £	Hi £	Low £pw	Hi £pw	Low	Hi
Flats & maisonettes	59,200	88,800	134	181	10.6%	11.8%
Terraced	50,400	75,600	147	198	13.2%	15.2%
Semi-detached	75,200	112,800	151	204	9.4%	10.4%
Detached	107,200	160,800	209	282	9.1%	10.1%

Percentage above the national average:	0%		
	Actual		**National Average**
Capital growth last 12 months:	21%		18%
Capital growth last 5 years:	60%		74%
Large employers in the area:	Halifax plc, Yorkshire Electricity Group, BT, Leeds NHS Trust, University of Leeds, Leeds Metropolitan University, William Hill, Walker Morris, Leeds City Council, HSBC, Direct Line, Green Flag		
Demand for letting:	**Excellent**		
Average void period:	2 weeks		

Our rating:	**Capital Growth** (out of 5) 5	**Yield** (out of 5) 5	**Total** (out of 10) **10**
Summary:	One of few locations that can promise a full score card. Students, working families, professional lets, and high yield terraced properties all in a few square miles. Add to this the dynamic regeneration plans and the newly commissioned tram system to reduce congestion and Leeds is well worth a good look. Best returns may come just a mile or two from the main centre as prices for acquisition drop but tenant demand soars.		
Description:	An energetic and strong business city, Leeds has undergone enormous renewal in recent years. The growth of the financial services and professional services sectors has created strong demand for city centre apartments, and even an experiment into 'microflats' for midweek		

▶

dwellers and tenants. Funding for urban regeneration has seen the rise of new information technology parks in former heavy industry sites. The phenomenon of telephone call centres has seen large employment in Leeds with more than 70 such centres in and around the city. The size of the university population creates yet another tenant group for landlords and investors in property.

Between Leeds City Council and Yorkshire Forward, the development of an area known as Holbeck Urban Village intends to create a new mixed use residential and business quarter. It will support existing businesses, affordable and luxury housing developments, office space, transport links and access to the city. Similarly, the Aire Valley Employment Area (AVEA) is a seven year programme funded with government support. This 1000 hectare area runs south east of the city to the enhanced M1-A1 link road. It contains 350 hectares of possible development land targeted to provide a major portion of the city's employment growth for the next ten years

Where the general economy of Leeds as a city is seen to be healthy and thriving, there are a number of areas where empty properties have become more common as businesses choose against investing in the area. In Holbeck and Beeston programmes for regeneration of such areas have enjoyed a success which is being gradually replicated elsewhere in the town. Leeds City Council has also launched 'The Property Shop' to enable council tenants to move between properties across the city.

The Supertram concept for travel within and across the city is to have a profound impact on future values. It has received the funding permission required from government. It will have a 28km rail network connecting the suburbs and the city centre. Major sites such as the Royal Armouries and Clarence Dock, the Seacroft Centre, the Bodington site at Headingly, the universities and St James's Hospital. Park & Ride sites at the end of each route will relieve the city of the pressure caused by many thousands of cars. The trams themselves will carry up to 270 people at a time, opening up many parts of the city to potential for developers, new business, retail sites, and housing.

The University of Leeds is home for just under 28,000 undergraduate students. In addition, a further 28,000 people are enrolled on short programmes. This has to be an enormous opportunity for landlords serving the student population with shorthold tenancies on individual houses and flats.

Transportation
The M62, M1 and A1(M) road networks mean Leeds is well placed in Central Northern England for easy access to the surrounding towns and cities. Train services to London and Edinburgh are around two hours. The Leeds-Bradford Airport out between Yeadon and Bramhope serves both national and international flights.

Mainline railway station:	25 minutes to York

Road access:	Main access M1 & M62 45 miles north east of Manchester 5 miles from M1			
Local newspaper:	Yorkshire Evening Post 0113 243 2701			
Estate agents:	**Name**	**Address**	**Tel**	**Web**
	Manning Stainton	30 Marsh St Rothwell Leeds LS26 0BB	0113 282 4353	www.manning stainton.co.uk
	Pickerings	16 St Annes Rd Hedingley Leeds LS6 3NX	0113 274 6746	www.pickering homes.com
	Walker Smale	The Old Smithy The Cross Bramhope Leeds LS16 9AX	0113 203 7777	www.walker- smale.co.uk
	City Living (Leeds)	28 Otley Rd Headingley Leeds LS6 2AD	0113 217 9090	www.cityliving. co.uk
	A.W.S.	Killingbeck Dr York Road Leeds LS14 6UF	0113 235 1362	www.awsltd. co.uk
	Hunters	15 York Place Leeds LS1 2SJ	0113 218 2449	www.hunters net.co.uk
	APS Estate Agents	96 Queen Street Morley Leeds LS27 9EB	0113 253 1133	www.askaps. co.uk
Letting agents:	**Name**	**Address**	**Tel**	**Web**
	Williams H Brown	112 New Road Side Horsforth Leeds LS18 4QB	0113 258 3476	www.sequence home.co.uk
	Gibson Twaites	3 Oxford Place Leeds LS1 3AX	0113 243 3961	
	Adair Paxton	33 Great Geoge Street Leeds LS1 3BB	0113 391 7100	www.adair paxton.co.uk

Area:	**Leicester, Leicestershire**						
Category:	C						
Investor profile:	Pension, Retirement, University, Business, Downshifter and Cash&Equity						
Population aged 15+:	276,613						
	Actual				**National Average**		
Percentage Class ABC1:	41%				44%		
Crime:	**Violence**		**Sexual**		**Burglary**		**Motor**
Per 1000 population:	21		1		12		7
Yield range:	4.5% – 13.7%						
Price ranges:	**Low £**	**Hi £**	**Low £pw**	**Hi £pw**	**Low**		**Hi**
Flats & maisonettes	44,000	66,000	116	157	12.4%		13.7%
Terraced	48,800	73,200	98	133	9.4%		10.4%
Semi-detached	78,400	117,600	100	135	6.0%		6.6%
Detached	125,600	188,400	114	164	4.5%		4.7%
Percentage above the national average:	0%						
	Actual				**National Average**		
Capital growth last 12 months:	34%				18%		
Capital growth last 5 years:	89%				80%		
Large employers in the area:	Leicester City Council, RF Brookes, Jacobs Bakery, Leicestershire Constabulary, Hays Customer Solutions, Royal Mail, Glenfield Hospital Trust						
Demand for letting:	Excellent						
Average void period:	1 week						
	Capital Growth (out of 5)		**Yield** (out of 5)		**Total** (out of 10)		
Our rating:	3		3		6		
Summary:	Major central England city with thriving local economy.						
Description:	Leicester is the largest city in the East Midlands and the tenth largest in the country. Its significance was first recognised by the Romans and then by the Danes, who used it to control the Midlands. Since then it has grown into a major commercial and manufacturing city, not reliant on one single industry, but known for a diverse range of industries. The diversity doesn't stop there – the city's ethnic minority community accounts for around 30% of Leicester's population which gives the city a certain cosmopolitan feel.						

Mainline railway station:	55 minutes to Birmingham New Street			
Road access:	Main access routes A6, M69 & M1 28 miles south of Nottingham 4 miles to M69 & M1			
Local newspaper:	Leicester Mercury 0116 2512512			
Estate agents:	**Name**	**Address**	**Tel**	**Web**
	Dales	13 Narborough Road Leicester Leicestershire LE3 0LE	0116 2541600	Website currently under development
	Osmonds	178 Melton Road Leicester Leicestershire LE2 1WX	0116 2613800	www.nation wide.co.uk
	Seths Estate Agents	157 Evington Road Leicester Leicestershire LE2 1QL	0116 2739090	www.seths.co.uk
	Andrew Granger & Co	8 Rutland Street Leicester Leicestershire LE1 1RA	0116 2538850	www.andrew granger.co.uk
	Rathods Property Centre	177 Melton Road Leicester Leicestershire LE4 6QT	0116 2666575	www.rathods. co.uk
	Peter James	68 Gramby Street Leicester Leicestershire LE1 1DJ	0116 2227575	www.peterjames web.co.uk
	Kendalls	27 Belvoir Street Leicester Leicestershire LE1 6SL	0116 2556800	kendalls@ madasafish.com
Letting agents:	**Name**	**Address**	**Tel**	**Web**
	Andrew Granger & Co	8 Rutland St Leicester Leicestershire LE1 1RA	0116 253 8850	www.andrew granger.co.uk

Letting agents:	Name	Address	Tel	Web
	Fallowell & Partners Ltd	51 Main St Broughton Ashley Leicester Leicestershire LE9 6RE	0116 247 0004	www.fallowells. co.uk
	Moore & York	83 Narborough Rd Leicester Leicestershire LE3 0LF	0116 255 9345	www.moore-york.co.uk
	Bradford & Bingley Frank Innes	48 Granby St Leicester Leicestershire LE1 1DH	0116 285 5455	www.bbg.co.uk
	Kendals Accommodation	27 Belvoir St Leicester Leicestershire LE1 6SL	0116 255 6800	www.kendals@ madasafish.com
	Norman Hope & Mann	74 Granby St Leicester Leicestershire LE1 1DJ	0116 285 5566	www.norman hopemann.co.uk

Area:	**Lincoln, Lincolnshire**					
Category:	A					
Investor profile:	Holiday Investor, Retirement Investor, University Investor, Downshifter Investor, Business Investor					
Population aged 15+:	68,724					

	Actual			National Average		
Percentage Class ABC1:	45%			44%		

Crime:	Violence		Sexual	Burglary		Motor
Per 1000 population:	14		1	12		4

Yield range:	6.2% – 12.1%					

Price ranges:	Low £	Hi £	Low £pw	Hi £pw	Low	Hi
Flats & maisonettes	41,600	62,400	97	132	11.0%	12.1%
Terraced	47,200	70,800	105	142	10.4%	11.6%
Semi-detached	65,600	98,400	87	118	6.2%	6.9%
Detached	97,600	146,400	140	189	6.7%	7.5%

Percentage above the national average:	0%		

	Actual	National Average
Capital growth last 12 months:	31%	18%
Capital growth last 5 years:	158%	74%
Large employers in the area:	Alstom, Rose Bearings, Dynex Power, Christian Salvesen, George Fischer, Lincoln & Louth NHS Trust, University of Lincoln, City of Lincoln Council	
Demand for letting:	Excellent	
Average void period:	2 weeks	

Our rating:	Capital Growth (out of 5) 5	Yield (out of 5) 5	Total (out of 10) 10

Summary:	I used to cycle out here as a teenager on a Saturday, watching the Cathedral loom ever larger on the horizon and would struggle up the cobbled streets to the top. Nowadays the architecture and the history is as present as ever, but the lower town is alive with dynamic architecture, a new marina in the town centre, and vast accommodation blocks for the growing university. I love the place. You can get some truly great yields and probably always will as this is a town largely off the beaten track and demand outstrips supply.
Description:	Commanding a strong presence on the skyline the cathedral and castle of Lincoln give a sense of the history of this very special city. The main shopping and business centre for the spacious county of Lincolnshire, there has been great redevelopment of the city and the housing stock in

recent years. For a high quality of life, supported by a thriving business community and excellent leisure facilities Lincoln offers various opportunities to the landlord and investor. The university looks to private sector landlords for accommodation, especially after the first year when a student can get a guaranteed place in halls of residence. For tourism too, there is more demand for good accommodation on short-term lets or as property that can be placed with a specialist holiday agency.

The older terraced housing in the "uphill" part of the town is hugely atmospheric, and always in demand for rentals. To the south around Boultham and Bracebridge larger properties can be multiple occupancies or family lets, and again will provide good returns. Ex local authority stock is spacious and can rent well.

Attractions to the area for tenants and visitors includes not just the beautiful cathedral (with its Airmen's' Chapel as a shrine to the thousands from Lincolnshire bomber bases who died in World War Two), or the castle atop the hill, but also to more modern and peaceful sites. There are two multi-facility leisure centres, each with their own swimming pool. Hartsholme Country Park and the Swanholme Lakes nature reserve provide beautiful countryside walks. Other activities include the Brayford Waterfront Festival, the Lincoln 10K run, and the Grand Prix Cycle Race. The calendar of rallies, shows and street theatre held in the city is also impressive.

Outside of town Horncastle, Wragby, Coningsby and Market Rasen all offer quiet living in a market-town environment where spacious properties can seem to be very good value and just 30 minutes drive from the city. Given that good state and public schools are well provided for around Lincoln these small communities can represent good opportunities for freehold rental, as well as potential sites for relocation of a small business that is non-dependent upon location or also for a retirement lifestyle. Closer in to Lincoln itself villages such as Brough, Haddington, Stapleford, Norton Disney and Brant Broughton all benefit from the swift access to the A1. The Western loop road from North Hykeham to Skellingthorpe and the North side of the city continues to reinforce prices of homes here, and new builds to the West of Lincoln are attractive to tenants seeking access to Newark, Nottingham, Gainsborough and Doncaster for work.

Transportation
Just 30 minutes along the A46 to Newark and the fast North-South A1 road, Lincoln is reasonably easy to get to. Long distance commuting though has to be done from the faster and more frequent trains out of Newark. It is an hour by car from the lengthy beaches at Mablethorpe, Chapel St Leonards, Ingoldmells and Skegness.

Mainline railway station:	55–60 minutes to Nottingham
Road access:	Main access routes A15 & A46 44 miles north east of Nottingham 35 miles from M1

Local newspaper:	Lincolnshire Echo 01522 525252			
Estate agents:	**Name**	**Address**	**Tel**	**Web**
	Pygott & Crone	36a Silver St Lincoln Lincolnshire LN2 1EW	01522 568822	www.pygott-crone.co,
	Walter's Estate Agents	44–45 Silver St Lincoln Lincolnshire LN2 1EH	01522 512513	www.walters-property.com
	Turner Evans Stevens Ltd	33 Silver St Lincoln Lincolnshire LN2 1EW	01522 511665	www.tes-property.co.uk
	King & Co	18 Guildhall St Lincoln Lincolnshire LN1 1TR	01522 525255	www.rightmove.co.uk
	Halifax Estate Agents	Unit 32 The Forum North Hykeham Lincoln Lincolnshire LN6 8HW	01522 698818	www.halifax.co.uk
	Mundys Estate Agents	29 Silver St Lincoln Lincolnshire LN2 1AS	01522 510044	www.mundy-uk.com
	Brogden Bews Brown	38–39 Silver St Lincoln Lincolnshire LN2 1EU	01522 531321	www.brewsbrown.com
Letting agents:	**Name**	**Address**	**Tel**	**Web**
	Hodgson Elkington & Co	343 High Street Lincoln LN5 7DQ	01522 533533	www.hodgsonelkington.co.uk/lettings
	Lincoln Lets	Brook House 32–33 Silver St Lincoln LN2 1EW	01522 888899	www.lincolnlets.co.uk
	Belvoir Lettings Lincoln	450 High Street Lincoln LN5 8HZ	01522 544999	www.belvoirlettings.com

Area:	**Liverpool City Centre, Lancashire**					
Category:	B					
Investor profile:	Pension, Retirement, University, Business, Downshifter and Cash&Equity					
Population aged 15+:	374,335					
	Actual			National Average		
Percentage Class ABC1:	41%			44%		
Crime:	Violence		Sexual	Burglary		Motor
Per 1000 population:	16		1	15		16
Yield range:	13.2% − 23.1%					
Price ranges:	Low £	Hi £	Low £pw	Hi £pw	Low	Hi
Flats & maisonettes	20,000	30,000	89	120	21.0%	23.1%
Terraced	29,600	44,400	93	126	14.8%	16.3%
Semi-detached	44,000	66,000	131	184	14.5%	15.5%
Detached	65,600	98,400	185	250	13.2%	14.7%
Percentage above the national average:	0%					
	Actual			National Average		
Capital growth last 12 months:	12%			18%		
Capital growth last 5 years:	52%			80%		
Large employers in the area:						
Demand for letting:	Excellent					
Average void period:	1 week					
	Capital Growth (out of 5)		Yield (out of 5)		Total (out of 10)	
Our rating:	2		5		7	
Summary:	A strong commitment from local government to make this city a Eurpoean city makes it a good bet for capital growth.					
Description:	The sixth largest city in the UK by population and in my estimation it is a mini-London. This city has it all − superb road and train links, large ports for export and import to and from the rest of the world and two international airports near the city centre. This is why so many businesses have located to Liverpool leading to the surge of the city's economy. And this trend can only continue, with the council committed to making Liverpool the most business-friendly city in Europe by 2006. Liverpool is one of six short-listed to be the European City of Culture for 2008. If Liverpool gets it there will be a major regeneration of the area and it will really put Liverpool on the map amongst our European partners. This can only mean that property prices will increase due to					

	the inward investment. Announcement of the winner will be in 2003 – I reckon Liverpool will be one of the favourites.

The university is in the heart of the city and has over 23,000 students. This keeps the city centre very busy on every night during term time. The students love to live in the city centre and the university cannot meet the students' accommodation demands. There are many professional landlords exclusively dealing with the student market but there is still room for others landlords as demand is so high. |
| **Mainline railway station:** | One hour 15 minutes to Manchester Piccadilly |
| **Road access:** | Main access M62 & M6
33 miles west of Manchester
1 mile from M62 |
| **Local newspaper:** | Liverpool Echo 0151 227 2000 |

Estate agents:	Name	Address	Tel	Web
	Dears Brack & Associates	24 North John Street Liverpool L2 9RP	0151 2421500	Website currently under development
	B E Property Services	663 West Derby Road Liverpool L13 8AG	0151 2201997	www.beproperty services.co.uk
	Roberts, Edwards & Worrall	321 Aigburth Road Liverpool L17 0BL	0151 7271814	www.worral. co.uk

Letting agents:	Name	Address	Tel	Web
	Whitegates Residential Letting	15 Church Rd Bebington Wirral CH63 7PG	0151 6456924	www.whitegates. co.uk
	Sequence (UK) Ltd	TBC	0151 2372350	www.sequence homesco.uk
	Andrew Louis	Muskers Building 1 Stanley St Liverpool L1 6AA	0151 2848888	www.andrew louis.co.uk
	Venmore Thomas & Jones	44 Stanley St Liverpool L1 6AL	0151 7342511	www.vtj.co.uk
	Bradford & Bingley	Marketplace 10 Allport Lane Bromborough Wirral Merseyside L62 7HP	0151 3345156	www.bbg.co.uk

Area:	**Luton, Bedfordshire**					
Category:	B					
Investor profile:	Pension, Business, University, Downshifter and Cash&Equity					
Population aged 15+:	138,028					
	Actual			National Average		
Percentage Class ABC1:	48%			44%		
Crime:	Violence		Sexual	Burglary		Motor
Per 1000 population:	13		1	10		10
Yield range:	5.6% – 9.4%					
Price ranges:	Low £	Hi £	Low £pw	Hi £pw	Low	Hi
Flats & maisonettes	52,000	78,000	94	127	8.5%	9.4%
Terraced	80,800	121,200	144	195	8.4%	9.3%
Semi-detached	105,600	158,400	143	201	6.6%	7.0%
Detached	144,800	217,200	174	235	5.6%	6.2%
Percentage above the national average:	0%					
	Actual			National Average		
Capital growth last 12 months:	24%			18%		
Capital growth last 5 years:	97%			80%		
Large employers in the area:	Luton Airport					
Demand for letting:	Excellent					
Average void period:	1 week					
	Capital Growth (out of 5)		Yield (out of 5)		Total (out of 10)	
Our rating:	3		4		7	
Summary:	Fast growing and expanding airport that can only spell long term potential for the town.					
Description:	Luton is the economic generator for Bedfordshire and surrounding counties. It is set to consolidate its current successes and to develop new opportunities for businesses and jobs, because it has all the main ingredients for future success. It has an excellent transport infrastructure. More and more passengers, especially business passengers, are choosing to use the airport (6.5m passengers now compared to 1.9m passengers five years ago). There is access to the M1 and the M25 and there is an excellent rail service – London–Luton Airport Parkway. The journey to Kings Cross takes less than 30 minutes					

▶

| | and there are up to 11 trains every hour to the capital. A free shuttle bus takes passengers to and from the terminal.

The airport is a huge generator of employment in the area and it will be a magnet for businesses – not only airport-related businesses, but the corporate headquarters that are moving to towns such as Luton. This is good news.

Prudential Insurance has invested millions of pounds in refurbishing the Arndale centre, which is the main shopping centre. The refurbishment has increased the centre's attractiveness to shoppers and has led to new retail outlets setting up there. Vauxhall has invested its money in Luton, preferring to stay there, rather than move to other European locations.

There are over 12,000 students at the University of Luton and there is limited student accommodation provided by the university, so there is a demand for private properties. The university welcomes landlords to approach them with their listings. |

Mainline railway station:	35 minutes to Kings Cross Thameslink
Road access:	Main access A6 & M1 35 miles north of Central London 2 miles from M1
Local newspaper:	Luton News & Dunstable Gazette 01582 700600

Estate agents:	**Name**	**Address**	**Tel**	**Web**
	Derek Wood Residential	599 Hitchin Road Stopsley Luton LU2 7UW	01582 31502	Website currently under development
	Burlingtons Estate Agents	5e Riddy Lane Luton LU3 2AD	01582 580500	www.luton-properties.com
	Taylors Estate Agents	27 George Street Luton LU1 2AF	01582 456622	www.rightmove.co.uk
	Kirkby & Diamond	1 Union Street Luton LU1 3AN	01582 738866	Website currently under development
	Nu Concept Estate Agents	54 New Bedford Street Luton LU1 1SH	01582 420202	nuconcept@dial.pipex.com
	Hartwell Estate Agents	34 Wellington Street Luton LU1 2QH	01582 729000	www.hartwell.uk.com

▶

Letting agents:	Name	Address	Tel	Web
	Lenwell Property Services	8, Wellington St Luton Bedfordshire LU1 2QH	01582 616263	www.lenwell.com

Area:	**Lymington, Hampshire**					
Category:	B					
Investor profile:	Holiday, Retirement, Downshifter					
Population aged 15+:	26,826					
	Actual			**National Average**		
Percentage Class ABC1:	64%			44%		
Crime:	**Violence**		**Sexual**	**Burglary**		**Motor**
Per 1000 population:	6		1	3		2
Yield range:	4.2% – 7.7%					
Price ranges:	Low £	Hi £	Low £pw	Hi £pw	Low	Hi
Flats & maisonettes	87,200	130,800	129	174	6.9%	7.7%
Terraced	137,600	206,400	141	192	4.4%	5.3%
Semi-detached	158,400	237,600	141	192	4.2%	4.7%
Detached	246,400	369,600	239	324	4.6%	5.0%
Percentage above the national average:	230%					
	Actual			**National Average**		
Capital growth last 12 months:	10%			18%		
Capital growth last 5 years:	222%			74%		
Large employers in the area:	Vosper Thornycroft, University of Southampton, Hampshire County Council, Brockenhurst College, Mole Valley Farmers, Beaulieu Motor Museum, Lymington – Wight Ferry Company, De La Rue Systems, New Forest District Council					
Demand for letting:	Normal					
Average void period:	2 weeks					
	Capital Growth (out of 5)		**Yield** (out of 5)		**Total** (out of 10)	
Our rating:	5		3		**8**	
Summary:	Popular and pretty place with big seasonal variations for holiday lets, but also good for year round rental income. Steady money and no big surprises. Great as a lifestyle base.					
Description:	Tired of the rat race and looking for something a little more peaceful, with year-round tourism and the New Forest as your back garden? It has to be Lymington, an ever busy Georgian market town sitting on the edge of the Solent with its own ferry service over to Yarmouth and the Isle of Wight. While the yields are decent at just over 7% the capital growth is extraordinary until you visit the place and understand its appeal.					

	Heaving with holiday-makers during the summer, Lymington offers a perfect lifestyle base for the landlord who perhaps seeks a portfolio of New Forest holiday cottages or seafront cottages let for a summer season. On the other hand, if you can put together a couple of dozen high yield traditional terraces then the New Forest might appeal to your desire for a tranquil existence if the letting agent will handle all the management!
	Lymington boasts good leisure facilities and shopping at all levels from quality boutiques to national supermarket group facilities. As you might expect for a town catering to the demands of the weekend boating and yachting fraternity the town is awash with excellent hostelries and restaurants, most of them just a matter of a few minutes walk from the Town Quay, which has moorings for 150 vessels. The two marinas and chandlers add to the impression of a sea going town. Several small boatyards add to the scene.
	Housing here is hellishly expensive and you may have a wait to get what you want. This demand though, works very well for rentals ensuring very small void periods between changes. Pricing is fuelled by the difficulty of building new housing locally due to the status of the New Forest as an area of beauty. A double-edged sword, this means that yields will continue to fall as a percentage of the amount required to make the initial investment. To enhance the yield look to properties away from the water front, perhaps to the far side of the A337.
Mainline railway station:	1 hour 50 minutes to London Waterloo
Road access:	Main access M27, then A337 19 miles south west of Southampton 12 miles from M27
Local newspaper:	Hants Advertiser & Times 01425 613384

Estate agents:	Name	Address	Tel	Web
	Caldwells	Beaufort House 69 High Street Lymington SO41 9AL	01590 675875	www.caldwells.uk.com
	Paul Jackson	14 Quay Hill Lymington SO41 3AR	01590 674411	www.pauljackson.co,uk
	John D Wood & Co	53 High Street Lymington SO41 9ZB	01590 677233	www.johndwood.co.uk
	Bishop Pyke	74 High Street Lymington SO41 9AL	01590 674222	www.bishoppyke.co,

Estate agents:	Name	Address	Tel	Web
	Burkmar Estate Agents	Anchor House 96 High Street Lymington SO41 9AP	01590 676111	www.burkmar. com
	Fells Gulliver Estate Agents	125 High Street Lymington SO41 9AQ	01590 671711	www.fells gulliver.com
Letting agents:	Name	Address	Tel	Web
	Godrey Charles	23 New Street Lymington SO41 9BH	01590 671744	
	J R Hill	Stanford House 12 Stanford Rd Lymington SO41 9GF	01590 679200	www.rightmove .co.uk
	Ridgeway Rents	4 Quay Hill Lymington SO41 3AR	01590 679655	www.newforest cottages.co.uk

Area:	**Manchester, Lancashire**					
Category:	B					
Investor profile:	Pension, Retirement, University, Downshifter, Business and Cash&Equity					
Population aged 15+:	345,705					
	Actual			National Average		
Percentage Class ABC1:	41%			44%		
Crime:	Violence		Sexual	Burglary		Motor
Per 1000 population:	25		2	21		15
Yield range:	6.9% – 14.3%					
Price ranges:	Low £	Hi £	Low £pw	Hi £pw	Low	Hi
Flats & maisonettes	44,800	67,200	123	166	12.8%	14.3%
Terraced	47,200	70,800	114	155	11.4%	12.6%
Semi-detached	72,800	109,200	148	201	9.6%	10.6%
Detached	132,800	199,200	195	264	6.9%	7.6%
Percentage above the national average:	0%					
	Actual			National Average		
Capital growth last 12 months:	8%			18%		
Capital growth last 5 years:	40%			80%		
Large employers in the area:	British Airways, Tesco, BP, Vodafone, Virgin and Manchester Airport.					
Demand for letting:	Excellent					
Average void period:	1 week					
	Capital Growth (out of 5)		Yield (out of 5)		Total (out of 10)	
Our rating:	1		5		6	
Summary:	The Jewel of the North West.					
Description:	During the past ten years, over 7,000 people have chosen to live in the city centre, with areas such as Castlefield, the Northern Quarter, Canal Street and Piccadilly Basin being amongst the most desirable locations. Manchester has the fastest growing city centre in Britain, with 2,314 flats planned and 852 of these currently under construction. Over half of the households in the city centre are single occupancy and males outnumber females by two to one. 42% earn over £20,000 per annum, 60% own a car and 59% work in the city centre itself. Main attractions to residents are cited as the lifestyle of city living, leisure facilities and the nightlife offered by a city centre.					

Research has shown that an estimated 20,000 people will live in the city by 2005, compared to just 1,000 in 1990.

Luxury apartments and penthouses, in styles ranging from Manhattan lofts to converted warehouses are in constant demand. Many of the apartments, both new build and converted/renovated, are centred around the Canal Basin area. In recent years, more and more people have chosen to move into city centre Manchester. House prices in regenerated Northern areas are set to outstrip rates in London as finance, IT and service sectors expand.

Manchester City Council's housing strategy aims to build on the successful partnerships which are transforming the Hulme and East Manchester areas. In Hulme, 2,800 flats were demolished and replaced by 1000 desirable new homes and flats available for rent and for sale, in and around the Stretford Road area. Hulme has been transformed by these new developments and the area now attracts investment and people from around the country who wish to live in Manchester. A further 1000 homes are being constructed by private sector firms, such as Bellway.

Elsewhere, housing ranges from stone terraced cottages on the West Pennine Moors to half-timbered houses along the banks of the Bridgewater Canal. There are modern family houses close to all amenities available in all parts of Manchester. To the north of the city lie Bolton, Bury, Rochdale and Oldham, once thriving centres of the cotton industry, now busy and vibrant local shopping centres with excellent leisure facilities.

The east of the city, soon to be connected to the centre by Metrolink as well as road and rail, is home to the Commonwealth Games City of Manchester Stadium and has seen a rise in popularity by home-hunters as a result. To the south lie the more traditional affluent areas such as Altrincham and Hale. Closer to the city centre are older suburban residential areas such as Withington and Didsbury, and the predominantly student 'villages' of Fallowfield and Rusholme.

Despite the rise in the number of homes being built, supply still appears to match demand in the city centre. Salford however has seen slowly rising prices as demand begins to grow, and in Stockport, the lack of supply has seen a sharp rise in bulk land values. Stockport has also seen a mini jobs boom as more firms move into the borough, collectively creating over 500 new positions in 6 months.

Property in the North West is still considerably cheaper than further south. It is possible to pay under £30,000 for a property closer to the centre or pay over £500,000 for a detached house in Bowden, just 10 miles outside the centre. Average house prices vary considerably from postcode to postcode; for example the lowest priced houses in 'M11–4' are under £15,000 whilst the highest priced houses are located in 'WA14–3' at an average cost of £350,000. The city's first £1,000,000 property in Century Buildings, Parsonage Gardens, was sold in late 2000 and a second was due for completion in 2002 in Deansgate.

▶

Mainline railway station:	One hour and 15 minutes to Liverpool Central			
Road access:	Main access M6, M62 & M56 33 miles east of Liverpool 6 miles to M62			
Local newspaper:	Manchester Evening News 0161 832 7200			
Estate agents:	**Name**	**Address**	**Tel**	**Web**
	Pad Residential	5th floor John Dalton House 121 Deansgate Manchester Lancashire M3 2AB	0161 202 2442	www.getapad. co.uk
	Carr & Hume	7 Memorial Rd Worsley Manchester Lancashire M28 3AQ	0161 799 0901	www.carrand hume.co.uk
	Jordan Fishwick Wadden	757 Wilmslow Rd Didsbury Manchester Lancashire M20 6RN	0161 445 4480	www.jordan fishwick.co.uk
	Ash Residential	180 Wilmslow Rd Manchester Lancashire M14 5LQ	0161 225 2500	www.ash residential.co.uk
	Suttons City Living	50 Granby Row Manchester Lancashire M1 7AY	0161 236 7001	www.suttons cityliving.co.uk
	Alex Dines & Co	29 Bury New Rd Prestwich Manchester Lancashire M25 0JU	0161 798 6633	www.alexdines. com
Letting agents:	**Name**	**Address**	**Tel**	**Web**
	Suttons City Living	50 Granby Row Manchester Lancashire M1 7AY	0161 236 7001	www.suttons cityliving.co.uk
	Robert Jordan & Associates	42 Brazennose St Manchester M2 5EB	0161 834 3444	www.robert jordan.co.uk

Letting agents:	Name	Address	Tel	Web
	Chesters	South Court Sharston Rd Manchester Lancashire M22 4SN	0161 902 0202	www.chesters-uk.com
	ABC Estates	35 Barlow Moor Rd Didsbury Manchester Lancashire M20 6TW	0161 434 2000	www.abc-estates.co.uk
	Barlow Costley Property Services	46 Chorley Rd Swinton Manchester Lancashire M27 5AF	0161 728 3358	www.barlow costley.co.uk

Area:	**Milton Keynes, Buckinghamshire**			
Category:	A			
Investor profile:	Pension, Business, and Cash&Equity			
Population aged 15+:	139,866			

	Actual		National Average	
Percentage Class ABC1:	56%		44%	

Crime:	Violence	Sexual	Burglary	Motor
Per 1000 population:	11	1	6	7

Yield range:	6.5% – 12.6%					
Price ranges:	Low £	Hi £	Low £pw	Hi £pw	Low	Hi
Flats & maisonettes	56,000	84,000	136	184	11.4%	12.6%
Terraced	72,800	109,200	117	158	7.5%	8.4%
Semi-detached	91,200	136,800	127	172	6.5%	7.2%
Detached	154,400	231,600	297	402	9.0%	10.0%

Percentage above the national average:	0%	
	Actual	National Average
Capital growth last 12 months:	10%	18%
Capital growth last 5 years:	83%	80%
Large employers in the area:	Open University, Tesco, Royal Mail, Milton Keynes Council and Abbey National	
Demand for letting:	Good	
Average void period:	2 weeks	

	Capital Growth (out of 5)	Yield (out of 5)	Total (out of 10)
Our rating:	4	3	7

Summary:	A rapidly expanding town in the last 5 years and shows no sign of slowing down.
Description:	I have chosen Milton Keynes as it has been chosen by the Government to be 1 of 3 major areas marked for considerable expansion over the next 25 years. We are talking £400m of private investment alone for Milton Keynes and surrounding areas – 100 extra stores, cafés, restaurants, improvements to car parks and public transport. The best bit is a retractable glass sunroof over the local court, Queens Court, which closes in poor weather and opens up when sunny, I'm sure this will attract a lot of interest.

	3,000 jobs will be created due to this expansion and should really put Milton Keynes on the map. The vision is of 'stimulating, bustling regional shopping districts linked to the cultural and leisure districts through pedestrianised piazzas and quality public spaces, which will help create a dynamic new Heart to the City'.
	Milton Keynes' unemployment is very low at 1.8%. Milton Keynes is also part of the new 'hubs & spokes' strategy for transport, the hubs being the major economic activity areas such as Milton Keynes and the spokes being the transport routes. These routes will be improved becoming the East–West rail link, the upgrading of the A421 and an extra lane on the M1 down to the M25.
Mainline railway station:	40–50 minutes to London Euston
Road access:	Main access A5 & M1 53 miles north of London miles from M1
Local newspaper:	Milton Keynes Citizen 01908 371133

Estate agents:	**Name**	**Address**	**Tel**	**Web**
	John Woollett & Co	3 Radcliffe Street Wolverton Milton Keynes Buckinghamshire MK12 5DQ	01908 222020	www.rightmove.co.uk
	Michael Anthony & Partners	Northgate House 500 Silbury Boulevard Milton Keynes Buckinghamshire MK9 2AX	01908 393553	www.michaelanthony.co.uk
	Alexander Stephens Estate Agents	Sovereign Court 213 Witan Gate East Milton Keynes Buckinghamshire MK9 2HP	01908 607787	www.alexanderstephens.co.uk
	Ryan Daniel Estate Agents	Ashton House 401 Silbury Boulevard Milton Keynes Buckinghamshire MK9 2AH	01908 234111	www.ryandaniel.co.uk
	Beasley & Partners	6 High Street Woburn Sands Milton Keynes Buckinghamshire MK17 8RL	01908 282820	www.beasley-partners.co.uk

▶

	Name	Address	Tel	Web
	Mortimers Estate Agents	317 Upper Fourth Street Witan Court Milton Keynes Buckinghamshire MK9 1EH	01908 398980	www.mortimers.uk.com
	Key Estate Agents	Regency Court Ground Floor 216 Upper Fifth Street Milton Keynes Buckinghamshire MK9 2HR	0870 7487990	www.key estateagents.com
Letting agents:	**Name**	**Address**	**Tel**	**Web**
	Castle Estates	Middle Bank House 211 Queensway Bletchley Milton Keynes Buckinghamshire MK2 2EQ	01908 641131	www.castle-estates.co.uk
	Brown & Merry	672 Silbury Boulevard Central Milton Keynes Buckinghamshire MK9 3AE	01908 661601	www.sequence home.co.uk
	Faulkner Property Rentals	4 Aspley Hill Woburn Sands Milton Keynes Buckinghamshire MK17 8NJ	01908 585551	www.Faulkner Property.co.uk

Area:	**Newark, Nottinghamshire**				
Category:	C				
Investor profile:	Cash&Equity investor, Pension investor, Downshifter investor, Business investor				
Population aged 15+:	20,165				
	Actual			**National Average**	
Percentage Class ABC1:	63%			44%	
Crime:	**Violence**	**Sexual**		**Burglary**	**Motor**
Per 1000 population:	11	1		7	3
Yield range:	2.7% – 9.1%				
Price ranges:	Low £ Hi £	Low £pw Hi £pw		Low	Hi
Flats & maisonettes	37,600 56,400	66 89		8.2%	9.1%
Terraced	48,000 72,000	66 89		6.4%	7.2%
Semi-detached	64,800 97,200	79 106		5.7%	6.3%
Detached	108,000 162,000	83 112		2.7%	3.6%
Percentage above the national average:	0%				
	Actual			**National Average**	
Capital growth last 12 months:	33%			18%	
Capital growth last 4 years:	62%			74%	
Large employers in the area:	Seven Trent Water				
Demand for letting:	Good				
Average void period:	3 weeks				
Our rating:	**Capital Growth** (out of 5) 4	**Yield** (out of 5) 3		**Total** (out of 10) 7	
Summary:	I love the way that Newark has been redeveloped and has grown in energy since the high speed rail links and the influx of new high quality housing estates. Look out for impressive development of the riverside warehouses. Some great restaurants for the foodies!				
Description:	Simply because this is home territory for one of us it is very tempting to say good things about Newark! Yet they should really be said because of the changes brought about in the town through wise planning and the total regeneration of the waterside areas.				
	The growth of the rail network and improvements in commuting times means there is a very active and lively community of commuters who				

▶

	will rise early and work in Nottingham, Doncaster, London and York, returning home at the end of the day. The commuting option has opened up the access to higher salaries and Newark has seen a lot of disposable income being spent in its shops and restaurants. The growth of good quality housing estates along the A1 brings people into the town at weekends, forcing up the requirement for better and better facilities. Higher quality supermarkets have come on the scene. The conversions of former warehousing or factory buildings into decent apartments have also raised the standard for development and brought a different investor into the town, over and above the local portfolio investors. Stay in the town for the higher yields, venturing into the villages for the two-bed commuter units. Consider the communities on the Nottingham side of Newark as being attractive for people working there. The A46 out to Bingham and on to Nottingham can be very fast to the point of dangerous, so be careful if you are thinking of buying a house with access on to this road. The beautiful town of Southwell just fifteen minutes to the North can be a good place for conversions and refurbs of older housing and a source of a slower pace of life. Lincoln is close at hand and villages such as Brough, Coddington, Collingham, Hawton and Carlton on Trent can provide demand with reasonable rents.
Mainline railway station:	25–30 minutes to Nottingham
Road access:	Main access routes A1, A46 & A617 26 miles north east of Nottingham 26 miles from M1
Local newspaper:	Nottingham Evening Post 0115 948 2000

Estate agents:	Name	Address	Tel	Web
	Smith-Woolley	Collingham Newark Nottinghamshire NG23 7LG	01636 892456	www.smith-woolley.co.uk
	St Marks Properties	42 Kirk Gate Newark Nottinghamshire NG24 1AB	01636 678008	www.stmarks properties.co.uk
	Gascoine's	Picture House Buildings Forest Road New Ollerton Newark Nottinghamshire NG22 9PL	01623 860328	Website currently under development
	Alasdair Morrison	26 Kirkgate Newark Nottinghamshire NG24 1AB	01636 700888	www.amorrison.co.uk

Estate agents:	Name	Address	Tel	Web
	Richard Watkinson & Partners	35 Kirk Gate Newark Nottinghamshire NG24 1AD	01636 611811	www.richard watkinson.co.uk
	Ian Sandy	Old Bank Chambers Sherwood Drive New Ollerton Newark Nottinghamshire NG22 9PP	01623 835252	www.iansandy. co.uk
Letting agents:	**Name**	**Address**	**Tel**	**Web**
	Richard Watkinson & Partners	17 North Gate Newark Nottinghamshire NG24 1EX	01636 677154	www.richard watkinson.co.uk
	Humberts Hill & Hill	Beaumond Chambers London Road Newark Nottinghamshire NG24 1TN	01636 674879	www.hill prop.co.uk
	Hodgson Elkington & Co	24 Carter Gate Newark Nottinghamshire NG24 1UB	01636 672780	www.hodgson elkington.co.uk/ lettings

Area:	**Newquay, Cornwall**			
Category:	C			
Investor profile:	Holiday investor, Retirement investor, Downshifter investor			
Population aged 15+:	19,720			
	Actual		National Average	
Percentage Class ABC1:	51%		44%	
Crime:	Violence	Sexual	Burglary	Motor
Per 1000 population:	7	1	4	3
Yield range:	4.6% – 7.2%			

Price ranges:	Low £	Hi £	Low £pw	Hi £pw	Low	Hi
Flats & maisonettes	56,800	85,200	92	125	6.5%	7.2%
Terraced	80,000	120,000	110	149	5.8%	5.8%
Semi-detached	90,400	135,600	127	172	6.5%	7.2%
Detached	146,400	219,600	136	184	4.6%	5.1%

Percentage above the national average:	0%	
	Actual	National Average
Capital growth last 12 months:	29%	18%
Capital growth last 4 years:	78%	74%
Large employers in the area:	Mainly tourist related small businesses and local government, i.e. schools, hospitals and councils. Few large employers locally.	
Demand for letting:	OK	
Average void period:	4 weeks	

	Capital Growth (out of 5)	Yield (out of 5)	Total (out of 10)
Our rating:	3	3	6

Summary:	Massive youth scene here across the summer with all the surfers hanging round the town at night. Great for family holidays and as a result for seasonal lets. The beach is just a few hundred yards from the town centre and the countryside all around. More exciting town than the simple scoring mechanism might suggest.
Description:	In a county where holiday homes as a proportion of local housing have reached some of the highest levels in Britain, the local council here have a job on their hands to support local people and to provide strategies for affordable housing. It is an uphill battle in such beautiful surroundings, yet with sensitivity to local needs and by working with the local community there is good opportunity here.

The council is at the end of its 2002/2003 survey of the condition of private sector housing and has also launched an HMO logbook to begin enforcement of new standards. The static population of Newquay is just below 21,000 but massively multiplied through the inflow of tourism over a long summer period that stretches from Easter until late September. Unemployment might seem high at c.a. 12% but is largely a function of the seasonal nature of much of the work here through tourism. In order to ensure the housing needs of the community are well met the councils of Newquay, Restormel and Caradon districts are clear about the need for the Housing Units to work closely with private sector landlords as an aspect of their strategies.

The power of tourism and its impact upon the area is profound. Of the approximately 4 million visitors to Cornwall each year, as many as 20% stay in Newquay! As a result the town has the strongest concentration of visitor accommodation. For you as the investor this could mean lifestyle shifts such as running a small hotel or B & B, or the acquisition of homes for secure holiday lets. Newquay has a busy trade in short lets throughout the year so three or four homes here would provide a living business while gathering some capital growth in property values.

The effect of The Eden project has been a strong force on local accommodation and will push up visitor numbers to Cornwall as new domes and experience zones are added to this astounding and very successful attraction for the South West. There is a big need for enhancements to the transport infrastructure and as these are made to support the strength of the tourist industry property prices will increase, fuelled by the easier access created by the transport links.

The harbour offers a focal point to the town and properties overlooking this or with sea views will obviously command higher prices for the short lets, but the downside is that they will also cost you more and reduce the yield. For better revenue look to the traditional stock in town, and to the more normal AST opportunities. Given the unemployment figures there is scope to consider providing good quality accommodation for those receiving housing benefit. For higher income but less frequency of occupation do consider the national as well as regional agencies promoting country and coastal holidays. There is a strong demand, and often repeat stays by the same guests, for these holiday lets.

Mainline railway station:	1 hour 50 minutes to Plymouth			
Road access:	Main access route M5, then A30 48 miles west of Plymouth 83 miles from M5			
Local newspaper:	Cornish Guardian 01208 781338			
Estate agents:	**Name**	**Address**	**Tel**	**Web**
	Towan Properties	21 Crantock St Newquay Cornwall TR7 1JJ	01637 878708	www.towan properties.com

Estate agents:	Name	Address	Tel	Web
	Newquay Property Centre	40 East St Newquay Cornwall TR7 1BH	01637 875161	www.newquay property.co.uk
	Miller & Co	1–3 Berry Road Newquay Cornwall TR7 1SF	01637 871242	www.rightmove. co.uk
	Webbers Property Services	Cliff Road Newquay Cornwall TR7 1SE	01637 873888	www.webbers. co.uk
Letting agents:	**Name**	**Address**	**Tel**	**Web**
	Stratton Creber	70 East Street Newquay Cornwall TR7 1BE	01637 876275	www.bbg.co.uk
	Lewis & Co Property Management	9–10 Market St Austell Cornwall PL25 4BB	01726 77900	lewiscoprop@ aol.com

Area:	**Norwich, Norfolk**				
Category:	A				
Investor profile:	Pension, Retirement, University, Downshifter, Business, Holiday and Cash&Equity				
Population aged 15+:	151,442				
	Actual			**National Average**	
Percentage Class ABC1:	42%			44%	
Crime:	**Violence**		**Sexual**	**Burglary**	**Motor**
Per 1000 population:	15		1	10	4
Yield range:	6.9% – 9.4%				

Price ranges:	Low £	Hi £	Low £pw	Hi £pw	Low	Hi
Flats & maisonettes	48,000	72,000	87	118	8.5%	9.4%
Terraced	64,800	97,200	103	140	7.5%	8.3%
Semi-detached	94,400	141,600	165	224	8.2%	9.1%
Detached	120,800	181,200	179	242	6.9%	7.7%

Percentage above the national average:	0%	
	Actual	**National Average**
Capital growth last 12 months:	38%	18%
Capital growth last 4 years:	112%	74%
Large employers in the area:	Norwich Union, Virgin Direct, the hospital, MARSH, BBC TV East and Anglia Television	
Demand for letting:	Good	
Average void period:	2 weeks	

	Capital Growth (out of 5)	Yield (out of 5)	Total (out of 10)
Our rating:	5	3	8

Summary:	The current dualling of the A11 highway makes this city a good growth target.
Description:	I used to work in Norwich and I loved it there. The only thing I didn't like about Norwich was the journey in and out of the city as it was single carraige all the way till you entered Suffolk! This is going to change when the A11 is converted to a dual carriageway due to be completed by the end of 2003. This will really open up Norwich. Its population is growing at a greater rate compared to the rest of the UK and there is already excess demand for good quality rental properties.

▶

	Many of the city's major employers have been in Norwich for at least 20 years and the city is famous for its financial services, electronics and engineering which are all expanding industries. Every major high street bank, insurance company and building society has a presence in Norwich as well as some of the major accountancy and law firms, recruitment, advertising and marketing agencies. Overall Norwich's unemployment rate is consistently lower than the national average at around 3%.
	This creates a high demand for rental properties from typically a younger than average workforce due to the type of industries they are in as mentioned above. Sharing a property is not uncommon and the 'Golden Triangle' area properties are very desirable amongst the 20–40 age group. Properties outside this area represent better value as they do not carry the premium for being in the area and are of equivalent standard – if not better! The University of East Anglia has a site at Norwich which creates further demand for rental properties.
	Tourism is also one of the Norwich's fastest growing industries which has helped employment in the city as well as created demand for good clean B&Bs.
Mainline railway station:	2 hours to Liverpool Street, London
Road access:	Main access routes A47, A11 64 miles north east of Cambridge 68 miles to M11
Local newspaper:	Norwich Evening News 01603 628311

Estate agents:	Name	Address	Tel	Web
	Tops Property Services	15–17 Princes Street Norwich Norfolk NR3 1AF	01603 767050	www.tops-property.co.uk
	Ewings	Marketplace Reepham Norwich Norfolk NR10 4JJ	01603 870473	www.ewings.co.uk
	Haart Estate Agents	18 Queen Street Norwich Norfolk NR2 4SQ	01603 761600	www.haart.co.uk
	Robert Wells Property Agents	2 Duke Street Norwich Norfolk NR3 3AJ	01603 660368	No website
	Potter & Co	2 Prince of Wales Road Norwich Norfolk NR1 1LB	01603 627201	www.teamprop.co.uk

▶

Estate agents:	Name	Address	Tel	Web
	Irelands	2 Harford Centre Hall Road Norwich Norfolk NR4 6DG	01603 250808	www.irelands. co.uk
	Gainsfords Estate Agents	Church Road Hoveton Norwich Norfolk NR12 8LG	01603 782978	www.gainsfords. co.uk

Letting agents:	Name	Address	Tel	Web
	William H Brown	5 Bank Plain Norwich Norfolk NR2 4SF	01603 627877	www.sequence home.co.uk
	FPD Savills plc	8–10 Upper King St Norwich Norfolk NR3 1HB	01603 229229	www.fpdsavills. co.uk
	Bush Property Management	Bridge House 1 Bridge Court Norwich Norfolk NR3 1UF	01603 614004	www.bush management. co.uk
	Elliots Residential Lettings	37 St Andrews St Norwich NR2 4TP	01603 454550	www.elliots estateagents. co.uk
	J S M Property Management	Eloise House 14 St George's St Norwich Norfolk NR3 1BA	01603 630671	www.jsm property.co.uk
	Brown & Co	Old Bank of England Court Queen St Norwich Norfolk NR2 4TA	01603 629871	www.brown-co.com
	Tops Property Services	11 Ring Rd Norwich Norfolk NR7 0XJ	01603 632244	www.tops-property.co.uk

Area:	**Oxford, Oxfordshire**					
Category:	C					
Investor profile:	Pension, Retirement, Downshifter, Business and Cash&Equity					
Population aged 15+:	163,766					
	Actual			**National Average**		
Percentage Class ABC1:	62%			44%		
Crime:	**Violence**	**Sexual**		**Burglary**	**Motor**	
Per 1000 population:	13	1		9	7	
Yield range:	3.5% – 8.3%					
Price ranges:	**Low £** **Hi £**	**Low £pw**	**Hi £pw**	**Low**	**Hi**	
Flats & maisonettes	117,600 176,400	187	253	7.5%	8.3%	
Terraced	160,000 240,000	158	213	4.6%	5.1%	
Semi-detached	172,000 258,000	256	347	7.0%	7.7%	
Detached	276,000 414,000	280	379	3.5%	5.3%	
Percentage above the national average:	66%					
	Actual			**National Average**		
Capital growth last 12 months:	20%			18%		
Capital growth last 5 years:	112%			80%		
Large employers in the area:	Electrocomponents, The Post Office, Vodafone, Regus & BT.					
Demand for letting:	**Excellent**					
Average void period:	1 week					
	Capital Growth (out of 5)	**Yield** (out of 5)		**Total** (out of 10)		
Our rating:	5	2		7		
Summary:	A world famous city to invest in – a safe bet.					
Description:	Oxford is the beefed up version of Cambridge. Again plenty of old historic buildings, tree lined avenues and large Victorian semis & terraces like Cambridge but Oxford simply has more of them! The city centre has everything – all the high street chains, indoor and outdoor markets, cinemas, boutiques, trendy and classy restaurants & bars, the list goes on. The prestige of Oxford as a university city masks what really is a good and varied local economy with significant bioscience, health, tourism, IT, publishing and creative media sectors. However, the student community is as large as Cambridge's in proportion, totalling around 30,000 and has a strong presence.					

	As an investment you can always rely on the student market. Oxford is one of the oldest universities of Great Britain so the inflow of students is consistent. Many private schools and publishers have been established because they can cash in on the 'Oxford' name. We also shouldn't forget Oxford Brookes University which has limited student accommodation, thus further increasing demand from the student sector.			

There are plenty of up and coming surrounding areas, the ones to look for being Sandford-on-Thames, Cowley & Greater Leys which are all in commuting distance and have high demand from the young professional sector. One area to avoid is Blackbird Leys as it is predominantly council housing and will only attract DSS claimant tenants or low paid workers.

The Oxford Business Park which totals 88 acres is located to the south east of the city and is next to the ring road with excellent commuter links to London, Heathrow Airport and the Midlands. Businesses are attracted to Oxford because of the highly skilled workforce it provides.

Mainline railway station:	One hour to London Paddington
Road access:	Main access routes A40, A44, A34, A420 59 miles north west of London 7 miles from M40
Local newspaper:	Oxford Mail 01865 425262

Estate agents:	Name	Address	Tel	Web
	Holyfield Estates Ltd	1 Walton Well Road Oxford Oxfordshire OX2 6ED	01865 515000	www.thomas merryfield.co.uk
	Finders Keepers Ltd	226 Banbury Road Oxford Oxfordshire OX2 7BY	01865 311011	Website currently under development
	Gilbert Walker	Eden House St Aldates Court St Aldates Oxford Oxfordshire OX1 1BN	01865 723551	Website currently under development
	E Gordon Hudson & Co	24 Friars Entry Oxford Oxfordshire OX1 2DB	01865 244089	Website currently under development
	David Tompkins Estate Agents	6 Chapel Way Botley Oxford Oxfordshire OX2 9LS	01865 436455	www.david tompkins.co.uk

Estate agents:	Name	Address	Tel	Web
	Premier	207 Cowley Road Oxford Oxfordshire OX4 1XF	01865 792299	Website currently under development
	Bradford & Bingley Buckell & Ballard	186 Banbury Road Summertown Oxford Oxfordshire OX2 7BY	01865 516201	www.bbg.co.uk
	Breckon & Breckon	5 King Edward Street Oxford Oxfordshire OX1 4HN	01865 244735	Website currently under development
	Oliver James	37 Park End Street Oxford Oxfordshire OX14 5BD	01235 553777	www.sequence home.co.uk
	Bradford & Bingley Adkin	12–13 St Clements Oxford Oxfordshire OX4 1YG	01865 727276	www.market place.co.uk
	Chancellors	215 Cowley Road Oxford Oxfordshire OX4 1XF	01865 240842	www.chancellors. co.uk
	Andrews Estate Agents	7 Elms Parade Botley Oxford Oxfordshire OX2 9LG	01865 790079	www.andrews online.co.uk
	Lear & Lear	263 Cowley Road Oxford Oxfordshire OX4 1XQ	01865 244833	Website currently under development
	James Penny	113 Walton Street Oxford Oxfordshire OX2 6AJ	01865 554422	www.jamesc penny.co.uk

Letting agents:	Name	Address	Tel	Web
	The Chancellors Group	107 London Rd Headington Oxford Oxfordshire OX3 9HZ	01865 292999	www.chancellors. co.uk
	Buckell & Ballard	7 St Aldates Oxford Oxfordshire OX1 1BS	01865 792888	www.bbg.co.uk
	John D Wood & Co	235 Banbury Rd Summertown Oxford Oxfordshire OX2 7HN	01865 311522	www.johnd wood.co.uk
	Cluttons	13 Beaumont St Oxford Oxfordshire OX1 2LP	01865 728000	www.cluttons. com
	Carter Jonas	Anchor House 269 Banbury Rd Summertown Oxford Oxfordshire OX2 7JF	01865 511444	www.carter jonas.co.uk
	Q B Management	114 London Rd Headington Oxford Oxfordshire OX3 9AX	01865 764533	www.qbman. co.uk
	Lifestyle Residential Lettings	267 Cowley Rd Oxford Oxfordshire OX4 1XQ	01865 244666	www.lifestyle- lettings.co.uk
	Hamptons International	1–4 The Plain Oxford Oxfordshire OX4 1AS	01865 723557	www.hamptons. co.uk
	Andrews Letting & Management	103 High St Oxford Oxfordshire OX1 4BW	01865 200401	www.andrews online.co.uk

Area:	**Padstow, Cornwall**				
Category:	C				
Investor profile:	Holiday Investor, Retirement Investor, Downshifter Investor				
Population aged 15+:	4,737				
	Actual			**National Average**	
Percentage Class ABC1:	53%			44%	
Crime:	**Violence**	**Sexual**		**Burglary**	**Motor**
Per 1000 population:	6	1		2	1
Yield range:	3.8% – 6.2%				

Price ranges:	Low £	Hi £	Low £pw	Hi £pw	Low	Hi
Flats & maisonettes	73,600	110,400	87	118	5.6%	6.1%
Terraced	92,000	138,000	91	124	4.7%	5.1%
Semi-detached	100,000	150,000	119	121	4.2%	6.2%
Detached	167,200	250,800	136	184	3.8%	4.2%

Percentage above the national average:	32%	
	Actual	**National Average**
Capital growth last 12 months:	47%	18%
Capital growth last 4 years:	88%	74%
Large employers in the area:	Mainly tourist related small businesses and local government, i.e. schools, hospitals and councils. Few large employers locally.	
Demand for letting:	OK	
Average void period:	5 weeks	

Our rating:	**Capital Growth** (out of 5) 4	**Yield** (out of 5) 3	**Total** (out of 10) 8

Summary:	Ignore the critical description of 'Kensington by the Sea' and look beyond to a hard working community with many seasonal changes to the population. Great town where it can be hard to buy due to the number of second homes. Good schools and the influence of the sea everywhere. Opportunities for buying more profitably just in outlying villages. A great base for a lifestyle investor pulling in rents from higher yield towns. My uncle and his family loved it and I can now understand why Padstow took him back to the sea.
Description:	The cream of the North Cornwall coastal communities, Padstow has a reputation that is hard to beat. It has seen enormous capital growth in recent years. Renting here has been very difficult given the number of

holiday homes in the area and the effect this has on supply for residents. On the other hand once you have been here – provided you can find the money – you may well want to come back and buy a slice of the place. It has restaurants, coffee bars, and small shops galore. Access to the rest of the West Country is quick and a train service to London is easily accessible.

The harbour area is probably too expensive for a new landlord to get involved in and a cottage or small flat will be a long time paying itself off from the rent. This will be made meagre by the high pricing. Yet, if you can access the monies from your portfolio of properties somewhere else, then regardless of whether you want to stay for the summer or come here at weekends throughout the year as a 'getaway' location, then this will be a shrewd investment. To get anywhere near a reasonable yield, step out of the town for a few minutes and look at the villages several miles away. Ten minutes in the car can save you a lot of money on the next investment. Simply by virtue of being further away from the sea, there will be a drop in pricing that makes a holiday home for you a more realistic option, especially if you can bear to rent it out commercially when you are not using it.

The regular boat from Padstow harbour in the summer months will take you across to Rock, or you can drive via the top road and St Minver. Rock is the place that has attracted the Sloane label as more people from London have bought family summer homes here. Certainly the prices have climbed steeply here, even more than Padstow, and the requirements for good eating and drinking have been well met by establishments that have risen to meet the challenge.

If you like what you see here, then stay a few days to get your research done well, but don't be too tempted by the summer holiday fantasy of buying the holiday home that you will use every weekend. Money invested in high yields elsewhere may be the route by which you get yourself a piece of Rock or Padstow!

Mainline railway station:	1 hour 40 minutes to Plymouth			
Road access:	Main access M5, then A30, then A389 39 miles west of Plymouth 66 miles from M5			
Local newspaper:	Cornish Guardian 01208 781338			
Estate agents:	**Name**	**Address**	**Tel**	**Web**
	Jackie Stanley	1 North Quay Padstow Cornwall PL28 8AF	01841 532555	www.jackie-stanley.co.uk
	Cole, Rayment & White	3 Duke Street Padstow Cornwall PL28 8AB	01841 533386	www.rightmove.co.uk

Estate agents:	Name	Address	Tel	Web
	Stratton Creber	8 The Strand Padstow Cornwall PL28 8AJ	01841 532230	www.market place.co.uk
Letting agents:	**Name**	**Address**	**Tel**	**Web**
	IPM	Bridge House Bridge End Wadebridge Cornwall PL27 6DA	01208 813888	Website currently under development

Area:	**Peterborough, Cambridgeshire**					
Category:	A					
Investor profile:	Pension, Business and Cash&Equity					
Population aged 15+:	107,987					
	Actual			**National Average**		
Percentage Class ABC1:	39%			44%		
Crime:	**Violence**		**Sexual**	**Burglary**		**Motor**
Per 1000 population:	17		1	10		8
Yield range:	4.5% – 8.8%					
Price ranges:	Low £	Hi £	Low £pw	Hi £pw	Low	Hi
Flats & maisonettes	44,800	67,200	76	103	8.0%	8.8%
Terraced	44,800	67,200	68	92	7.1%	7.9%
Semi-detached	69,600	104,400	106	143	7.1%	7.9%
Detached	116,000	174,000	111	150	4.5%	5.0%
Percentage above the national average:	0%					
	Actual			**National Average**		
Capital growth last 12 months:	22%			18%		
Capital growth last 4 years:	70%			74%		
Large employers in the area:	Coca Cola & Schweppes Beverages, British Sugar, ACCO UK, Freemans, Pearl Assurance, Peterborough Council & Royal Mail					
Demand for letting:	Good					
Average void period:	2 weeks					
Our rating:	**Capital Growth** (out of 5) 4		**Yield** (out of 5) 4	**Total** (out of 10) 7		
Summary:	Good population growth predicted so likelihood of above average property price growth.					
Description:	Peterborough is located 80 miles (128 kilometres) north of London and 40 miles (64 kilometres) north-west of Cambridge. The city benefits from frequent high-speed train services on the main East Coast rail line. Adjacent roads such as the A1(M), A14 and A47 provide swift access to the national road network. There are rapid connections with major airports such as Heathrow, Gatwick, Stansted, Luton, East Midlands and Birmingham. Peterborough is within easy reach of major East Coast sea ports such as Felixstowe, Harwich and Hull.					

	Peterborough's status as a dynamic business centre has been underlined by research that ranks the city as one of the four most productive non-metropolitan locations in Britain, along with Norwich, St Albans and Southampton. The 2002 UK Competitiveness Index – compiled by Robert Huggins Associates, a research-based economics consultancy and think-tank – places Peterborough in 15th position out of the country's top 56 city areas for overall competitiveness. The index benchmarks a range of economic factors including: Productivity, gross domestic product per person, economic activity, business density, proportion of knowledge-based businesses, unemployment rates and average earnings.
	Peterborough's projected population growth accelerates from 6.6% for the period 1996 – 2006 To 11% for the period 2006 – 2016
	Peterborough was designated a 'New Town' in 1968, and the Peterborough Development Corporation was established to double the city's population in close partnership with the city council. The master plan was to concentrate development in four new residential townships, each with a full range of social and economic facilities. The last of these, Hampton, is now being built to the south of the city, which will continue the city's growth into the next century with the development of over 5,000 houses and industry and commercial space for 12,000 jobs.
	The city centre has developed into a regional shopping centre. The indoor Queensgate centre, voted amongst the best in Europe, complements the older, tree-lined pedestrianised shopping area.
	Peterborough is a major centre for sport and recreation. Among its open spaces are the Nene Country Park and Ferry Meadows, with extensive sporting facilities. There are ten golf courses within 20 miles, and Peterborough is a centre for major shows and displays, including the East of England Show – Britain's second-largest agricultural show.
	Peterborough was designated an Environment City in 1992, one of only four cities in Britain to be given this status. A unique environment partnership exists between public, private and voluntary sectors, centred on the Peterborough Environment City Trust, which takes a lead role in many environmental initiatives in the area.
	A university for Peterborough has just been established, by a partnership involving the city council, a number of private and voluntary sector partners and Loughborough University.
Mainline railway station:	One hour to London Kings Cross
Road access:	Main access A47 & A1 55 miles south east of Nottingham 33 miles from M11
Local newspaper:	Peterborough Evening Telegraph 01733 555111

▶

Estate agents:	Name	Address	Tel	Web
	Cook & Ward	44 Cowgate Peterborough Cambridgeshire PE1 1NA	01733 774444	www.cook andward.com
	City & County Estate Agents	Brittanic House 11–13 Cowgate Peterborough Cambridgeshire PE1 1LZ	01733 563965	www.city-and-county.co.uk
	Dickens Watts & Dade	Saxon House Cross Street Peterborough Cambrdigeshire PE1 1XA	01733 344464	www.dwd property.com
	Woodcock Holmes Estate Agents	347 Lincoln Road Peterborough Cambridgeshire PE1 2PF	01733 557365	www.woodcock holmes.co.uk
Letting agents:	**Name**	**Address**	**Tel**	**Web**
	Covehome Ltd	85 Park Rd Peterborough Cambridgeshire PE1 2TN	01733 890044	www.cove home.co.uk
	Countrywide Residential Lettings	1 Queen St Peterborough Cambridgeshire PE1 1PA	01733 341888	www.rightmove. co.uk
	William H Brown	7–9 Cowgate Peterborough Cambridgeshire PE1 1LR	01733 553545	www.sequence home.co.uk

Area:	**Poole Harbour, Dorset**			
Category:	A			
Investor profile:	Holiday Investor, Retirement Investor, Downshifter Investor			
Population aged 15+:	111,169			
	Actual		**National Average**	
Percentage Class ABC1:	55%		44%	
Crime:	**Violence**	**Sexual**	**Burglary**	**Motor**
Per 1000 population:	8	1	5	5
Yield range:	6.9% – 14.5%			

Price ranges:	Low £	Hi £	Low £pw	Hi £pw	Low	Hi
Flats & maisonettes	75,200	112,800	209	284	13.1%	14.5%
Terraced	98,400	147,600	144	195	6.9%	7.6%
Semi-detached	115,200	172,800	200	271	8.2%	9.0%
Detached	157,600	236,400	289	391	8.6%	9.5%

Percentage above the national average:	25%	
	Actual	**National Average**
Capital growth last 12 months:	25%	18%
Capital growth last 4 years:	119%	74%
Large employers in the area:	Barclays Bank, Hugh Symons Group, Liverpool Victoria Assurance, Abbey Life Assurance, Dorset Healthcare Trust, Wessex Water, Borough of Poole, Bournemouth & Poole College	
Demand for letting:	Good	
Average void period:	3 weeks	

	Capital Growth (out of 5)	Yield (out of 5)	Total (out of 10)
Our rating:	4	5	9

Summary:	Busy, and mixed community from the high yielding decent investments to the Millionaires' Row properties out by the waters edge. Poole has plenty of opportunity. Stick with the high yield traditional stock and watch it rise to a better level. Can be hideously busy in summer season. You can buy well just a few miles out.
Description:	With the admission recently that Poole is short of 1000 housing units, the town represents a great opportunity for the landlord and investor. There are plenty of high priced units around the town including the expensive detached homes and apartments out on the Sandbanks, which surely represent some of the most glamorous, albeit most

expensive, properties in Dorset. However, the highest yields are found closer to the town centre and on the North side, as well as on the estates coming in from Wimborne Minster and Broadstone, as well as from Ferndown via Dudsbury and Ensbury.

The role that Bournemouth plays is crucial since it not only has more large companies where the tenants earn their salaries, but also has a much larger selection of housing available. As with most coastal communities the properties with the views and the easiest access to the shoreline or to the sea views will command the best prices. Running along the coast from Christchurch means that Southbourne, Boscombe, Westbourne, Canford and Parkstone offer good easy letting potential. Within the apartment blocks around both towns there is always a unit you can pick up at a better price than others, yet where the rent levels are still as high. Stick with these rather than be tempted by the best of everything at a high price with only the average rent.

The traffic through the urban areas can be slow particularly in the summer months as the hotels fill with visitors, and the A35 becoming the A338 can be pure drudge at these times. As a downshifting proposition being a landlord here with strong residual income offers you the scope for a way of life that comes at a lesser price than it might in Brighton, yet with the same facilities or better.

Unemployment in Poole and Dorset in general is very low and falling at faster rates than the country average.

The average age of residents in the coastal towns is above the UK average and Poole is of the same trend. You may find that the right properties will appeal to the retired affluent tenant group who have sold up elsewhere and may spend a year in a property of yours while they house hunt for themselves in a leisurely fashion. On the other hand the large number of financial services businesses spread between Poole and Bournemouth will also provide tenants with above average incomes, who will be seeking and expecting high quality rental accommodation.

Mainline railway station:	90 minutes to London Waterloo
Road access:	Main access route M27, then A31 5 miles west of Bournemouth 26 miles to M27
Local newspaper:	Bournemouth Daily Echo 01202 554601

Estate agents:	**Name**	**Address**	**Tel**	**Web**
	Greys Estate Agents	7 The Triangle Upton Poole Dorset BH16 5PG	01202 622101	www.greys estateagents. com
	Frost & Co	2 Station Road Poole Dorset BH14 8UB	01202 778855	www.frost-estateagents. co.uk

▶

Estate agents:	Name	Address	Tel	Web
	Sibbett Gregory	6 Winchester Place North Street Poole Dorset BH15 1NX	01202 661177	www.sibbett gregory.com
	Haven Estate Agents	11 Haven Road Canford Cliffs Poole Dorset BH13 7LE	01202 706888	www.haven estateagents .co.uk
	Herrings	23b Church Road Lower Parkstone Poole Dorset BH14 8UF	01202 747555	Website currently under development
	R & S Estate Agents	171 Alder Road Parkstone Poole Dorset BH12 4AN	01202 733016	Website currently under development
	Thomas & Rawson	461 Ashley Road Parkston Poole Dorset BH14 0AX	01202 721131	Website currently under development
Letting agents:	**Name**	**Address**	**Tel**	**Web**
	Quality Residential Management	1 Station Rd Parkstone Poole Dorset BH14 8UA	01202 716553	www.quality-residential.co.uk
	Palmer Snell	325 Wimborne Rd Oakdale Poole Doreset BH15 3DH	01202 677400	www.palmer snell.co.uk
	Goadsby & Harding	245 High St North Poole Dorset BH15 1DX	01202 673375	www.goadsby co.uk

Area:	**Portsmouth, Hampshire**					
Category:	A					
Investor profile:	Residential Cashflow Investment, Capital Appreciation Investment and Retirement.					
Population aged 15+:	157,311					
	Actual			**National Average**		
Percentage Class ABC1:	48%			44%		
Crime:	**Violence**		**Sexual**	**Burglary**		**Motor**
Per 1000 population:	16		1	6		6
Yield range:	7.0% – 16.4%					
Price ranges:	Low £	Hi £	Low £pw	Hi £pw	Low	Hi
Flats & maisonettes	54,400	81,600	191	258	12.2%	16.4%
Terraced	79,200	118,800	146	197	8.6%	9.6%
Semi-detached	96,800	145,200	144	195	7.0%	7.7%
Detached	101,600	152,400	156	211	7.2%	8.0%
Percentage above the national average:	0%					
	Actual			**National Average**		
Capital growth last 12 months:	24%			18%		
Capital growth last 5 years:	106%			80%		
Large employers in the area:	Mainly tourist related small businesses and local government, i.e. schools, hospitals and councils. Few large employers locally.					
Demand for letting:	**Excellent**					
Average void period:	2 weeks					
Our rating:	**Capital Growth** (out of 5) 4		**Yield** (out of 5) 5		**Total** (out of 10) **9**	
Summary:	I was here for my degree and lived in Southsea and then on neighbouring Hayling Island. The navy and the students were in roughly equal numbers, now the university has its own way and offers great income for good landlords. Also a good place for a family seeking good options for schools while bringing in strong rental income. And because it's an island you can see there is only so much competition from other housing!					
Description:	A bustling town surrounded by modern and traditional industrial estates and business parks and with a huge university demand for housing, Portsmouth represents consistent opportunity. The city has worked hard to make a new identity for itself in replacing the former focus solely on naval activity.					

▶

	The Gunwharf Quays development provides a range of leisure facilities, bars and restaurants set in magnificent harbour surroundings and is only 15 minutes' walk from the main University campus.
	Southsea is Portsmouth's Victorian seaside resort and offers four miles of coastline flanked by open spaces, gardens and public parks. This is the ideal place for students to live and many landlords concentrate their properties around here, working closely with the Student Accommodation Office.
	The closure of the former Royal Marines barracks has created some high quality investment opportunities in a community space. Elsewhere classic homes are available in Old Portsmouth at a premium and around the broad and friendly streets of Southsea. Further from the centre of the island Milton, Somerstown, Fratton and North End offer good opportunities for regular lettings to the student market which in this town is the biggest rental sector audience.
	The University has established a 2 tier registration scheme for private landlords. It begins at the Standard level of £48 per week plus food and bills and rises slightly for their Premium designated properties offering a higher quality. Even with the best value three bed properties around the South and centre of the island going for more than £110,000 – £125,000 you can make decent yields with these figures. The further North you move up the island the cheaper the housing becomes. For these look in and around Hilsea and North End, or just onto the mainland at Cosham. To the East look to Milton and then at Eastney, where prices can climb again because of the developments at this side of the island.
	In early September the Students' Union and the University provide a two day housing experience designed to help students find accommodation in the city's private rented sector. These Secure-a-Home days are unique to the University of Portsmouth, offering new students the chance to find both their housemates and their first home. Students stay in university accommodation overnight and then spend a day looking at properties. This gives the landlord the opportunity to have the equivalent of an open-day at each property and be confident of letting the property.
	The A3 is the fast route up to London, passing the attractive town of Petersfield which is worth exploring for good rental opportunities to professional tenants. The quality of life here is high with the area also being well served by a good Farmers' Market, boutiques, office services and all levels of education provision. Look also at villages such as Ramsdean, East Meon, High Cross, the Hartings, and Buriton.
	Southampton hosts the closest local airport, but fast motorway links mean that Heathrow is similarly accessible. The train to central London takes just 85 minutes. Motorways such as the M275 and M27 get you off the island and up to Southampton and then the New Forest.
Mainline railway station:	1 hour 40 minutes to London Waterloo

Road access:	Main access route M27, then M275 19 miles south east of Southampton 6 miles from M27			
Local newspaper:	Portsmouth News 023 9266 4488			
Estate agents:	**Name**	**Address**	**Tel**	**Web**
	Jeffries & Partners	112–114 London Road North Portsmouth Hampshire PO2 0LZ	023 9266 1662	www.jeffries.uk.com
	Vail Williams	1 The Quarterdeck Port Solent Portsmouth Hampshire PO6 4TP	023 9220 3200	www.vailwilliams.com
	Mann & Co (South East)	101b High St Cosham Portsmouth Hampshire PO6 3AZ	023 9238 1244	www.rightmove.co.uk
	Stevens & Partners	99 London Road Portsmouth Hampshire PO2 0BN	023 9266 0888	www.stevenspartners.co,uk
	Mitchell & Perrye	212 London Road Portsmouth Hampshire PO2 9JE	023 9266 3060	No website
	Whymark Estate Agents	146 London Road Portsmouth Hampshire PO2 9DJ	023 9269 0044	www.whymarkgroup.co.uk
Letting agents:	**Name**	**Address**	**Tel**	**Web**
	Bradford & Bingley Marketplace Ltd	74 Palmerston Rd Southsea Hants PO5 3PT	02392 737121	www.bbg.co.uk
	Your Move	194 Havant Rd Drayton Portsmouth Hampshire PO6 2EH	023 9269 9095	www.your-move.co.uk/lettings

▶

Letting agents:	Name	Address	Tel	Web
	Fox & Sons	126 London Rd Portsmouth Hampshire PO2 9DE	023 9267 1212	www.sequence home.co.uk
	Countrywide Residential Lettings	127 London Rd North End Portsmouth Hampshire PO2 9AA	023 9265 0101	www.rightmove .co.uk
	Leaders Limited	132–134 London Rd Portsmouth Hampshire PO2 9DE	023 9266 6111	www.leaders .co.uk
	Veness Ltd	107 High St Cosham Portsmouth Hampshire PO6 3BB	023 9221 0071	www.veness .co.uk

Area:	**Reading, Berkshire**			
Category:	C			
Investor profile:	Pension, University and Cash&Equity			
Population aged 15+:	178,448			
	Actual		**National Average**	
Percentage Class ABC1:	60%		44%	
Crime:	**Violence**	**Sexual**	**Burglary**	**Motor**
Per 1000 population:	13	1	13	10
Yield range:	5.3% – 8.3%			

Price ranges:	Low £	Hi £	Low £pw	Hi £pw	Low	Hi
Flats & maisonettes	92,800	139,200	148	201	7.5%	8.3%
Terraced	111,200	166,800	150	203	6.3%	7.0%
Semi-detached	146,400	219,600	165	224	5.3%	5.9%
Detached	206,400	309,600	293	396	6.7%	7.4%

Percentage above the national average:	42%	
	Actual	**National Average**
Capital growth last 12 months:	17%	18%
Capital growth last 4 years:	93%	74%
Large employers in the area:	BG(HQ), Compaq, Energis, Foster Wheeler, Scottish Courage Brewing, Gillette, ICL, JD Edwards, Microsoft (HQ), Oracle (HQ), Prudential Assurance, Racal (HQ), Seagate Software (HQ), Thames Water, Thorn UK, Yellow Pages	
Demand for letting:	**Excellent**	
Average void period:	1 week	

	Capital Growth (out of 5)	**Yield** (out of 5)	**Total** (out of 10)
Our rating:	5	3	**8**

Summary:	The UK's future version of Silicon Valley
Description:	Reading, at the centre of the Thames Valley, is a fast growing city. It is one of the fastest growing in the UK for retail, businesses, transportation and leisure – and there is no evidence of a slow down. The recent dramatic expansion of Reading's shopping facilities by the creation of The Oracle Shopping & Leisure Destination has led to Reading being the 13th top shopping centre in the UK. It is predicted they will go top 10 by 2004 with over 100 retailers queuing to get through the door!

	Reading intends to go international and it has already attracted several major international hi-tech companies, including Microsoft, Compaq and Worldcom. Also due to Reading's large catchment area (around 1.7m people) and great transportation links it has successfully attracted the national headquarters of a number of financial and commercial organisations.
	Under expansion is a major business park, Green Park, which will make this one of the largest in the UK providing 2.25m sq ft of office space.
	Reading's workforce is predominantly business services or finance thus attracting a higher earning individual with 35% of the workforce holding down a managerial or professional job. The University of Reading also produces a highly skilled workforce who usually stay on and live in the area due to the excellent facilities the city provides.
	Unemployment is extremely low, at around 1.7%, the population is growing and so is the local GDP – so all the key statistics point in the right direction!
Mainline railway station:	30 minutes to London Paddington
Road access:	Main access A4, A33, A329(M) & M4 41 miles west of London 4 miles from M4
Local newspaper:	Reading Evening Post 0118 9183000

Estate agents:	Name	Address	Tel	Web
	Warmingham & Co	4 & 5 High Street Reading Berkshire RG8 9AT	01491 874144	Website currently under development
	Patrick Williams	303–305 Oxford Road Reading Berkshire RG30 1AU	0118 957 3579	www.patrick williams.co.uk

Letting agents:	Name	Address	Tel	Web
	Parkers Lower Earley	34 Maiden Lane Centre, Kilnsea Drive Lower Earley Reading Berkshire RG6 3HD	0118 935 1700	www.parkers properties.co.uk

Letting agents:	Name	Address	Tel	Web
	Kings Property Management	46 Prospect St Caversham Reading Berkshire RG4 8JL	0118 946 2323	www.kings-lettings.co.uk
	Jon Hallett Ltd	2 Kings Walk Reading Berkshire RG1 2HG	0118 959 5858	www.jon hallett.com
	Romans	23 Market Place Wokingham Berkshire RG40 1AP	0118 953 8710	www.romans .co.uk
	Countrywide Residential Lettings	147 Friar St Reading Berkshire RG1 1EX	0118 950 9901	www.rightmove .co.uk

Area:	**Ripon, North Yorkshire**					
Category:	A					
Investor profile:	Cash & Equity Investor, Holiday Investor, Downshifter Investor					
Population aged 15+:	20,860					
	Actual			**National Average**		
Percentage Class ABC1:	52%			44%		
Crime:	Violence		Sexual	Burglary		Motor
Per 1000 population:	8		1	5		3
Yield range:	4.4% – 10.9%					
Price ranges:	Low £ Hi £	Low £pw	Hi £pw	Low		Hi
Flats & maisonettes	80,800 121,200	170	230	9.9%		10.9%
Terraced	78,400 117,600	117	158	7.0%		7.8%
Semi-detached	108,800 163,200	124	169	5.4%		5.9%
Detached	204,800 307,200	191	258	4.4%		4.8%
Percentage above the national average:	0%					
	Actual			**National Average**		
Capital growth last 12 months:	29%			18%		
Capital growth last 4 years:	79%			74%		
Large employers in the area:	Mainly tourist related small businesses and local government, i.e. schools, hospitals and councils. Few large employers locally.					
Demand for letting:	**Excellent**					
Average void period:	3 weeks					
Our rating:	**Capital Growth** (out of 5) 4		**Yield** (out of 5) 4		**Total** (out of 10) 8	
Summary:	Old and quaint hides behind a new ring road and an improving waterways network. Expensive terraces pushing yields down as commuters can now reach Leeds and the Northeast from here.					
Description:	On our very first night in Ripon I had to get down to the Market Square at 9.00pm to watch a ceremony that has been going on every night for more than 1,000 years. It is the 'setting the watch' custom in which a gentleman 'hornblower' sounds the hour at each corner of an obelisk in the centre of town. This tradition gives you a sense of the history pervading the town, whether it is the inspiring cathedral just south of the town centre, or the World Heritage site of Fountains Abbey and Studley Royal just three miles from town.					

Modern commuters love the place too, placed as it is between Leeds and Middlesbrough. As Leeds has seen the growth of its financial district and the M1 extension around to Harrogate and beyond has improved, so to have the prices of property. The terraced houses to the north west of the Square have begun to trip over into almost six figures and a small two bed flat overlooking the canal basin can hold a far higher price. The improvements to the partial ring road on the west side have helped push prices, but the road down to Harrogate can still be a dangerous one.

The impact of the good schooling in town has been strong on the market, with many looking for quality of life and rethinking the cost of a private education. There is strong competition to get children into Ripon Grammar School for its excellent teaching methods and good staff. Close by in Harrogate and Knaresborough the picture is similar in respect of schooling and good results. The North Yorkshire Moors National Park and the Pennines are on your doorstep.

If prices here seem too high for starters look instead to the towns of Masham, Knaresborough, Northallerton and Thirsk, where there is still good scope for the capital growth that has already happened in Ripon and driven rental yields down as a result. Many of the surrounding villages can also give good scope for capital growth, particular those out to the east side of town and the easy access to the road networks.

Mainline railway station:	50 minutes to York – 2 hours plus to London Paddington
Road access:	Main access A1, then A61 27 miles north of Leeds 5 miles from A1
Local newspaper:	Harrogate Advertiser 01423 564321

Estate agents:	Name	Address	Tel	Web
	Beadnall Copley	10 Fishergate Ripon North Yorkshire HG4 1DY	01765 698100	www.beadnall copley.com
	Halifax Estate Agents	37 Market Place South Ripon North Yorkshire HG4 1DG	01765 552913	www.rightmove. co.uk
	Dacre Son & Hartley	10 Queen St Ripon North Yorkshire HG4 1ED	01765 605151	www.bakers. co.uk
	Joplings	10 North St Ripon North Yorkshire HG4 1JY	01765 694800	Website currently under development

▶

Letting agents:	Name	Address	Tel	Web
	Carrington Property Management	40 North St Ripon North Yorkshire HG4 1HJ	01423 323100	www.lcproperty. free-online.co.uk
	Belvoir Lettings Teeside	22 Skelldale View Ripon North Yorkshire HG4 1UJ	01765 606601	www.belvoir lettings.com
	Premiere Estates	3a Westgate Ripon North Yorkshire HG4 2AT	01765 690059	Website currently under development

Area:	**Romford, Essex**					
Category:	A					
Investor profile:	Pension, Business and Cash&Equity					
Population aged 15+:	51,624					
	Actual			**National Average**		
Percentage Class ABC1:	62%			44%		
Crime:	**Violence**		**Sexual**	**Burglary**		**Motor**
Per 1000 population:	14		1	5		8
Yield range:	4.1% – 9.7%					
Price ranges:	Low £	Hi £	Low £pw	Hi £pw	Low	Hi
Flats & maisonettes	82,400	123,600	153	207	8.7%	9.7%
Terraced	119,200	178,800	175	236	6.9%	7.6%
Semi-detached	145,600	218,400	193	262	6.2%	6.9%
Detached	243,200	364,800	214	289	4.1%	4.6%
Percentage above the national average:	5%					
	Actual			**National Average**		
Capital growth last 12 months:	22%			18%		
Capital growth last 5 years:	95%			80%		
Large employers in the area:	Retail – Lakeside and Bluewater complexes locally.					
Demand for letting:	Good					
Average void period:	2 weeks					
Our rating:	**Capital Growth** (out of 5) 4		**Yield** (out of 5) 4		**Total** (out of 10) **8**	
Summary:	Good inner M25 area that hasn't seen a ridiculous surge in property prices.					
Description:	The shopping capital of the south east! It has more retail space than both Lakeside and Bluewater (two large self-contained shopping complexes located on the London borders) and is ranked as one of the top five shopping centres in Greater London. People travel from surrounding areas including the east of London to enjoy the range of shops Romford provides. I predict that Romford will be the largest shopping complex within the M25 within 5 years thus providing a large employment requirement.					

	This strong retail side of Romford attracts further businesses to locate to this area and is home to more than 7,000 businesses employing around 70,000 people. There are many Head Offices located in Romford tending to be insurance companies for a reason that is unknown to me.
	Areas such as Gidea Park, Harold Wood and Upminster will always be good investments as they all have mainline railway connections to Liverpool Street Station in the city. Areas to avoid are Harold Hill and Collier Row as these are predominantly council housing.
	This is the only area I have mentioned that is within the M25 because it is really the only area that is good value. Flats are readily available under the £90,000 mark which represents an excellent return on your investment. I have only one property in Romford and I am currently looking to invest further, as I predict that this town will experience a medium to long term gain in excess of most areas neighbouring the city of London.
Mainline railway station:	25–30 minutes to Liverpool Street Station, London
Road access:	Main access route A12 18 miles east of Central London 4 miles from M25
Local newspaper:	Romford Recorder Series 01708 771500

Estate agents:	Name	Address	Tel	Web
	Porter Glenny	77 Main Road Romford Essex RM2 5ER	01708 764418	www.porter glenny.co.uk
	Keys & Lee	215 Pettits Lane North Romford Essex RM1 4NU	01708 723658	www.keys andlee.com
	Ashton & Perkins	30 Victoria Road Romford Essex RM1 2JH	01708 723700	www.ashton perkins.co.uk
	Hilbery Chaplin	Atlanta House 148 South Street Romford Essex RM1 1SX	01708 767676	www.hilbery chaplin.co.uk
	Payne & Co	30–32 Station Road Chadwell Heath Romford Essex RM6 4BE	020 8597 7555	www.payne andco.co.uk
	Beresford Estate Agents	52 Collier Row Road Romford Essex RM5 3PA	01708 730707	www.beresfords group.co.uk

▶

Estate agents:	Name	Address	Tel	Web
	Glenisters Estate Agents	32 Victoria Road Romford Essex RM1 2JH	01708 747470	www.glenisters direct.co.uk

Letting agents:	Name	Address	Tel	Web
	Andrews Letting & Management	20, North St Romford Essex RM1 1BH	01708 753521	www.andrews online.co.uk
	Hilbery Chaplin Residential	Atlanta House 148 South Street Romford Essex RM1 1SX	01708 737373	www.hilbery chaplin.co.uk
	Beresfords Letting Division	52 Collier Row Road Romford Essex RM5 3PA	01708 738100	www.beresfords group.co.uk

Area:	**Salisbury, Wiltshire**					
Category:	C					
Investor profile:	Cash&Equity, Holiday, Retirement, Downshifter					
Population aged 15+:	37,119					
	Actual			**National Average**		
Percentage Class ABC1:	53%			44%		
Crime:	**Violence**		**Sexual**	**Burglary**		**Motor**
Per 1000 population:	7		1	4		2
Yield range:	3.5% – 7.6%					
Price ranges:	**Low £**	**Hi £**	**Low £pw**	**Hi £pw**	**Low**	**Hi**
Flats & maisonettes	74,400	111,600	109	148	6.9%	7.6%
Terraced	110,400	165,600	131	178	5.6%	6.2%
Semi-detached	136,800	205,200	147	200	5.1%	5.6%
Detached	208,800	313,200	156	211	3.5%	3.9%
Percentage above the national average:	29%					
	Actual			**National Average**		
Capital growth last 12 months:	21%			18%		
Capital growth last 5 years:	72%			74%		
Large employers in the area:	Mainly tourist related small businesses and local government, i.e. schools, hospitals and councils. Few large employers locally.					
Demand for letting:	Good					
Average void period:	6 weeks					
Our rating:	**Capital Growth** (out of 5) 4		**Yield** (out of 5) 3		**Total** (out of 10) 7	
Summary:	As a gorgeous place for living and working Salisbury is hard to beat. Seasonal rentals are good with the opportunity for high quality tourist lets. The average yields are exceeded by strong capital values. Big demand in the villages within a 15 minute drive.					
Description:	Sitting elegantly between the West Country and the New Forest, Wessex and the Coast, Salisbury occupies a unique and beautiful location for residents and investors alike. Easily one of the most charming small towns in England it can also be expensive. Don't expect huge yields here except perhaps on some of the older estates and among former ex local authority properties. There is strong demand for detached commuter homes with ease of access to the road network. With much					

effort made each year to promote the now thirty year old and ever famous Salisbury Festival, and the strong pull of the medieval Cathedral, it comes as no surprise that Salisbury attracts more than 600,000 visiting tourists each year. Most of these are day trippers but many will locate themselves in the area for as much as a week. Hardly the opportunity for an AST bonanza but offering plenty for the B & B or mini serviced lets to the affluent. Also consider the issues of traffic, parking and general congestion before you think about moving down here for the ease of access to the Downs and the Plain.

But step away from the Cathedral and its famed Close, and enter the main town and you see a different picture. Many smaller communities within a short drive are existing without the same shops and suppliers they had as recently as this is a magnet for shopping from many outlying areas, not all of which are prosperous. Rural villages locally can often appear to have lost much of their heart, in exchange for access to the shopping centres that Salisbury has to offer.

The Ministry of Defence has two of its four largest garrisons nearby, and housing for this huge force has been increasing as a problem for several years. Most recently the announcement of a Public & Private Partnership initiative for technical, administrative and domestic accommodation for forces in the Salisbury Plain area and nearby Aldershot has attracted investors with long-term thinking. The biggest need as identified by the review is for single persons accommodation and much of it is off camp provision, creating interesting potential for the private landlord/developer close to these garrisons.

With the estimated contract value being around £1 billion over 25 years, the results of the PPP/PFI initiative and competitive tendering exercise will be awaited later in 2003 with keen interest. Of the 10,700 bed spaces as many as 2,500 will be within an hour of Salisbury.

In the town a thriving Charter Market continues to trade regardless of the weather, featuring a daily farmers section, as well as the regular stalls providing residents and visitors with the staples of a good life. At the top end of the market you can enjoy a coffee at an outside table café as you watch the crowds go by.

Elsewhere in town the Maltings Shopping Centre features a Sainsbury supermarket and local stores providing the usual array of retail goods. It helps that the Maltings and the adjoining Central Car Park provide over 1600 parking spaces. Further along the river the Wilton Shopping Village offers a broad range of the factory outlet type of shop.

Mainline railway station:	85 minutes to London Waterloo
Road access:	Main access A30 & A36 22 miles north west of Southampton 15 miles from M27
Local newspaper:	Salisbury Journal 01722 412525

Estate agents:	Name	Address	Tel	Web
	McKillop & Gregory	44 Castle Street Salisbury Wiltshire SP1 3TS	01722 414747	www.mckillop andgregory.co.uk
	Myddelton & Major	49 High St Salisbury Wiltshire SP1 2PD	01722 337575	www.myddelton major.co.uk
	Simon Colligan Estate Agents	2 High St Amesbury Salisbury SP4 7DL	01980 625173	www.rightmove. co.uk
	Clifford & Drew	62 Castle St Salisbury Wiltshire SP1 3TS	01722 329795	www.rightmove. co.uk
	Connell Estate Agents	46–50 Castle St Salisbury Wiltshire SP1 3TS	01722 328562	www.connells. co.uk
	Knapman & Bament	St Thomas's Square Salisbury Wiltshire SP1 1TW	01722 325125	Website currently under development
	Symonds & Sampson	89 Crane St Salisbury Wiltshire SP1 2PU	01722 336944	www.symonds andsampson. co.uk
	Austin & Wyatt	54 Castle St Salisbury Wiltshire SP1 3TS	01722 338444	www.rightmove. co.uk
Letting agents:	**Name**	**Address**	**Tel**	**Web**
	Woolley & Wallis	51–61 Castle St Salisbury Wiltshire SP1 3SU	01722 424535	www.w-w.co.uk
	Goadsby & Harding	31 Castle St Salisbury Wiltshire SP1 1TT	01722 323444	www.goadsby .co.uk
	Strutt & Parker	41 Milford St Salisbury Wiltshire SP1 2BP	01722 328741	www.struttand parker.com

Area:	**Selby, North Yorkshire**					
Category:	B					
Investor profile:	Capital Growth, Cashflow Investment and Retirement					
Population aged 15+:	30,896					
	Actual			**National Average**		
Percentage Class ABC1:	50%			44%		
Crime:	**Violence**		**Sexual**	**Burglary**		**Motor**
Per 1000 population:	9		1	5		3
Yield range:	6.5% – 14.0%					
Price ranges:	**Low £**	**Hi £**	**Low £pw**	**Hi £pw**	**Low**	**Hi**
Flats & maisonettes	22,400	33,600	60	81	12.5%	14.0%
Terraced	37,600	56,400	69	94	8.7%	9.5%
Semi-detached	54,400	81,600	81	110	7.0%	7.5%
Detached	79,200	118,800	110	149	6.5%	7.2%
Percentage above the national average:	0%					
	Actual			**National Average**		
Capital growth last 12 months:	16%			18%		
Capital growth last 4 years:	32%			74%		
Large employers in the area:	Major industry from cities nearby					
Demand for letting:	**Excellent**					
Average void period:	2 weeks					
	Capital Growth (out of 5)		**Yield** (out of 5)		**Total** (out of 10)	
Our rating:	3		5		**8**	
Summary:	Ever since I was a kid on family holidays in Yorkshire I have enjoyed the town and its regular market. Good opportunities here and in the villages offering easy commutes to York and/or the M62.					
Description:	Enjoying an important location between York and Doncaster, Leeds and the Humber, Selby has been ignored by investors for a long time. Now, however, it stands to benefit from the finishing of the new bypass which will speed up traffic flow around the outside of the town, leaving more peace for the town centre.					
	Scope here for capital growth as well as good current cashflow investment. Employment is good with several decent towns and cities being within a 45 minute commute. As a result there is good demand					

▶

	for new build on estates springing up around the outskirts of town and the new road structure will add significantly to their values. Look to surrounding villages just off the bypass as well as those between Selby and York to give good growth. Barlby, Osgodby, Escrick, Appleton Roebuck, Riccall, Camblesforth and Drax can all offer value to investors serving the York/Leeds commuter market, while some provide potential for retirement within a community. A good place to live for work/life balance Selby district is surrounded by idyllic rural scenery and three thriving market towns. It also benefits from excellent business parks and training facilities, and enjoys a skilled workforce. This has attracted big name employers to the area. **Transportation** Good infrastructure links allow for a good business relationship with nearby economies in Leeds (A63) and York (A19). The enhanced and widened A1M is just 10 miles to the West and the M62 lies only 8 miles South of the town, affording fast access to Scunthorpe and Kingston upon Hull. The Selby Bypass has an intended completion date for Spring of 2004. It is for a single carriageway road 6.25 miles long that passes to the south of Selby from Thorpe Willoughby in the west to Barlby in the east. Roundabouts will be built at each end and at the Al9 and the Al041 where they are crossed by the route.
Mainline railway station:	35 minutes to Leeds
Road access:	Main access A19 & A63 30 miles east of Leeds 8 miles from M62
Local newspaper:	Evening Press 01904 653 051
Estate agents:	**Name** · **Address** · **Tel** · **Web**

Name	Address	Tel	Web
APS Estate Agents	11 Finkle Street Selby North Yorkshire YO8 4DT	01757 213832	www.askaps.co.uk
Keith Taylor	56 Gowthorpe Selby North Yorkshire YO8 4ET	01757 709457	www.keithtaylorproperty.co.uk
Stephensons	43 Gowthorpe Selby North Yorkshire YO8 4HE	01757 706707	www.stephensons4property.co.uk
Ashtons Estate Agents	17 Finkle Street Selby North Yorkshire YP8 4DT	01757 213999	www.ashtonsnet.com

Estate agents:	Name	Address	Tel	Web
	Park Row Properties	14 Finkle Street Selby North Yorkshire YP8 4DS	01757 241124	www.parkrow properties.co.uk
Letting agents:	**Name**	**Address**	**Tel**	**Web**
	West Yorkshire Property Rentals	PO Box 93 Selby YO8 3YS	01757 269265	Website currently under development

Area:	**Southampton, Hampshire**			
Category:	A			
Investor profile:	Cash&Equity Investor, Holiday Investor, Retirement Investor, University Investor, Business Investor			
Population aged 15+:	184,131			
	Actual		**National Average**	
Percentage Class ABC1:	52%		44%	
Crime:	Violence	Sexual	Burglary	Motor
Per 1000 population:	14	2	6	8
Yield range:	3.4% – 12.7%			

Price ranges:	Low £	Hi £	Low £pw	Hi £pw	Low	Hi
Flats & maisonettes	75,200	112,800	162	219	11.4%	12.7%
Terraced	99,200	148,800	178	241	7.1%	7.8%
Semi-detached	113,600	170,400	147	198	4.0%	4.5%
Detached	228,000	342,000	198	269	3.4%	3.8%

Percentage above the national average:	5%	
	Actual	**National Average**
Capital growth last 12 months:	30%	18%
Capital growth last 5 years:	119%	80%
Large employers in the area:	Southampton City Council, The Ordnance Survey, Vosper Thornycroft, University Hospitals Trust, Skandia, The Stationery Office, University of Southampton, UK Air Traffic Control Centre	
Demand for letting:	Excellent	
Average void period:	3 weeks	

	Capital Growth (out of 5)	Yield (out of 5)	Total (out of 10)
Our rating:	4	5	9

Summary:	So many investment styles are catered for here. Which one do you want? Huge student community and a massive demand from professional tenants across many industries. Do your research here and come out with some tremendous yields.
Description:	Despite being 30 miles inland from the English Channel, Southampton has built a powerful and well deserved reputation as a city of seafarers, and the names of Walter Raleigh, Francis Drake, the *Titanic*, The Whitbread Round the World Race, and the Southampton Boat Show are known around the world. Southampton Water flows out to the Solent

and past the Isle of Wight providing the busiest waterway on the UK coast. While the beauty of the New Forest may also serve to encourage people to want to live in this city, Southampton also lays claim to being a centre of learning, through the University and through the several hundred small research businesses based in and around the city.

The maritime industry fuels a good part of the employment market here and the potential to develop the Port of Southampton with a self-contained terminal at Dibden on the western shore will create more work and with this, more demand for housing.

The Service sector is strong with nearly 25% of employees in Southampton working in banking, insurance, property and land and other business services. This tenant group has specific requirements in housing stock and represents good opportunities for landlords in the city.

A third big user of accommodation is the University of Southampton which provides and manages 5,000 spaces within Halls of Residence but also goes out to the private landlord to accommodate a further 6,000 students each year.

Development and regeneration programmes in the city affect areas such as West Itchen, Outer Shirley, Weston Shore and Thornhill. Buying in and close to these areas can result in good capital growth over an extended period while providing good yields on standard rent.

Just off the M3 between Winchester and Southampton, there is always strong demand for rental housing around Chandlers Ford, and Eastleigh. Also look to Bassett, Swaythling, Thornhill, and Hedge End as places where tenants want easy access to the motorway East to Fareham, Cosham, Havant and Portsmouth for work. Closer to the city centre new waterside apartments are commanding good prices off plan and may represent strong capital growth benefits and above average rents.

Mainline railway station:	75 – 90 minutes to London Waterloo
Road access:	Main access routes M3, then M27, then M271 80 miles south west of Central London 8 miles to M3
Local newspaper:	The Southern Daily Echo 023 8042 4777

Estate agents:	Name	Address	Tel	Web
	Home from Home	60 Oxford Street Southampton SO14 3DL	023 8088 1000	Website currently under development
	London Clancy	2 Carlton Crescent Southampton SO15 2EY	023 8033 0442	www.london clancy.com
	Primmer Olds	61 Cromwell Road Southampton SO15 2JE	023 8022 2292	www.primmer olds.co.uk

Estate agents:	Name	Address	Tel	Web
	Vail Williams	Meridians House 7 Ocean Way Ocean Village Southampton SO14 3TJ	023 8082 0900	www.vail williams.com

Letting agents:	Name	Address	Tel	Web
	Pearsons Residential Letting	58 London Rd Southampton Hampshire SO15 2AH	023 8023 2909	www.pearsons .com
	Fox & Sons	390c Bitterne Villages Bitterne Rd Southampton Hampshire SO18 5RS	023 8036 2000	www.sequence home.co.uk
	Your Move	4 West End Rd Bitterne Southampton Hampshire SO18 6TG	023 8033 9983	www.your-move.co.uk/ lettings

Area:	**Southend-on-Sea, Essex**				
Category:	A				
Investor profile:	Pension, Retirement, B&B, Business, Holiday and Cash&Equity				
Population aged 15+:	152,617				

	Actual		**National Average**		
Percentage Class ABC1:	57%		44%		

Crime:	**Violence**	**Sexual**	**Burglary**	**Motor**
Per 1000 population:	11	1	8	6

Yield range:	4.9% – 10.6%					

Price ranges:	Low £	Hi £	Low £pw	Hi £pw	Low	Hi
Flats & maisonettes	51,200	76,800	104	141	9.5%	10.6%
Terraced	88,800	133,200	137	186	7.3%	8.0%
Semi-detached	98,400	147,600	170	230	8.1%	9.0%
Detached	182,400	273,600	191	258	4.9%	5.4%

Percentage above the national average:	0%	

	Actual	**National Average**
Capital growth last 12 months:	25%	18%
Capital growth last 4 years:	85%	74%
Large employers in the area:	Mainly tourist related small businesses and local government, i.e. schools, hospitals and councils. Few large employers locally.	
Demand for letting:	Average	
Average void period:	3 weeks	

	Capital Growth (out of 5)	**Yield** (out of 5)	**Total** (out of 10)
Our rating:	3	4	7

Summary:	Plenty of potential for capital growth due to inward investment to the town.
Description:	I remember Southend as the cool place to be when I was a teenager. Now as a property investor I still think it's the place to be but for different reasons! Southend is the largest town in Essex and now has a glitzier feel to the place than before. Its theme park operates all year round and attracts families looking for a day out from a 1 hour travelling distance radius. For this reason alone the tourism industry in Southend is its biggest revenue generator.

Southend has had its problems though. Unemployment is higher than average for the east of England as it relies heavily on the tourist trade |

and its fishing industry. However this is about to change.

The number of visitors is set to rise due to investment of £17 million on the Southend sea front, high street and pier-enhancement project. The project will radically change the appearance of the town's central corridor, from the entrance in Prittlewell through the high street and along the 1.5 mile pier, which is being redeveloped following the fire 3 years ago.

Works to be undertaken as part of the project include cycle tracks, themed quarters in the high street and the updating of ugly and old-fashioned eye-sores. Southend is already visited by 1.6 million people a year. The aim of the project is to double that number.

This should boost jobs and therefore boost demand for rental properties for the lower and average paid workers and for rooms at hotels and B&Bs from the increased visitors. 150 new jobs were created by London Clubs International alone, which opened a new Casino at the Kursal building earlier this year. The airport provides 1,300 jobs for Southend and surrounding areas and the outlook for the airport looks strong.

There are two major developments at Shoeburyness, at the eastern periphery of the borough, both of which are former Ministry of Defence ranges and are considered crucial to the regeneration of the area. One development, at Shoeburyness garrison, will result in 600 jobs as the result of the creation of a mini-town comprising 465 new homes, a school, shops, leisure centre and health centre.

The A127 and A13 trunk roads link Southend to the national motorway network via the M25, which is 20 minutes' drive from the town. However, both trunk roads are overloaded but will be seeing a £14.5 million investment to improve passenger transport and reduce congestion on the A13 and A127. In addition, Southend received an increase in transport block funding of £4.6 million for 2001–02, against funding of £2.3 million in the previous financial year.

Mainline railway station:	One hour to Liverpool Street, London or Fenchurch Street, London
Road access:	Main access along A13 then A127 (dual carriageway). 48 miles east of Central London. 23 miles from M25
Local newspaper:	Basildon Evening Echo 01268 522792

Estate agents:	Name	Address	Tel	Web
	Tudor	257–261 Victoria Avenue Southend on Sea Essex SS2 6NE	01702 346818	www.tudor estates.co.uk
	Dedman Property Services	375 Southchurch Road Southend on Sea Essex SS1 2PQ	01702 461100	Website currently under development

Estate agents:	Name	Address	Tel	Web
	Hopson Property Services	39 Alexandra Street Southend on Sea Essex SS1 1BW	01702 334353	www.hopson property.co.uk
	Hair & Son	200 London Road Southend on Sea Essex SS1 1PJ	01702 394959	Website currently under development
	Belle Vue Property Services	501 Southchurch Road Southend on Sea Essex SS1 2PH	01702 611299	Website currently under development
	Wilsons Bureau	82 London Road Southend on Sea Essex SS1 1PG	01702 348400	Webiste currently under development
	Barbara Zialor Estate Agents	601 Southchurch Road Southend on Sea Essex SS1 2PN	01702 619618	Website currently under development
	H V & G Sorrell	40 Clarence Street Southend on Sea Essex SS1 1BD	01702 342225	www.sorrell estates.co.uk
Letting agents:	**Name**	**Address**	**Tel**	**Web**
	Countrywide Residential Lettings Ltd	21 Clifftown Rd Southend on Sea Essex SS1 1AB	01702 434334	www.right move.co.uk
	Regis Group plc	16–18 Warrior Sq Southend on Sea Essex SS1 2JH	0800 300700	www.regis plc.com

Area:	St. Albans, Hertfordshire					
Category:	C					
Investor profile:	Pension, Retirement, Downshifter,and Cash&Equity					
Population aged 15+:	63,208					
	Actual			**National Average**		
Percentage Class ABC1:	66%			44%		
Crime:	**Violence**		**Sexual**	**Burglary**		**Motor**
Per 1000 population:	4		1	4		3
Yield range:	3.6% – 7.8%					
Price ranges:	Low £	Hi £	Low £pw	Hi £pw	Low	Hi
Flats & maisonettes	103,200	154,800	155	210	7.1%	10.6%
Terraced	152,000	228,000	171	232	5.3%	8.0%
Semi-detached	195,200	292,800	219	296	5.3%	9.0%
Detached	300,000	450,000	229	310	3.6%	5.4%
Percentage above the national average:	126%					
	Actual			**National Average**		
Capital growth last 12 months:	16%			18%		
Capital growth last 4 years:	78%			74%		
Large employers in the area:	Hertfordshire County Council, KPMG Accountants, GlaxoSmithKline, John Lewis plc, Norwich Union, Sun Bank, HM Land Registry, Oscar Faber plc, Post Office Counters Ltd, J Sainsbury plc, St Albans City & District Council					
Demand for letting:	**Excellent**					
Average void period:	1 week					
	Capital Growth (out of 5)		**Yield** (out of 5)		**Total** (out of 10)	
Our rating:	4		2		6	
Summary:	A superb place to live, work and commute, making this place a safe investment, but property prices are high.					
Description:	The St Albans area is the place to be in Hertfordshire. It is famous for being full of affluent and prosperous professionals – 1 in 3 people resident in St Albans is in a managerial or professional occupation. Unemployment is incredibly low at sub 1%, the lowest in Hertfordshire, and compare that to London at 7%! They're a brainy lot too – GCSE results for St Albans schools showed 63% of pupils achieving 5 A* – C grades, compared with a national average of around 46%.					

▶

| | The area is very close to London due to the excellent rail and road links which have a major effect on the area's economy. 20% of the population commutes to London but St Albans is not simply another commuter town – and this is important in terms of future land use planning. The area has a booming local economy, which provides over 45,000 jobs, nearly half of which are filled by people outside of the area.

It is also home of the entrepreneur – 15% of the workforce is self-employed compared to 12% nationally and the trend is set to continue upwards. People working from home is on the increase and where better to work from home than a St Alban's home! This entrepreneurial blood runs through the veins of the local economy.

The area also has two prestigious research centres – Rothamstead Experimental Station at Harpenden, and the Building Research Establishment in Bricket Wood.

St Albans is dripping with history and this is apparent when walking through the high street. There is a lively street market and plenty of national chain stores to give you a blend of the past and the present. Everywhere you turn in the town there is a little quaint shop specialising in something. |

Mainline railway station:	20–30 minutes to Kings Cross Thameslink
Road access:	Main access M25 & M1
25 miles north of Central London
5 miles from M1 & M25
Local newspaper:	St Albans Observer 01727 834477

Estate agents:	Name	Address	Tel	Web
	Frosts Estate Agents	4 Chequer Street St Albans Hertfordshire AL1 3XZ	01727 861166	www.frosts.co.uk
	Richard Gibbs	6 Holywell Hill St Albans Hertfordshire AL1 1BZ	01727 868111	No website
	Brading & Harmer	69 High Street Redbourn St Albans Hertfordshire AL3 7LW	01727 793165	Website currently under development
	Collinsons Estate Agents	9–11 Victoria Street St Albans Hertfordshire AL1 3UB	01727 843222	www.collinsons.co.uk

Estate agents:	Name	Address	Tel	Web
	Daniels Estate Agents	104a London Road St Albans Hertfordshire AL1 1NX	01727 836561	www.daniels .uk.net
	Druce & Partners	12 London Road St Albans Hertfordshire AL1 1NG	01727 855232	www.druce-partners.co.uk
Letting agents:	Name	Address	Tel	Web
	Aitchisons	2 Holywell Hell St Albans Hertfordshire AL1 1BZ	01727 866686	www.aitchinsons .co.uk
	Your Move	2 High St St Albans Hertfordshire Al3 4EL	01727 840258	www.your-move.co.uk/ lettings

Area:	**St Andrews, Fife**					
Category:	A					
Investor profile:	Holiday, University, Downshifter					
Population aged 15+:	21,306					
	Actual			**National Average**		
Percentage Class ABC1:	61%			44%		
Crime:	**Violence**		**Sexual**	**Burglary**		**Motor**
Per 1000 population:	3		1	10		4
Yield range:	4.4% – 8.7%					
Price ranges:	Low £ Hi £		Low £pw	Hi £pw	Low	Hi
Flats & maisonettes	89,000 134,000		110	175	4.9	6.4%
Terraced	92,000 142,000		125	240	3.7%	7.5%
Semi-detached	122,000 285,000		105	320	5.83%	4.4%
Detached	130,250 340,000		165	400	5.9%	6.5%
Percentage above the national average:	151%					
	Actual			**National Average**		
Capital growth last 12 months:	21%			18%		
Capital growth last 5 years:	94%			74%		
Large employers in the area:	The University of St Andrews					
Demand for letting:	Excellent					
Average void period:	5 weeks					
	Capital Growth (out of 5)		**Yield** (out of 5)		**Total** (out of 10)	
Our rating:	4		3		8	
Summary:	In the Kingdom of Fife this place is a real treasure. An isolated village by the coast, the houses are those of a more expensive community by far! Buy cautiously, given the age of the usual stock in the town centre and buy with equity growth in mind rather than yield.					
Description:	One of the most globally famous locations in this listing St Andrews is known for its connections with golf, with the University, and its historic links. The University here is sometimes described as 'England's northernmost university' purely because of the numbers of students here from south of the border. Such a high proportion of students here come from private education that the opportunity to rent a property to affluent tenants is very high.					

	Former local authority property here can achieve very decent yields that the smarter homes cannot reach. The preference for flats is strong and most buildings have already been divided up into these smaller units of space.
	The small size of the community (15,000 residents and around 6,000 students) reinforces the romantic notion of the place, but does not help when winter storms from the sea remind you how remote this town is.
	The University is the largest employer in the town by far and enjoys a well developed relationship with the town. Halls of Residence take care of virtually all the newcomer students, with second year students finding their own places and tending to hang onto what they really like across the summer in exchange for a retainer paid to the landlord. Even one bed apartments command good rents and the yields can be decent to average.
	If one half of the temporary population is students, then the other half is tourists and golfers. Keen to play the Royal and Ancient Course, these visitors will stay in B&B places all over the town or in the better hotels close by the course.
	Outside the town rental opportunities can be found in places such as Leuchars, Kincaple, Cameron, Cellardyke and Guardbridge. These might be cottages or small farm buildings that have enjoyed good conversions.
Mainline railway station:	One hour to Edinburgh
Road access:	Main access A91 & A915 12 miles south east of Dundee 29 miles from M90
Local newspaper:	Daily Record 0141 309 3000

Estate agents:	Name	Address	Tel	Web
	Pagan Osborne	106 South St St Andrews Fife KY16 9QD	01334 475001	www.all-about-homes.com
	Drummond Cook & Mackintosh	33 Bell St St Andrews Fife KY16 9UR	01334 472152	www.drummondcook.co.uk
	Murray Donald & Caithness	17 Bell St St Andrews Fife KY16 9UR	01334 474200	www.md-c.co.uk
	Bradburne & Co	139 South St St Andrews Fife KY16 9UN	01334 479479	www.bradburne.co.uk

Letting agents:	Name	Address	Tel	Web
	Inchdairnie Properties	50 Argyle St St Andrews Fife KY16 9BU	01334 477011	Website currently under development

Area:	**Stansted, Essex**					
Category:	C					
Investor profile:	Pension, Retirement, Downshifter, Business and Cash&Equity					
Population aged 15+:	10,320					
	Actual			**National Average**		
Percentage Class ABC1:	65%			44%		
Crime:	**Violence**		**Sexual**	**Burglary**		**Motor**
Per 1000 population:	6		1	3		2
Yield range:	4.1% − 6.4%					
Price ranges:	**Low £**	**Hi £**	**Low £pw**	**Hi £pw**	**Low**	**Hi**
Flats & maisonettes	78,400	117,600	96	129	5.7%	6.4%
Terraced	121,600	182,400	155	210	6.0%	6.6%
Semi-detached	154,400	231,600	182	247	5.5%	6.1%
Detached	216,800	325,200	189	256	4.1%	4.5%
Percentage above the national average:	40%					
	Actual			**National Average**		
Capital growth last 12 months:	17%			18%		
Capital growth last 5 years:	93%			80%		
Large employers in the area:	Stansted Airport					
Demand for letting:	Excellent					
Average void period:	1 week					
	Capital Growth (out of 5)		**Yield** (out of 5)		**Total** (out of 10)	
Our rating:	3		4		7	
Summary:	With Stansted Airport being one of the fastest growing airports in Europe and related industries moving to Stansted because of this, tenant demand can only be strong.					
Description:	There is only one thing you think about when you think of Stansted − Stansted Airport! It has been granted permission to nearly double its passenger handling capacity from 14m to 25m by 2010. It will be the home for all the low cost European airlines such as Easyjet & Ryanair. Stansted will be therefore the gateway to Europe and will see a flow in both directions of travellers leaving or visiting. Governmental investment must follow the expansion of Stansted Airport into the town					

▶

	itself to make the place attractive, considering it will be the first landing point for all our European visitors. The expansion of the airport it will bring further industries, thus creating more jobs for the town resulting in strong tenant demand. I suggest B&B accommodation will be highly sought after as well as good quality homes for professional staff such as pilots.			
Mainline railway station:	45 minutes to Liverpool Street, London			
Road access:	Main access M20 29 miles south east of Central London 2 miles from M20			
Local newspaper:	Herts & Essex Star Observer 01992 586401			
Estate agents:	**Name**	**Address**	**Tel**	**Web**
	Intercounty Estate Agents	8 Cambridge Road Stansted Essex CM24 8BZ	01279 814400	www.inter country.co.uk
	Genesis Property Services	18 Silver Street Stansted Essex CM24 8HD	01279 817700	Website currently under development
Letting agents:	**Name**	**Address**	**Tel**	**Web**
	Front Door Property Management	Rowe House 4 Emson Close Saffron Walden Essex CB10 1HL	01799 525136	www.fdpm.co.uk

Area:	**Swansea, Glamorgan**				
Category:	B				
Investor profile:	Cash&Equity Investor, Holiday Investor, University Investor, Business Investor				
Population aged 15+:	127,032				

	Actual		National Average		
Percentage Class ABC1:	47%		44%		

Crime:	Violence	Sexual	Burglary	Motor
Per 1000 population:	13	1	6	15

Yield range:	4.2% − 6.3%					

Price ranges:	Low £	Hi £	Low £pw	Hi £pw	Low	Hi
Flats & maisonettes	41,600	62,400	50	67	5.6%	6.3%
Terraced	52,800	79,200	51	69	4.5%	5.0%
Semi-detached	69,600	104,400	63	86	4.3%	4.7%
Detached	114,400	171,600	102	139	4.2%	4.6%

Percentage above the national average:	0%					

	Actual	National Average
Capital growth last 12 months:	16%	18%
Capital growth last 5 years:	41%	80%

Large employers in the area:	3M, Addis, Alberto Culver, Alcoa GB, Admiral Insurance, City and Council of Swansea, DVLA, Gorseinon College, HM Land Registry, NHS Direct, Crown House Engineering, BT, Dwr Cymru − Welsh Water, EDS, Walkers Snack Foods, INCO Europe, Asda, Boots, BHS Ltd, Morganite Electrical Carbon, EDS.
Demand for letting:	Good
Average void period:	3 weeks

	Capital Growth (out of 5)	Yield (out of 5)	Total (out of 10)
Our rating:	4	3	7

Summary:	Lots of traditional stock around a more modern city centre with its redevelopment and regeneration initiatives of recent years. Buy wisely and you can still hope to pick up good equity growth.
Description:	Busy, bustling and confident. Swansea as a city and as a community should give confidence to a variety of investors. It is a great location for business both small and large, has a productive workforce and still manages to qualify as a city that welcomes tourism and is on the

▶

doorstep of fantastic countryside. A city with a young approach some 24% of the population are aged 19 and under, with around 18% over the age of 65. With the marina, the beaches and seaside communities of Mumbles, Rhossili Bay, Brandy Bay and Oxwich all so close to the city, it is no surprise that Swansea loves to cite its own high scoring in a survey of lifestyle cities within the UK.

Investment and regeneration into this city over the past twenty plus years has created a newly structured and freshly dynamic location. Big on new business parks with swift access to the M4, places such as Swansea Vale with its 110 acres, and Swansea Enterprise Park offer good reasons for business relocation and represent decent yields for investors in commercial premises.

The working population of 95,000 are predominantly employed in the service sectors and this reflects in the major employers category. A third of this service sector is made up of work in distribution, hotels and restaurants and illustrates the role played by Swansea as the regions shopping and service centre. Manufacturing though, is still a strong force with around 11,000 jobs. The largest employer locally is the City Council and County Council with some 12,000 people on the books.

Other major employers are the hospitals and also Swansea university with 10,000 students attracted by the high academic standards as well as the enviable lifestyle opportunities offered by the city. Between these staff figures and the student numbers across the city the scope for small and portfolio landlords to find clients is very high. You might also explore the possibilities for accommodation provision around the higher education colleges with their campus locations at Mount Pleasant, Gorseinon and Swansea itself. These three sites cater to the requirements of at least 8,000 students.

Look to the maritime quarter and the business district for apartment sites and some new developments where good capital appreciation can be expected, and where good serviced lets are feasible. For the student community stay close by the campus locations mentioned previously. There are large numbers of ex local authority stock with the better yields in a broad sweep around the city, and good holiday cottage type accommodation which is easily let and place through the more specialist agencies. For high yields relatively close by also explore the availability of properties at Porthcawl, Maesteg, Port Talbot, Skewen, Neath and Llanelli. Swansea offers good investment opportunities both below the mid-market prices of £40,000 - £60,000 and also in the new housing estates and apartment living opportunities closer to business parks, call centre operations and enterprise zones.

Mainline railway station:	55 minutes to Cardiff Central
Road access:	Main access M4 40 miles west of Cardiff 6 miles to M4
Local newspaper:	South Wales Evening Post 01792 650841

Estate agents:	Name	Address	Tel	Web
	Peter Alan	14 West St Gorseinon Swansea SA6 8AL	01792 796767	www.remax-wales.co.uk
	Simpson Evans	21 Walter Rd Swansea SA1 5NQ	01792 476111	www.simpson evans.co.uk
	Bishell Brothers	18 Springfield Avenue Upper Killay Swansea SA2 7HW	0845 6032901	Website currently under development
	Clee, Tompkinson & Francis	35 Herbert St Pontardawe Swansea SA8 4EB	01792 865042	Website currently under development
	Graham J Price & Co	91 Sterry Rd Gowerton Swansea SA4 3BN	01792 874777	Website currently under development
	Richards Estate Agents	74 St Teilo St Swansea SA4 8ST	01792 884444	Website currently under development
	John Francis	76 Newton Rd Mumbles Swansea SA3 4BE	01792 360060	Website currently under development
Letting agents:	Name	Address	Tel	Web
	Homehunters Property Management	140 Walter Road Swansea SA1 5PW	01792 645355	www.home-hunters.co.uk
	Dawsons	419 Gower Rd Killay Swansea SA2 7AN	01792 367301	www.dawsons property.co.uk

Area:	**Swindon, Wiltshire**					
Category:	C					
Investor profile:	Pension, Business and Cash&Equity					
Population aged 15+:	118,456					
	Actual			**National Average**		
Percentage Class ABC1:	44%			44%		
Crime:	**Violence**		**Sexual**	**Burglary**		**Motor**
Per 1000 population:	11		1	5		3
Yield range:	4.7% – 7.1%					

Price ranges:	Low £	Hi £	Low £pw	Hi £pw	Low	Hi
Flats & maisonettes	65,600	98,400	90	121	6.4%	7.1%
Terraced	84,800	127,200	106	143	5.8%	6.5%
Semi-detached	102,400	153,600	113	152	5.1%	5.7%
Detached	144,800	217,200	147	198	4.7%	5.3%

Percentage above the national average:	0%	
	Actual	**National Average**
Capital growth last 12 months:	15%	18%
Capital growth last 5 years:	96%	80%
Large employers in the area:	BP Castrol, Honda, Intel, Lucent Technologies, Motorola, WH Smith, Zurich, BMW, Arval PHH, Woolworths & Tyco Industries	
Demand for letting:	Good	
Average void period:	2 weeks	

	Capital Growth (out of 5)	**Yield** (out of 5)	**Total** (out of 10)
Our rating:	3	3	**6**

Summary:	Businesses will always locate here due to its location so tenant demand will always be strong.
Description:	The reason I have recommended this town is simply due to its location. It is dead centre on the M4 between London & Bristol, has improved access to the M5 via the A419 to go north and has unrivaled accesability to a significant number of air and seaports: ■ Heathrow Airport (it is quicker by car from Swindon than it is from central London!) ■ Bristol Airport ■ Southampton Airport

▶

	■ Avonmouth Docks ■ Southampton Docks ■ Cardiff Docks. This is why so many companies have located to Swindon to take advantage of its accessability, especially distribution centres. People continue to relocate to Swindon at consistent rates to meet the demand from employers in the local economy. With a low unemployment rate and the varied skills base of the local population, Swindon is the first choice for many national and international businesses.		
Mainline railway station:	30–40 minutes to Bristol Parkway		
Road access:	Main access A419 & M4 40 miles east of Bristol 4 miles from M4		
Local newspaper:	Swindon Evening Advertiser 01793 528144		

Estate agents:	**Name**	**Address**	**Tel**	**Web**
	Ridgeway Estate Agents	Tritton House 14 Bath Road Old Town Swindon Wiltshire SN1 4BA	01793 431000	www.roderick wightman.co.uk
	Cecil Pike & Partners	5–6 Commercial Road Swindon Wiltshire SN1 5NF	01793 614868	Website currently under development
	Chappells Estate Agents	76 Victoria Road Swindon Wiltshire SN1 3BB	01793 618080	Website currently under development
	Dewhurst & Co	23 Commercial Road Swindon Wiltshire SN1 5NS	01793 430200	www.dewhurst andco.co.uk
	Philip Andrews Estate Agents	62 Devies Road Old Town Swindon Wiltshire SN1 4BD	01793 431432	www.philip andrews.co.uk

▶

Letting agents:	Name	Address	Tel	Web
	Ridgeway Estate Agents	21–22, Commercial Rd Swindon Wiltshire SN1 5NS	01793 530167	www.ridgeway estateagents .co.uk
	Home Choice	167, Victoria Rd Swindon Wiltshire SN1 3BU	01793 431725	www.home choice-uk.com
	Dreweatt Neate	28, Wood St Swindon Wiltshire SN1 4AB	01793 489303	www.dreweatt-neate.co.uk
	Peter Long & Partners	16, High St Old Town Swindon Wiltshire SN1 3EP	01793 615555	www.peterlong andpartners .co.uk
	Joy Sherwood Property Management	25, Commercial Road Swindon Wiltshire SN1 5NS	01793 538616	www.joy sherwood.co.uk

Area:	**Taunton, Somerset**					
Category:	C					
Investor profile:	Cash&Equity Investor, Pension Investor, Holiday Investor, Retirement Investor, Downshifter Investor					
Population aged 15+:	50,164					
	Actual			**National Average**		
Percentage Class ABC1:	51%			44%		
Crime:	**Violence**	**Sexual**		**Burglary**		**Motor**
Per 1000 population:	12	1		7		2
Yield range:	3.2% – 6.6%					

Price ranges:	Low £	Hi £	Low £pw	Hi £pw	Low	Hi
Flats & maisonettes	60,800	91,200	98	133	6.0%	6.6%
Terraced	77,600	116,400	90	121	3.6%	4.1%
Semi-detached	94,400	141,600	127	172	4.8%	5.3%
Detached	170,400	255,600	136	185	3.2%	3.6%

Percentage above the national average:	6%	
	Actual	**National Average**
Capital growth last 12 months:	29%	18%
Capital growth last 4 years:	86%	74%
Large employers in the area:	Avimo, The Charity Commission, UK Hydrographic Office, Debenhams (Admin. & Computer Centre), Wincanton Logistics, Hatcher & Sons, Kennedy & Donkin, Lloyds TSB (HR), Nat West (Voucher Processing), Somerset County Council, Taunton & Somerset NHS Trust	
Demand for letting:	Good	
Average void period:	5 weeks	

	Capital Growth (out of 5)	**Yield** (out of 5)	**Total** (out of 10)
Our rating:	5	3	**8**

Summary:	A true lifestyle or downshift move, Taunton is a strong town with a sense of the traditional. Great Farmers' Market, good schools, restaurants and properties that will at least give good average yields. Easy access to the countryside and quick to the motorway. We love it!
Description:	With yields of only average proportion, Taunton features here for the lifestyle investor, the downshifter and the person who recognises that Taunton is a gateway into and out of the West Country. With the M5 running right past the edge of town and the A358 cutting across from

▶

North Somerset to Dorset, Taunton is a place that has always drawn the traffic to it. If you want to find a place for yourself where you can also develop a portfolio of steady income and steady capital growth Taunton may fit the bill.

The rural setting of the Blackdown and Quantock Hills, combined with Taunton's role as the county town for Somerset, means that lifestyle and leisure considerations are well met. Walking, country pursuits, the racing, and the market are here. There is a tremendous choice of both state and independent schools around the town.

But Taunton can also offer decent housing to landlords looking for stable stock. The new developments growing up to either side of the M5 around junctions 25 and 26 are there primarily for people seeking a quick commute to either Exeter or Bristol and prices here mean savings on both of those larger cities. Buying these recent builds can reduce the likelihood of large annual maintenance bills and provide good scope for equity growth as the motorway access adds to the values of those units you buy.

Wellington just to the south offers strong capital appreciation and a similarly traditional community, albeit smaller. The upmarket address carries with it some small additional pricing and scores highly in terms of lifestyle or work/life balance opportunity. There are too many lovely and rural villages within twenty minutes to the west and south of Taunton to attempt to mention, but get down there quickly and snap up something good. As well as the commuting set and regular workers as tenants, you are sufficiently in the country here to be able to invest in decent holiday accommodation lets and have them managed through the specialist cottage holiday organisations. Watch out for their expensive charges though. That said, they could find you holiday makers virtually all year round.

Village living can be had within twenty minutes of any part of Taunton, enhancing the potential of the wider Taunton Deane area to attract new businesses and new residents. Business parks and support services from the local council are seeing a steady inflow of companies and new start-ups. The College of Arts has a link with the University of Plymouth and potentially can require accommodation for its students.

Mainline railway station:	One hour to Bristol Temple Meads
Road access:	Main access M5 47 miles south of Bristol 2 miles from M5
Local newspaper:	Somerset County Gazette 01823 725045

Estate agents:	Name	Address	Tel	Web
	Lucas & Sloman Estate Agents	43–44 High Street Taunton Somerset TA1 3PN	01823 253000	www.lucas sloman.co.uk

Estate agents:	Name	Address	Tel	Web
	Gibbins Richards Ltd	50 High Street Taunton Somerset TA1 3PR	01823 332828	www.gibbins richards.co.uk
	Darlows	51 & 52 High Street Taunton Somerset TA1 3PR	01823 326444	www.tmxhaart. co.uk
	Greenslade Taylor Hunt	13 Hammet Street Taunton Somerset TA1 1RN	01823 277121	Website currently under development
	Bradleys Estate Agents	49 & 50 East Street Taunton Somerset TA1 3NA	01823 351351	www.bradleys-estate-agents. co.uk
Letting agents:	Name	Address	Tel	Web
	Martin & Co	12 Middle St Taunton Somerset TA1 1SH	01823 275804	www.martinco .com
	Austen Barton	46 Bridge St Taunton Somerset TA1 1UD	01823 331396	www.austen barton.co.uk
	Sherlock Homes	1 Church Square Taunton Somerset TA1 1SA	01823 276111	Website currently under development

Area:	**Tetbury, Gloucestershire**					
Category:	A					
Investor profile:	Holiday, Retirement, Downshifter					
Population aged 15+:	7,212					
	Actual			**National Average**		
Percentage Class ABC1:	57%			44%		
Crime:	**Violence**		**Sexual**	**Burglary**		**Motor**
Per 1000 population:	5		1	5		2
Yield range:	2.6% – 10.6%					
Price ranges:	Low £	Hi £	Low £pw	Hi £pw	Low	Hi
Flats & maisonettes	66,400	99,600	135	182	9.5%	10.6%
Terraced	118,400	177,600	136	185	5.4%	6.0%
Semi-detached	170,400	255,600	144	195	4.0%	4.4%
Detached	274,400	411,600	153	208	2.6%	2.9%
Percentage above the national average:	49%					
	Actual			**National Average**		
Capital growth last 12 months:	37%			18%		
Capital growth last 4 years:	96%			74%		
Large employers in the area:	Mainly tourist related small businesses and local government, i.e. schools, hospitals and councils. Few large employers locally.					
Demand for letting:	**Excellent**					
Average void period:	4 weeks					
Our rating:	**Capital Growth** (out of 5) 5		**Yield** (out of 5) 4	**Total** (out of 10) **9**		
Summary:	Traditional yet very stylish with it, this small town has very expensive property for reasons that will be clear when you visit. Expect competition from others when you try to buy here. Good schools of variety. The planners and others of influence will make sure the place remains as attractive as it is.					
Description:	On a busy Saturday morning this tiny town comes alive with the mixing of residents and those who just visit for the weekend. Tetbury is a classic Cotswolds community where the pressure on the housing stock shows in pricing, as well as in the slow movement of traffic through the narrow streets.					

	Largely unchanged in layout for around 300 years, the centre of the town features a beautiful stilted Market Hall and the commanding features of St Mary's church. From the tower you can see west across to the Highgrove Estate and to the National Arboretum at Westonbirt. Recent building has included expensive apartments in the former food factory. A new supermarket on the eastern edge of town vies with the more specialist produce shops and delicatessens in the high street.
	Bustling with the mix of retailers offering antiques and provisions alongside each other, Tetbury is high on the index of expensive places to live. The quality of life is high when measured in terms of small community living, several public schools within a ten mile drive, decent train connections to London and Swindon from Kemble village. Bristol is just 30 miles away by car and the attractions of shopping or dining in Bath or Cirencester are even closer. The National Agricultural College at Cirencester creates further rental opportunity with its influx of students. Villages around the Cotswolds Water Park and Cricklade can provide good rental opportunities.
	Close neighbours in Malmesbury, Minchinhampton and Wotton under Edge all testify to the general affluence of this western end of the Cotswolds. Village prices are high all around and property sufficiently difficult to come by that rents can be quickly achieved. Longer holiday lets can also be successfully secured given the attraction of the area to visiting tourists, keen to soak up the atmosphere. Communities closer to the M4 offer good long term lets to those attracted by the quick commute times. Consider Codrington, Pucklechurch, Chipping Sodbury and the Somerfords. For those working in Bristol or Gloucester the villages with easy access to the M5 have seen strong price rises and good rental opportunities. Look to Tortworth, Thornbury and the smaller communities along the A38.
	Transportation Tetbury sits in the centre of a triangle of road networks formed by the M4, M5 and the A419 connecting quickly with Swindon, Bristol and Gloucester. Fast train service to London via Swindon.
Mainline railway station:	$1\frac{1}{2}$ hours to London Paddington
Road access:	Main access route A483 27 miles north of Bristol 11 miles to M4
Local newspaper:	Wilts & Glos Standard 01285 642642
Estate agents:	**Name** **Address** **Tel** **Web**
	Butler Sherborn 9 Market Place Tetbury Gloucestershire GL8 8DA 01666 505105 www.butler sherborn.co.uk

Estate agents:	Name	Address	Tel	Web
	Hibbard Farmer Estate Agents	21 Market Place Tetbury Gloucestershire GL8 8UD	01666 501900	Website currently under development
	R A Bennett & Partners	19 Market Place Tetbury Gloucestershire GL8 8DD	01666 502528	www.rightmove. co.uk

Letting agents:	Name	Address	Tel	Web
	Perry & Chambers	3 Church St Tetbury Gloucestershire GL8 8JG	01666 500250	Website currently under development

Area:	**Welwyn Garden City, Hertfordshire**					
Category:	C					
Investor profile:	Pension, Business and Cash&Equity					
Population aged 15+:	43,257					
	Actual			**National Average**		
Percentage Class ABC1:	53%			44%		
Crime:	Violence		Sexual	Burglary		Motor
Per 1000 population:	5		1	7		4
Yield range:	3.7% – 7.5%					
Price ranges:	Low £ Hi £		Low £pw	Hi £pw	Low	Hi
Flats & maisonettes	85,600 128,400		123	166	6.7%	7.5%
Terraced	116,800 175,200		127	172	5.1%	5.7%
Semi-detached	140,000 210,000		138	187	4.6%	5.1%
Detached	224,800 337,200		179	242	3.7%	4.1%
Percentage above the national average:	27%					
	Actual			**National Average**		
Capital growth last 12 months:	23%			18%		
Capital growth last 4 years:	84%			74%		
Large employers in the area:	SmithKline Beecham, Roche, Schering Plough, UCB Films, Stafford Miller, Sika, Catomance and Serono Laboratories					
Demand for letting:	Excellent					
Average void period:	1 week					
	Capital Growth (out of 5)		**Yield** (out of 5)		**Total** (out of 10)	
Our rating:	3		3		6	
Summary:	A growing affluent area with low unemployment – a safe bet.					
Description:	When I trained as an accountant I used to do an audit here and I was always so impressed with the whole vibe of the area. The shopping centre is well spaced out – the outside square for the whole town cente probably covers around 22,500sqm with various roads leading off it. WGC is definitely affluent and you can tell this from the shops. There are the usual John Lewis and Marks & Spencer but also the niche boutiques and customary Waitrose Supermarket – the choice for any self-respecting middle class person. Welwyn Garden City's history as a garden city and Hatfield's position as a New Town means that businesses have been housed in well-thought-					

of and easily reached locations. Welwyn Garden City is not far from London, and is crossed by the A1M and M25. Rail links to London and Cambridge are superb, and the area is close to both Luton and Stansted airports. The number of businesses and people employed in the district are growing rapidly. The business areas are well-planned and thus continue to attract new busiensses.

In 1997 there were 3,600 businesses, compared to 2,100 in 1991. During this period the number of businesses grew faster in WGC than in the country as a whole – 69% compared to 53%. In 1997 51,000 people were employed in the Welwyn-Hatfield Area, compared to 43,000 in 1991. Employment growth was faster than the county average: 19% in Welwyn-Hatfield compared to 11% in Hertfordshire itself. The service sector has created more jobs than any other; financial and business services employed an additional 6,000 people in this period and are now the largest sector in the area. Financial and business services have a higher concentration in the district than in Great Britain as a whole. They comprise mainly small companies and professional firms and branches of large financial institutions, such as banks.

Other significant sectors with a high concentration in Welwyn-Hatfield include manufacturing of chemicals, manufacturing of medical, precision instruments, etc., computing and related activities and other business activities. Welwyn-Hatfield has a higher concentration of high-tech sectors than the regional and county averages, although the numbers employed are relatively small and are dominated by the pharmaceuticals industry.

Healthcare companies have played a leading role in the manufacturing history of Welwyn Garden City. The first major healthcare firm to locate here was Roche Products in 1937. Pharmaceutical company Schering-Plough and Vega the software and systems engineering group have moved into WGC in recent years and are based at the Shire Park Business Park. Other large companies based in Welwyn Garden City include Rank Xerox who opened a multi million pound technical centre in Bessemer Road in 1995 the first of its kind in the UK.

Mainline railway station:	30 minutes to London Kings Cross 45–50 minutes to Moorgate, London			
Road access:	Main access A1(M) & A414 28 miles north of Central London 1 mile from A1(M)			
Local newspaper:	Welwyn & Hatfield Times 01727 866166			
Estate agents:	Name	Address	Tel	Web
	Wrights	36 Stonehills Welwyn Garden City Hertfordshire AL8 6PD	01707 332211	www.team prop.co.uk

Estate agents:	Name	Address	Tel	Web
	Country Properties	3 Bridge Road Welwyn Garden City Hertfordshire AL8 6UN	01707 339146	www.greenrose network.co.uk
	Ashtons Estate Agents	33 Wigmores North Welwyn Garden City Hertfordshire AL8 6PG	01707 331100	Website currently under development
	Haart	23 Stonehills Welwyn Garden City Hertfordshire AL8 6NA	01707 322222	www.tmxhaart. co.uk
	Putterills of Hertfordshire	34 Wigmores North Welwyn Garden City Hertfordshire AL8 6PH	01707 393333	www.putterills. co.uk
Letting agents:	Name	Address	Tel	Web
	Halcyon House Management	43 High St Welwyn Hertfordshire AL6 9EE	01438 712712	www.halcyon house.com

Area:	**Wisbech, Cambridgeshire**					
Category:	A					
Investor profile:	Pension, Business, Retirement, Holiday, Downshifter and Cash&Equity					
Population aged 15+:	16,889					
	Actual			**National Average**		
Percentage Class ABC1:	36%			44%		
Crime:	**Violence**		**Sexual**	**Burglary**		**Motor**
Per 1000 population:	11		1	4		4
Yield range:	7.2% – 14.3%					
Price ranges:	**Low £**	**Hi £**	**Low £pw**	**Hi £pw**	**Low**	**Hi**
Flats & maisonettes	32,800	49,200	90	123	13.0%	14.3%
Terraced	45,600	68,400	87	118	9.0%	9.9%
Semi-detached	65,600	98,400	109	148	7.9%	8.6%
Detached	111,200	166,800	170	231	7.2%	8.0%
Percentage above the national average:	0%					
	Actual			**National Average**		
Capital growth last 12 months:	22%			18%		
Capital growth last 5 years:	92%			80%		
Large employers in the area:	Mainly tourist related small businesses and local government, i.e. schools, hospitals and councils. Few large employers locally.					
Demand for letting:	**Excellent**					
Average void period:	1 week					
	Capital Growth (out of 5)		**Yield** (out of 5)		**Total** (out of 10)	
Our rating:	4		4		**8**	
Summary:	Isolated town with a good local economy and strong tenant demand.					
Description:	I have 9 properties in this area. What I love about this area is that it is quite tucked away from other towns and is at least a good 50 mins' drive down a single carriageway to any of the neighbouring cities. Because of this, any sensible person working in the town would like to live in the town.					
	I put an advert in the local press detailing my properties available to rent and I received at least 40 calls that week – tenant demand is high!					
	The town is a pretty town, there is a river running through, it is quite close to the coast, and there are several new development areas being					

▶

	constructed. The port has been renovated thanks to a £1m development fund set up by the local council, English Partnerships & the European Regional Development Fund, The port has reintroduced its use as a tourist and leisure facility. Currently the area is used for moorings, but the surrounding land will be used for industrial purposes thus providing jobs.			
Mainline railway station:	1 hour and 40 minutes to London Kings Cross (with one change)			
Road access:	Main access route A47 43 miles north of Cambridge 40 miles to M11			
Local newspaper:	Cambridgeshire Times & Standard 01354 652621			
Estate agents:	**Name**	**Address**	**Tel**	**Web**
	Spicer McColl Ltd	10 York Row Wisbech Cambridgeshire PE13 1EF	01945 467555	www.tmx spicer.co.uk
	John Jordan Estate Agents	12 Union Street Wisbech Cambridgeshire PE13 1DJ	01945 588301	www.rightmove. co.uk
	Principal Estate Agents	5 Church Terrace Wisbech Cambridgeshire PE13 1BJ	01945 581234	www.principal homes.co.uk
	Harrison Murray Ltd	9–10 Bridge Street Wisbech Cambridgeshire PE13 1AE	01945 465432	www.harrison murray.co.uk
	Bairstow Eves Estate Agents	9 Union Street Wisbech Cambridgeshire PE13 1DJ	01945 581085	www.rightmove. co.uk
Letting agents:	**Name**	**Address**	**Tel**	**Web**
	Holmes	9 Union Street Wisbech Cambridgeshire PE13 1DJ	01945 588875	www.holmes 2rent.co.uk
	A1 Property Rentals	17–18 Church Mews Wisbech Cambridgeshire PE13 1HL	01945 466951	Website currently under development

Area:	**York, Yorkshire**			
Category:	A			
Investor profile:	Cash&Equity, Pension, Holiday, Retirement, Downshifter, Business			
Population aged 15+:	159,232			
	Actual		**National Average**	
Percentage Class ABC1:	51%		44%	
Crime:	**Violence**	**Sexual**	**Burglary**	**Motor**
Per 1000 population:	9	1	13	5
Yield range:	5.4% – 14.5%			

Price ranges:	Low £	Hi £	Low £pw	Hi £pw	Low	Hi
Flats & maisonettes	52,800	79,200	147	200	13.1%	14.5%
Terraced	81,600	122,400	96	131	5.6%	6.1%
Semi-detached	89,600	134,400	129	174	6.7%	7.5%
Detached	152,800	229,200	160	217	5.0%	5.4%

Percentage above the national average:	2%	
	Actual	**National Average**
Capital growth last 12 months:	31%	18%
Capital growth last 5 years:	96%	80%
Large employers in the area:	DEFRA; Norwich Union Life; British Telecom; CPP Card Protection Plan; TSYS Europe (payment-processing company); Nestle UK Headquarters	
Demand for letting:	Excellent	
Average void period:	2 weeks	

	Capital Growth (out of 5)	**Yield** (out of 5)	**Total** (out of 10)
Our rating:	4	5	9

Summary:	A tremendous mixture of heritage and modern industry, York provides the landlord with steady rents and some very good yields within a few areas of the city. Very much a lifestyle decision to live and work here for many of your tenants and perhaps for you too!
Description:	In a time when the world pace is increasing daily York provides a lesson in combining history with technology and learning. However busy life can be in the work context a twenty minute walk – high above the bustle and along the city walls that encircle the core of this ancient city – will put you back into a great state of mind.

For quality of life, ease of communication and the business facilities available, York is a big plus for many small and large companies. More than 20% of the working population of York is employed inside the information economy. This could include many of your tenants in this town. Urban development projects and business parks have created the need for more family housing on the outskirts of town and for good apartments close to the city walls.

Science City York is a funded partnership project for the development of science and technology in and around the city, with participants from over 230 technology companies – often small niche sector businesses – but employing around 7,000 people. This is typical of the activity going on in this industrious city which appears only to present a Heritage front to the strong tourist industry which has a year round need for accommodation.

The pull of well paying companies means that tenant demand for good housing stock from the landlords is high and you can get good yields, not just around the city but also in local villages and neighbouring towns. Close in look to Acomb, Clifton and South Bank for rents. There are many good returns to be had with flats in the centre and close to the walls. Consider larger housing developments of new builds and village homes as far east as Malton on the A64 which is just 18 miles away, or many of the communities between York and Wetherby 10 miles to the west, or between York and the town of Knaresborough.

The role of the university is also strong in creating demand for shared housing and small terraced properties commanding decent returns. Buy with care to avoid overpriced property, while there is still plenty around that you can make a decent return on.

Mainline railway station:	York has its own mainline station with a fast $2\frac{1}{2}$ hour service to London.
Road access:	Main access A1, then A64 25 miles north of Leeds 12 miles from A1
Local newspaper:	Evening Press – York 01904 653 051

Estate agents:	Name	Address	Tel	Web
	Hunters the Estate Agents	47 York Road Acomb York YO24 4LN	01904 780640	www.hunters net.co.uk
	Claude H Elmer	45 Front St Acomb York YO24 3BR	01904 787900	www.caludeh elmer.co.uk
	Chris Clubley & Co	52 Market Place Pocklington York YO42 2AH	01759 304040	www.chris clubley.co.uk

Estate agents:	Name	Address	Tel	Web
	Jonathan P Morley	Penleys House 59a Monkgate York YO31 7PA	01904 631013	www.jonathan morley.co.uk
	Quantum	6 Walmgate York YO1 9TJ	01904 631631	www.quantum estateagency .com
	Stephensons	10 Colliergate York YO1 8BP	01904 625533	www.stephensons 4property.co.uk
	Churchills Estate Agents	57 The Village Haxby York YO32 2JE	01904 758858	www.churchills estateagents. co.uk
	Alan Black & Co	95 Main St Fulford York YO10 4PN	01904 679733	www.blacks property.com
	Halifax Estate Agents	45 The Village Haxby York TY32 2HU	01904 766030	www.halifax. co.uk
Letting agents:	Name	Address	Tel	Web
	White Rose Property Management	201 Acomb Rd York North Yorkshire YO24 4HD	01904 782022	Website currently under development
	Carter Jonas	82 Micklegate York North Yorkshire YO1 6LF	01904 627436	www.carter jonas.co.uk
	Countrywide Residential Lettings	72 Low Petergate York North Yorkshire YO1 7HZ.	01904 652158	www.right move.co.uk

Other Services from the Authors

The authors also offer a portfolio building service to clients of all sizes. They will help with:

- Sourcing the right properties tailored to your own strategy
- Raising the cheapest finance to purchase the properties
- Finding the right tenants
- The ongoing maintenance of the properties.

If you are thinking of building a portfolio or need help expanding your portfolio then contact:

Ajay Ahuja or Nick Rampley-Sturgeon
Tel: 01327 706622
Email: talk2nick@buyingtorent.com
Web: www.buyingtorent.com

Tel: 0800 652 3979
Fax: 01277 362563
Email: emergencyaccountants@yahoo.co.uk
Web: www.accdirect.co.uk

> **Subscribe to www.propertyhotspots.net for up to the minute information on property hotspots, property prices, rental yields, property search, estate agents, letting agents, auctions, 100% mortgage providers, buy-to-let mortgage providers, portfolio management, and much more.**

Index of Property Hotspots

Alnwick, Northumberland	3	Kettering, Northamptonshire	113
Anglesey	6	Kings Lynn, Norfolk	115
Ashford, Kent	9	Leamington Spa	118
Bath, Somerset	12	Leeds, Yorkshire	121
Beckenham, Kent	15	Leicester, Leicestershire	124
Bedford, Bedfordshire	17	Lincoln, Lincolnshire	127
Billericay, Essex	20	Liverpool City Centre, Lancashire	130
Birmingham City Centre,		Luton, Bedfordshire	132
West Midlands	22	Lymington, Devon	135
Bournemouth, Dorset	26	Manchester, Lancashire	138
Brentwood, Essex	31	Milton Keynes, Buckinghamshire	142
Brighton, Sussex	34	Newark, Nottinghamshire	145
Bristol, Somerset	39	Newquay, Cornwall	148
Cambridge, Cambridgeshire	42	Norwich, Norfolk	151
Canterbury, Kent	46	Oxford, Oxfordshire	154
Cardiff, South Glamorgan	49	Padstow, Cornwall	158
Cardigan, Dyfed	52	Peterborough, Cambridgeshire	161
Chelmsford, Essex	55	Poole Harbour, Dorset	164
Cleethorpes, Lincolnshire	58	Portsmouth, Hampshire	167
Colchester, Essex	60	Reading, Berkshire	171
Darlington, County Durham	63	Ripon, North Yorkshire	174
Durham, County Durham	66	Romford, Essex	177
Edinburgh, Lothian	69	Salisbury, Wiltshire	180
Epping, Essex	73	Selby, North Yorkshire	183
Exeter, Devon	75	Southampton, Hampshire	186
Fowey, Cornwall	78	Southend-on-Sea, Essex	189
Frome, Somerset	81	St Albans, Hertfordshire	192
Goole, North Humberside	84	St Andrews, Fife	195
Gosport, Hampshire	87	Stansted, Essex	198
Grantham, Lincolnshire	90	Swansea, Wales	200
Great Yarmouth, Norfolk	92	Swindon, Wiltshire	203
Guildford, Surrey	94	Taunton, Somerset	206
Harrogate, North Yorkshire	97	Tetbury, Gloucestershire	209
Hull, North Humberside	100	Welwyn Garden City,	
Ipswich, Suffolk	104	Hertfordshire	212
Isle of Wight	107	Wisbech, Cambridgeshire	215
Kendal, Cumbria	110	York, Yorkshire	217